The Arts Go To School

Classroom-based activities that focus on music, painting, drama, movement, media, and more

EDITED BY
David Booth
Masayuki Hachiya

Pembroke Publishers Limited

© 2004 Pembroke Publishers
538 Hood Road
Markham, Ontario, Canada L3R 3K9
www.pembrokepublishers.com

Distributed in the U.S. by Stenhouse Publishers
PO Box 11020
Portland, ME 04101
www.stenhouse.com

We acknowledge the financial support of the Government of Canada through the Book Publishing Industry Development Program (BDIDP) for our publishing activities.

We acknowledge the Government of Ontario through the Ontario Media Development Corporation's Ontario Book Initiative.

....

Library and Archives Canada Cataloguing in Publication

The arts go to school: classroom-based activities that focus on music, painting, drama, movement, media, and more / [edited by] David Booth, Masayuki Hachiya.

Includes index.
ISBN 1-55138-175-3

1. Arts—Study and teaching (Elementary) 2. Interdisciplinary approach in education. I. Booth, David. II. Hachiya, Masayuki, 1973-

LB1591.A787 2004   372.5'044   C2004-903660-2

....

Editor: Kate Revington
Cover Design: John Zehethofer
Cover Photography: Ajay Photographics
Typesetting: Jay Tee Graphics Ltd.

Printed and bound in Canada
9 8 7 6 5 4 3 2 1

Contents

FINALE Voices from the Arts Community *125*
By David Booth

Introduction

Riding on the Red Arts Wagon

By David Booth and Masayuki Hachiya

Today dozens, if not hundreds, of books and journals offer a bounty of ideas for teaching the arts. But creative ideas are not enough. We need to be clear about what we want to achieve with the children in our care for nine years of elementary school and how we will assess our progress in helping them to grow in arts experiences and arts knowledge. Our aim in developing this book was not to create a grab bag of every idea on the arts for classrooms, but rather to help classroom teachers construct arts programs and to offer a template that a school team can use in designing the curriculum that their school needs.

With these outcomes in mind, we approached a variety of author-educators, experts in their fields of arts education—visual arts, music, drama, dance, technology, film and television—and members of the program at the Ontario Institute for Studies in Education of the University of Toronto (OISE/UT). These contributors are our friends and colleagues, and we value their collective experiences and artful wisdom in promoting the arts as a means of learning and of contributing to our world.

Together, we hope to help teachers, as well as administrators, to design a thoughtful and effective approach to incorporating the many facets of arts education into their daily school programs. The modules that we and our colleagues have included are drawn from our own experiences as teachers and from research and continuing study. These modules are also drawn from observing and interacting with teaching associates, graduate students, and student teachers in our community who ground us in the classroom and in the joys of the possibilities of teaching inside the arts frame. The arts are all around us all the time, and we want to pull you onto our little red arts wagon and then race down the hill . . .

The Language of the Arts

In *The Arts Go to School*, we begin with a rationale for including the arts in our school lives, drawn from current research and from writers who have wisdom to share, and from curriculum documents that offer support for teaching the arts in education. We offer an overview of the arts in education and practical suggestions for implementing an arts-based approach to learning. We feature examples of how different schools have gone about designing an arts-based program. We outline various ways for building the arts into the curriculum, and know that many teachers will integrate different components of the arts disciplines so that they can create an arts environment that supports all kinds of learning.

Two mice were cowering in the mousehole when a cat approached. "Meow meow meow" they heard, then "woof woof woof," the sound of a furious dog, a spitting retreat, and thankful silence. Cautiously, the two mice crept out of the shelter and the cat pounced on them, remarking as he ate them up, "I always knew it would be useful to have a second language."

For this book, the second language is the language of the arts. We know it as a second way of thinking, another way of being in and of constructing our world.

Chapters 2 to 7 each present a brief rationale for one particular arts focus, along with model units that demonstrate a range of activities available to teachers who want to explore this mode of arts education. By focusing on each of these arts disciplines—visual arts, music, drama, dance, and media—we hope to help explore and expand the possibilities that all of the arts components offer in building a holistic program. However, even in these discrete expressions, you will find overlap and integration—the arts are a unique and unified force in children's lives.

Arts suggestions are explored alongside models of classroom experiences that we hope demonstrate how to make arts education happen for our students. The scope of the units includes examples from Grades 1 to 8, with approaches that would work for most grades. The classroom close-ups, which are integrated with the text, are augmented by a number of short features taking a wide-angle view of the arts and appearing near the end of the chapters.

In each of the chapters on arts education, you will find a chart which shows a spectrum of arts events that can be used in designing and implementing an arts curriculum. By reviewing these charts, you and your school may gain ideas for designing a school-based arts program. Which events will fit into your plans this year? How can you design a curriculum calendar that will be as rich as possible in experiences and in learning? What can you work towards implementing in the curriculum next year? Where do you need support from volunteers, from artists, from the neighboring secondary school, or from other classrooms? What resources are necessary? Which curriculum documents offer useful suggestions? What role will parents and community organizations play in your planning? Having a school-based arts program is the ideal.

The back-of-text matter provides additional theoretical and practical support. The appendices offer a framework for developing a school-based arts policy, along with a summary of research projects supporting an arts-enriched curriculum. A checklist for assessing progress in the arts appears as Appendix C. Finally, the references feature an annotated list of recommended resources to which each chapter author contributed.

And now, away we go in this book, as we share our experiences, our reflections, and our research about painting and playing and singing and dancing and role-playing and viewing with children, sometimes plugged in and sometimes covered in colored chalk. We are all inside the arts, with the children, and brightened by the virtual sunshine that illuminates an arts-enhanced world.

1 Implementing an Arts-based Curriculum

Why the Arts Matter

By David Booth

David Booth is professor emeritus at the Ontario Institute for Studies in Education of the University of Toronto. A well-known speaker on the arts in education internationally, he is the author of many books for teachers, parents and children.

The arts matter to children. We know this as parents. We know this as teachers. And we know this from our memories of our own childhood. And now we have writings by knowledgeable authorities, reports by government committees, curricula from ministries of education, and research from expert academics, that document and articulate the role and power of the arts in the lives of our children. *What we knew in our hearts was right all along.*

As caring and concerned members of our home and school communities, we want our children to grow into adulthood with arts-enhanced lives, engaging fully in the world's activities with their aesthetic, cognitive, physical, and emotional strengths—entwining these life processes as often as possible. We need to feel our thoughts, and we need to think about our feelings. Knowing that emotion is a powerful component of life's intellectual responses, we require opportunities to grow as whole beings, to fill our personal worlds with events and experiences that reveal as many shades of color as possible, that widen the possibilities inherent in everything we see and do.

Can our schools open up, even explode, the repertoire of artful choices that children could encounter each day, so that their knowledge expands, their senses grow, and their responses to life's situations become mindful and thoughtful? That is the real role of the arts in our lives—to help us construct our world in wonderful and meaningful ways, and at the same time, gain satisfaction from our expanded ways of knowing how to accomplish this lifelong process. We live holistically; everything matters. Schools need to support this vital way of becoming.

Sharing Gifts and Resources in the Arts

It would be wonderful if everyone on a school's staff were an expert in the teaching of all the arts. Most of us feel competent in some of the arts forms: perhaps we play the piano or took art lessons in college; maybe we majored in dance or drama in our undergraduate degrees; or we attended summer schools or in-service sessions devoted to arts in the classroom. But to handle each of the arts in our own classroom often leads to a sense of inadequacy or frustration. How should we address handling all of the arts in the curriculum?

As teachers, each of us brings particular gifts to the classroom program, and, as with every aspect of our professional lives, our abilities and experiences will vary. We will possess a different set of knowledge and strategies in each of the arts disciplines. The continuum of learning about the arts in education is complex, and each of us struggles to find effective ways and means of both engaging our students in arts events and helping them to acquire techniques and skills that will help them move into deeper and more affective interactions with each of the arts forms—as makers of the arts and as receivers of arts experiences.

On the other hand, what if we saw the whole school as the arts curriculum, where children experience a multiplicity of arts events throughout each year? How these would accrue over the nine years in elementary school in the growth of each child! These events could be coordinated throughout children's times in the different grades, so that they truly gain an education in the arts and through the arts. If we see this arts curriculum as school-wide and a decade long, rather than taking the bits-and-pieces approach where each of the arts disciplines is crowded into a year, each school could work towards an arts policy that would, in turn, lead towards a more comprehensive and integrated arts curriculum. Every member of the staff, the parents, the artists and the arts community could collaborate in creating a grounded, wide-ranging and interconnected arts curriculum.

By planning an arts program as a whole school or as a division, you and your colleagues can begin to create a comprehensive picture of what is happening in the arts with all the children; even more important, you can begin planning cooperatively to organize and implement a stronger, more varied, and inclusive arts curriculum. By simply listing the arts events and curriculum that the children will experience each week or month, everyone can begin to understand their own classroom dynamic. Individual teachers can hitchhike on the energy and ideas that occur from the revealing and articulating of what is happening by all of the teachers involved in the life of the school. And, of course, what could happen if we decide to expand our horizons? It may be that a small committee of teachers begins to lay out the arts plans so that others can add to and extend the list of opportunities. Some events will be special occasions with guests, performances and field trips adding power to our school program. Other events may be curriculum-based where we deliberately recognize the connections of the arts area in our planning for a unit of teaching. Still other occasions will evolve as we work on arts teams, each member adding a particular strength from individual backgrounds and talents. Each one of us will then be able to share with our students so much more than if we had struggled on alone.

Think of the resources that can be pooled—ideas, materials, themes, techniques and talents. For example, my limited teacher-knowledge of music is suddenly expanded by the shared experience of my team members. Some schools have music specialists to handle that aspect of the arts, but even then, we need to ensure that these experiences are part of the whole of the arts education that our children are receiving, and that we understand how this component fits into the larger frame of integrative and cumulative arts learning. Sometimes we can even combine or exchange classes in order to offer a specific experience that one of our colleagues wants to share.

The Life-affirming Power of the Arts

After the disaster of 9-11 in New York City, parents and schools were at a loss at what to tell children, how to frame the pain of this tragic and terrifying event for these vulnerable and shocked youngsters. What followed in New York is a metaphor for arts education, as thousands of schoolchildren turned to creating paintings and drawings and poems and stories and letters to somehow give form to their feelings, and to share in the sadness that enveloped their communities. As they engaged in arts responses, they revealed so much more than they could articulate in talk. They were able to find hope beyond the destruction. They were able to find catharsis, to seek out ways of demonstrating their compassion and anger. They were able to use art to construct a present reality and to recognize a better future. As parents and teachers and friends, we view their pictures and read their words, and recognize the depth of their feelings and the connections they have made to the human family. Their questions ring with anguish, and their observations seek out the smallest feathers of hope. It is so fulfilling to read this book, *Messages to Ground Zero*, and to stand alongside their attempts at understanding that which we can only weep over. We are better able to cope because of their artistic efforts.

At his grandmother's funeral, my son was particularly moved by a poem read aloud by his cousin, a poem his grandma had selected in preparation for this event. He asked for a copy that he would represent in calligraphy and frame for his bedroom. His grandmother had known what he and others would need to mediate their grief. Such wisdom.

At a wedding where the couple represented two cultures—Greek and Scottish—it was delightful to watch the women of Greek heritage, young and old, dancing again and again in an ever-widening circle, shoes off, participating in the folk art of the centuries. But most important, I watched the Scots women, and eventually the men, be drawn into the circle, and stiffly, to be sure, follow the steps of their mentors, until the rhythm and the energy took over and they danced, all of them.

My friends Mary and Harry drive downtown every Friday for tango lessons, to be part of a group of people who engage in a foreign art form that, as they become more adept at the steps and the movement, delights everyone involved. For the moment, they transcend the cold winter for the partnered warmth of Argentina.

Drawing has always been part of my son Jay's life. Even at 17 years old, he noticed that grandma's fridge door was empty of art, and quickly painted a goalie in full flight to affix to it. At 18, he prepared to finish his final high school year at a residential hockey school, and as he was packing for the first term, I noticed that he had included his paints. As he said: "There may be things I want to remember."

For me, the arts can resemble the paint chips we now find at the decorating store when we are ready to choose the colors of the walls in our homes: the names of the shades draw us into realms of knowing we had never even thought of, and faced with thousands of choices, we narrow our selection to those that lift or comfort our lives.
—D.B.

What Really Matters in the Arts

We all have refrigerators with kids' art on it. What do you do when your kids are grown? Why, grandchildren's art on that refrigerator! One night in our arts class at OISE/UT, the students had to bring in everything on their refrigerator doors. We could then begin our look at the arts in education with what really matters and what is most precious: art that is freed from judgment. Simply, what is there on the refrigerator door. Since my fridge has a cupboard door on it, due to some kitchen designer, that door has no magnetic quality. How to display art? I solved the problem with nails and a hammer, because you need to make a decision in life about what counts, and in my house, refrigerator art counts.

One cartoon that I like raises many questions about art. In it two Inuit are in an igloo carving a polar bear. *The one says, "What you're doing is art." The other says, "Everything we do is art."* What a complicated cartoon. But it brings out the central question of arts education: What *is* art? How do we know what children's art should look like? How do we know that we are promoting the arts with our students? How do we know what is worthwhile? Should it just be placed on the fridge—or be judged, valued, or rejected? All these questions about the arts every teacher faces each day.

Here's a pointed comment from a Peanuts cartoon: *"We've been reading poems in school, but I never understand any of them. How am I supposed to know which poems to like?"* And Charlie says, *"Somebody tells you."*

How do children ever come to grips with what they should like, if somebody is always telling them what they should like, what they should do, what they should read, what they should paint, what they should sing? Where is choice in all of this pedagogy?

In her book *Releasing the Imagination*, Maxine Greene paints a perfect picture of school life:

> *There are the worn-down, crowded urban classrooms and the contrasting, clean-lined spaces in the suburbs. There are the bulletin boards crammed with notices and instructions, here and there interlaced with children's drawings or an outspoken poem. There are graffiti, paper cutouts, uniformed figures in the city schools; official voices blaring in and around; sudden shimmers when artists visit; circles of young people writing in journals and attending to stories. There are family groups telling one another what happened the night before, describing losses and disappearances, reaching for one another's hands. Clattering corridors are like the backstreets of ancient cities, filled with folks speaking multiple languages, holding their bodies distinctively, watching out for allies and for friends. There are shouts, greetings, threats, the thump of rap music, gold chains, flowered leotards, multicolored hair.* (p. 10)

We mustn't forget what school looks like as we talk about the arts in education. We want to celebrate, be proud of school, and understand the enormous complexities of this particular village square and those streets behind. And for schools, teachers, and principals, believing in the arts in school is a complicated dream.

I don't want to be the one who tells you what the poem means. Not anymore. I want the children to tell *me* what they think about the poem and I will then engage in a dialogue with them. That is one quality that the arts possess: they open all kinds of avenues for discussion that we just can't explore any other way. A child, Juan, age six, said about the arts, "If you don't know what a wing is on a bird, and how it is made, you can draw it and then you'll know." Such a wonderful line. You don't know what something is until you try to draw it; you don't know what it is until you try to say it; you don't know what it is until you write it.

Just What Is Art?

With graduates in my arts in education class, we tried to create a list of all the arts from different reference books. We couldn't find a complete list—the arts are all over the place. Every category is on a different page. But I found a definition from *The National Endowment for the Arts*: "The Arts comprise literature, visual art and design, performing art and media arts." I think I can crowd everything into that.

But it's sometimes hard to recognize art. In the year 2004, people quilt. Why? You can buy a quilt at IKEA; you can even cover your table with one. But the quilt is about art. Every Saturday when I was seven years old, I had to help my grandmother set up the quilting frames when the women came to quilt at her house. I would leave the room as the women gathered around these huge frames. In an OISE/UT class, a teacher who came from California showed us the quilts made there; they were very different from the quilts of Toronto. The art is unique to a culture. A pioneer woman in 1850 was recorded as saying: "Quilt making, for me, is frightening. I can't believe how much that quilt knows about me." The arts live a long time.

What about advertising? How much of it is art? We watch more advertising than any other art form going. Are these workers artists, or have they sold out? Are they patrons? Did Shakespeare have a patron? What's the problem with art in advertising? There are more people involved in advertising than in any other arts field in our country. You watch, you laugh, and sometimes you buy.

That takes us to the next problem with the arts: taste. I love that word. Taste. The student who doesn't know about tables has none in table design. How could he? He hasn't begun that journey yet. What is taste? A young student told me, "Taste is what Coco Chanel gave design." I know who Coco is, because on *The Simpsons*, Marge Simpson has a dress by Chanel. Think how *The Simpsons* and their sardonic lifestyle mock the elitism of taste. Taste destroyed by Marge Simpson. When you use that word, think about this article in the *New Yorker* by John Seabrook: "There's high brow, there's low brow and there's no brow." And we have moved in our culture to "no brow" where the poor and the rich cannot be separated by what they wear. We now see the movie stars shopping at the same places where my son's friends shop. "No brow." "No brow art," where elitism disappears and connoisseurship arrives, where it's because of what we know and represent, and what we've considered and thought about, that we begin to understand what we value.

I value "now brow" culture, and so does my very favorite writer on the arts, Maxine Greene. Now in her eighties, she talks about youth:

> *The untapped diversity among North American youth. Its undefined talents and energies. Its differentiated modes of expression. Any why do we struggle to retain the familiar paradigms, and ignore or repress the need for alternative possibilities in the face of economic and demographic change? The Arts open new perspectives and identify alternatives. New connections we can make in our lives.* (pp. 17–18)

How could that woman tolerate youth so well? And believe in them. It's so easy to be a "put-down" elitist with young people who like certain art forms, from their navel rings to their music. My father wouldn't allow Elvis Presley music in our house. My son's music is allowed—I just don't listen. But my son knows more about his music than I know about mine. He possesses a deeper connoisseurship about his music than I have about mine. And he has a philosophy about the kind of music he likes. His music magazines are very complex. Very intricate. Very backgrounded. It's naive to think elitist art wins and the art enjoyed by youth loses.

The Arts Connected to Everything We Do and See

You learn art from doing it. When you pick up a brush, and dip it in the paint, a whole new set of fears enters. I was working in Ohio on a drama lesson with *The Monument* by Gary Paulsen. This Grade 4 class explored the book's issue of how to build a monument that celebrates and remembers those soldiers from a small town who died in Vietnam. This is a very tricky issue in Ohio. I watched those students sweat and work for two hours determining the kind of monument they wanted. As well, we were working with 60 teachers. (I want you to imagine 60 teachers and 30 children in a great big gym at the same time. That's how I like to work.) We needed to build a monument that would help us to remember those we had lost. The teachers, working in their groups with the children, decided that the monument should, of course, be a peace exhibit. The children, being wonderful Grade 4 students, came to me and said, "We're going to build a statue of peace."

Working in role as mayor, I told them: "Go back to those teachers and ask them why they don't want to celebrate my son as a soldier who fought in that war, and ask them why they think my son isn't worthy of a monument."

The children went back to the adults: "I don't think the mayor likes the idea of peace." It was a thrilling two hours. The adults shouted: "Go back and tell the mayor peace is what we believe in."

And back they would come and hear: "This is the last picture of my son when he left. He was wearing this uniform, his battle fatigues, his rifle, his kit, his helmet. I want to see it. I'm paying for it and I want to see it."

Now the kids were becoming passionate: "You see, he believes in his son. He wants . . . " The energy level in the room was rising and rising. The teachers were getting more determined. Two wonderful girls, wearing their confirmation dresses because they heard there would be a guest in the morning, came in and said, "We've decided that maybe we should make a compromise."

"I see. Just what kind of compromise will celebrate my son?"

This nine-year old said, "You're forgetting, sir, there were nurses killed too. And ambulance drivers. There were other people who were in that war, besides your son. We want to honor all of them."

"How will you go about it?" And this class in Ohio decided to build a garden.

"We will go to the garden and we will dream of the children we no longer have and somehow they will visit us every time we're in the garden." By now, of course, the teachers were quiet, staring at the Grade 4's.

After I had returned to Toronto, the teacher mailed me pictures of her class touring all the monuments they could find in Columbus, Ohio. The teacher's name is Donna. Don't you want to know her? She understands what we mean by the school arts, connecting them to everything we do and see.

We need to give children nothing but our best. Every single time we work with young people we will struggle to learn what "best" means. We will come to understand personal best within an art form. Teachers often say to me, "I can't teach music, or the visual arts, or drama and I can't dance. What am I going to do?" I can only reply, "What do you *like* to do? Start with that arts form."

If each of us had chosen our art form every year, by the end of nine years of elementary school, our children would have had experience with nine art forms! But there's hope for those who feel their gifts in the arts are limited. Some of us

I've learned that people will forget what you said, people will forget what you did, but people will never forget how you made them feel.
—*Maya Angelou*

can't sing like others; but some of us can *teach* singing like those of us who can sing can't. That's what's special about the arts. What changed my life was teaching a graduate course called "Arts Education." I thought it would all be about drama, for that is my world. The teachers in the course said: "Don't just talk about drama, talk about music, visual arts, movement, media." The graduate teachers changed me. I worry about schools in which some students won't have arts experiences, but I'm not worried for the whole world, because there will always be arts.

The arts are an imperative. In the concentration camps in the Second World War, the children drew and wrote poems. In the book *I Never Saw Another Butterfly*, you can actually read the poems and find the drawings of the children. Once in a class of one man and 29 women, the man said to me: "David, I'm having trouble coping with schools. I can't find the reason to go on and I can't find the joy. Because it's tough right now." I remembered this book and I shared it with him and through his tears he said, "I have to keep reading these books, I have to keep hearing the songs, I have to keep seeing the drawings and then I'll be all right."

The arts demand engagement. To begin with, you *mix* the paint, *play* the CD, *watch* the film, *wear* the mask, *join* the circle, *sing* the song. And then, the experience begins to pull you inside, either as participant or as audience, and often, as both. Even children who have entered the room determined not to become involved find themselves pulled into the activity physically, cognitively, and emotionally caught in the arts' net; struggling readers who feel they will never read, laugh and chant alongside their teacher as they "catch a rogue elephant deep in a jungle"; students with no music background create complex rhythms with the instruments from the music box. And as for attention-span problems, I have witnessed youngsters begging their teacher to let them miss the school bus so that they can continue their mural.

What if we thought of the arts as significant ways in which we make meanings, special kinds of meanings that involve the emotions, the affective component of thoughtful engagement? And sometimes, the meaning is conveyed and understood without words—with images or sounds. Since arts experiences offer other modes and ways of experiencing and learning, children will have opportunities to think and feel as they explore, problem solve, express, interpret, and evaluate the process and the results. To watch a child completely engaged in an arts experience is to recognize that the brain is on, driven by the aesthetic and emotional imperative to make meaning, to say something, to represent what matters.

The doors flew open one June day to a school transformed into a living Arts curriculum. More importantly, through the Arts Festival, the doors were also flung open to untold possibilities for improved student learning through the Arts.
—Kathy Fraumeni

Maxine Greene says, "We who are teachers would have to accommodate ourselves to lives as clerks or functionaries if we did not have in mind a quest for a better state of things for those we teach and for the world we share." That's why we teach. The eternal hope.

The Theory of Multiple Intelligences
—Shosh Brenner

My fascination with Howard Gardner's Theory of Multiple Intelligences started when I was a teacher candidate in the consecutive program at York University in 1995. By that time I already had over ten years of teaching experience in the parochial system and aspired to be certified and recognized in the public education system in the province of Ontario.

The introduction to the theory commenced with a self-inventory to determine our own dominant intelligence. I was not surprised to discover that my interpersonal intelligence was the most prevalent, but I was also happy to affirm that in my learning capacities I have a combination of other intelligences as well. Overall, my cognitive profile was dominantly a combination of the interpersonal, the intrapersonal, the linguistic and the mathematical intelligences. Four out of then seven intelligences were my strengths. I learned in that year that I needed to develop the other three: the bodily/kinesthetic, the visual/spatial and the musical/rhythmic intelligences. I was thrilled to discover that even though the latter three were not my dominant capacities, I could develop them as I further delved into the theory.

Frames of Mind by Howard Gardner (1983) posits seven intelligences, often referred to as the seven ways of knowing, that ultimately yield a cognitive profile for each individual. The quotient of any single intelligence in each person varies from one individual to another; therefore, the combination of all the intelligences differs from one person to the next. In a paper presented at the American Educational Research Association in Chicago, Illinois, on April 21, 2003, entitled "Multiple Intelligences after Twenty Years," Howard Gardner asserted that "not even identical twins possess exactly the same profile of intelligences." This fact makes every human being cognitively unique and different from one another in ways of teaching and learning.

Given that Howard Gardner is a psychologist, his book was intended initially for psychologists and humanists, but it was so well received by educators that many schools and districts in North America applied the theory in their classrooms following Key school in Indianapolis.

In 1994/1995 Howard Gardner found "ample evidence for a naturalist intelligence; and suggestive evidence as well for a possible existential intelligence—the intelligence of big questions . . . So far, I am sticking to my 8 intelligences but I can readily foresee a time when the list could grow, or when the boundaries among the intelligences might be reconfigured" (2003). There have been many suggestions for new intelligences such as the culinary, the technologist, the emotional, the spiritual, and many more, but they have not been approved by Howard Gardner.

It is important to note that in *Frames of Mind* Howard Gardner is interchanging the word "intelligences" with *faculties, capacities, competences, talents, abilities, realms, domains, propensities* and *endowments*, yet by 2003, Gardner considered the interchange of "intelligences" by some practitioners with "learning styles" a "misinterpretation" or a "confusion." I will revisit this misinterpretation later on in my summary.

Frames of Mind stems from a Dutch van Leer Foundation project titled Project on Human Potential. Howard Gardner was a member of the steering committee researching "the development of symbolic skills in normal and gifted children and the impairment of such skills in brain-damaged adults" (1983). Perhaps as a psychologist the term *normal* is permissible but as an educator, to be politically correct, I would use the term *average* instead.

Planning Units around the Intelligences

During my practicum, I was lucky to be placed in a Grade 2 classroom, where the host teacher was very supportive of planning units around the intelligences. I had

---

The Original Multiple Intelligences:
• Verbal/Linguistic
• Logical/Mathematical
• Visual/Spatial
• Bodily/Kinesthetic
• Musical/Rhythmic
• Interpersonal
• Intrapersonal

Howard Gardner's interest in the arts and the absence of it in academic psychology prompted him to be a founding member of Harvard's Project Zero and to serve as co-director from 1972 to 2000. The internationally renowned research group was founded by philosopher Nelson Goodman, whose intention was to improve education in the arts. "Goodman believed that arts learning should be studied as a serious cognitive activity, but that *zero* had been firmly established about the field; hence the project was given its name." (http://pzweb/Harvard.edu/History/History.htm)

Project Zero has offered teachers models of the use of multiple intelligences inside arts experiences for youngsters.

to plan the Structures unit in Science. Every activity centre was directly related to one intelligence. The unit was introduced over two weeks and allowed for independent rotation as soon as the performing tasks in the selected centre were completed. Students were allowed to prioritize their choices as long as they participated in all the centres. It was interesting to observe that students tend to prioritize their choices based on their strengths. Those who were highly spatial or kinesthetic preferred building a structure first. The students with linguistic dominant competence preferred to read facts about a structure and answer questions. The musical ones went to a listening centre to listen to songs about structures and the mathematical had to identify patterns in structural pictures. These are just some highlights of the multiple intelligences approach which took place during my practicum. It is helpful to know that not every centre can be based on one intelligence only. Many times resources force you to integrate intelligences. In music it would be challenging to separate the language from the rhythm and that is a positive instance. I recommend integrating two capacities at the most.

Whether we plan for Kindergarteners or for higher grades, whether in a centred approach or an individualized approach, it is essential to begin with the strengths of the student. We have to "hook" them and motivate them as educators. Usually the "hook" is done with greater ease through the arts. We can plan a unit in any discipline, bearing in mind to incorporate and embed performance tasks that accommodate all the formal eight competences in order to include all intellectual profiles.

As educators we all implement some elements of the Theory of Multiple Intelligences in one respect or another, but the significance of this approach is that it provides us with a planning tool for any curriculum development. This theoretical framework helps us meet the needs of every student in the classroom. It guides and facilitates us to further differentiate instruction and enhance the inclusionary perspective, culminating in high-quality education and improved levels of student achievement.

Picture Books: Images of Art
— Meguido Zola

What do some of our children's earliest and most important teachers—their first books—have to say to them about the arts, the artist, the artistic vision? Arnold Lobel's mythic *The Great Blueness* tells how art—writ large—first came into the world. Long ago, there were no colors: "almost everything was grey, and what was not grey was black or white"—until one day a bored wizard concocts something new and strange.

> "What is it?" asked the neighbors.
> "A color," said the wizard. "I call it blue."
> "Please," cried the neighbors, "please give us some."
> And that was how the Great Blueness came to be. After a short time everything in the world was blue.

But while this change yields momentary satisfaction, the people of the world soon yearn for change. The wizard replaces blue with a new color . . . and then another . . . and another. But the inhabitants of the world become only more frustrated and angry as one color only takes the place of the one before. In desperation, the wizard mixes the colors together, thus creating new colors:

It was a terrible mess. But when the wizard saw what was happening, he exclaimed, "That is the answer!"

The people now take all the colors and, most important, learn to keep and use all of them, finding "good places for each one."

Leo Lionni captures this notion in his classic *Frederick*, which tells how the field mice gather corn and nuts, and wheat and berries—all except Frederick, who does not work, appearing, instead, to dream the summer away. But, unlike the idle cricket whom the industrious ant sent away to starve, Frederick saves his friends from the long, cold winter, proving he had indeed done his share of work by gathering images and words, warmth and color—and now sharing from this supply as he spins his stories and poems:

When Frederick had finished, they all applauded. "But, Frederick," they said, "you are a poet!"
Frederick blushed, took a bow, and said shyly, "I know it."

....

An Arts-focused School: Queen Victoria

Milica O'Brien, Pria Muzamdar, and Denise Ng head the Arts committee at Queen Victoria Public School. In the following interview, they provide an overview of the arts-based initiatives at this Toronto school.

How is Queen Victoria an arts-focused school?
At Queen Victoria, we use the building blocks of the arts to help create meaningful events for our students as they learn within a variety of curricular areas. We have established an Arts committee of ten teachers that help promote arts learning throughout the school in a number of ways. Over the years, we have brought a variety of arts experiences to the students and made it accessible to all learners.

What do you think contributes to the success of Queen Victoria as an arts-focused school?
A majority of the staff lead arts-focused lives. We have teachers who participate in dance, choir, acting or visual arts activities in their own lives. Some teachers on staff have been instructors on educational arts courses. Because of this passion, there is a willingness to work with artists in the classroom, a commitment to expose the students to a range of performing arts events, inside and outside the school, and a recognition that the arts need to be woven into the curriculum throughout the week. Not only do teachers make time for the arts in their program, but they also take time to learn more about arts practice through professional development in the school, through board and university courses.

What are some of your goals in providing the arts as a framework for learning?

- The arts initiative gives the school a focus. Having a common goal provides a sense of community among staff members, administrators and the school community.
- The arts help build partnerships. Not only are partnerships built among teachers, but we are able to connect to artists and the arts community in meaningful ways. Another strong partnership is with families. The children are our best ambassadors for arts-based learning and families come to appreciate artistic product and recognize the cognitive, physical, emotional and social learning that can evolve through the arts.
- Queen Victoria is a school of great diversity. The arts can provide a meaningful thread to connect students with stories, songs, designs, expressions and identities from a range of cultures.
- As a staff, we have an opportunity to examine curriculum expectations in meaningful ways. Through the arts we also consider carefully the importance—and challenges—of integrating our programs.
- Through professional development and exposure to artists in the school, teachers increase their comfort level in infusing the arts in their program.
- The arts provide a vehicle for connection with ESL and Special Education students, strengthening their abilities to communicate and make meaning.

This experience connects to the thoughts in Chapter 7, where we celebrate the partnerships between artists and schools.

What advice might you give to schools interested in developing an arts-based focus?
It takes a passion and belief that the arts can make a difference. The arts should not be product-driven, but should promote a balance between process and product. The recognition of arts learning does not come quickly for a school-wide focus. It takes time to see tangible results, but the more you organize arts programming, the more you become committed to it, the more your arts programs will evolve. A positive attitude among the staff community needs to be in place. Also, schools need staff with a knowledge of the arts who consistently implement music, dance, visual arts and drama in their program, recognizing that all strands of the arts curriculum are significant.

Along with the staff commitment, our school administration is supportive of the arts, through commitment to funding and programming concerns. Administration needs to be understanding of the value of learning through the arts, recognizing that the arts reveal significant learning evidenced in the sharing.

What have some challenges been in developing a commitment to the arts?
Time is always a factor. With the current demands of teaching today, teachers need to set priorities about the content and methodologies they would like to introduce, and offer a meaningful balance to implementing the range of curriculum expectations. Though integration of the arts is encouraged, it is sometimes challenging to integrate the arts into an already-packed curriculum. It is challenging, too, for an Arts committee to find time to plan a variety of performing artists and artists in resident opportunities for a Kindergarten to Grade 6 school of more than 1,000 children. Sometimes, it is challenging to convince families that time given to the arts matters. Educational research supports success through arts-based learning, but some parents feel that more time needs to be devoted to language and mathematical programming rather than the arts.

How do you know the arts have produced meaningful learning for the students at Queen Victoria?

We hear it straight from the students themselves! All students can and do participate as audience members for music, dance, storytelling, and theatre performances. They enthusiastically take part in activities that allow them to create and explore ideas. Because the arts can support social growth, we see significant improvement in student behavior. We have an extensive ESL population in the school and each of the arts can provide a medium for success. Students can respond to a piece of music, create a painting, work in role with others in a drama. Our literacy scores and math scores have improved as a result of children expressing themselves, taking risks and experiencing a range of events that address the range of multiple intelligences.

If we see arts events as activities that engage children in making, viewing, or reflecting on experiences focusing on the various forms of arts in education, can you provide an overview of the arts events at Queen Victoria?

Act One: Performing Arts: We provide visits from dance, theatre, mask, puppet, music, or storytelling performing companies. For purposes of organization, we provide two performances each for the Kindergarten/Grade 1, Grade 2/Grade 3, and the junior divisions. An accompanying teacher's guide is always offered to each classroom teacher for exploration before and after a presentation.

Act Two: Visiting Artists: We have booked ten artists to visit Queen Victoria this year. Each artist is hosted by one member of the Arts committee. This teacher mentors other staff members through the process involving the artist in the classroom. It is important to have materials readily available and perhaps arrange the classroom to accommodate an artist visit, organize introductory and extension activities and facilitate a display of students' work.

Act Three: Arts Proposals from Teachers: Classroom teachers are encouraged to write proposals to the Arts committee. They can request up to $100 for specialized materials to complete larger projects such as a quilt or canvas mural.

Act Four: Arts Proposals from Artists: We are often approached by artists to work in our school. These proposals are filtered through the Arts committee in order to obtain a balance of experiences in the classroom.

Act Five: Student Workshops: It is one of our goals to provide opportunities for performing artists (e.g., puppeteers, mime artists) to return to the school to provide workshops for classes who have seen their presentations.

Act Six: Professional Development
- Classroom teachers who are involved with a visiting artist learn new skills that can be infused in future programming.
- We have organized a book club for interested staff who meet once a month. In preparation, teachers read an assigned chapter.
- We offer a variety of workshops to support teacher practice. For example, Dan Yashinsky (storyteller), Kathy Lundy (drama consultant), and Cathy Clarke (artist) have presented sessions to the staff.
- Members of the Arts committee serve as mentors to new staff at the school.

2 Finding Yourself in the Painting

Visual Arts in Education

By Masayuki Hachiya

Masayuki Hachiya is an educator completing his Ph.D. in the Department of Curriculum, Teaching and Learning, at the Ontario Institute for Studies in Education of the University of Toronto. He is currently working on research about teacher interaction with students engaged in art-making.

Introducing elementary school students to a variety of art activities helps to broaden and represent their experiences in life. Art classes can motivate students to expand their worlds of imagination and give form and shape to their ideas and feelings.

The value of visual arts in education is now widely understood. Art educators and educational organizations have contributed to raising the public awareness of its power for child development. This chapter offers ideas and suggestions that will help to support and strengthen your art teaching, to help create new artistic paths for students to follow, and to illuminate their learning through a variety of art experiences. It aims to introduce various types of art activities in the context of elementary school classroom practices.

Art can reflect human needs and it plays an integral part in everyone's life. You can guide students in expressing and making sense of many things in the world through art experiences. The excitement of creating something new and original with the imagination can lead students into new ways of learning and give them a stronger sense of self.

A Dual Focus: Art-making and Art-viewing

Your art classes can involve both art-making and art-viewing. From representing visual images drawn from feelings and thoughts in painting, to viewing artwork and studying art history, your art program can provide different types of experiences, balancing a variety of art activities, such as drawing, painting, modelling, printmaking, design, and crafts, and incorporating a number of domains (e.g., advertising, architecture, folk art, functional art, fine art, popular art, primitive art, and religious art). The key to art-viewing activities is not to have students memorize images and information, but to help them ask meaningful questions about artists and their work by using prints, posters, and photographs available at local museums, bookstores and libraries and on the Internet. Students will be interested in learning details about artists' lives and descriptions of their works. For example, when you bring your students to museums and galleries, you can prepare a folder for students that contains prompts relating to the exhibit, as well as blank paper and pencils for sketches, so that the experiences of art-making and art-viewing can happen together.

Teachers can offer students opportunities to participate in exciting, innovative activities. Try not to rush them in the class; allow them enough time to finish their artwork while they are learning to develop new ideas and work with new materials. Students will soon learn to share with others their individual perspectives and experiences. Your teaching can also connect the subject matter of your art lessons to events taking place in the curriculum.

An Overview of Teaching Art

1. *Learning Objectives for Each Art Class*

It is necessary to set learning objectives for each art class so that you can plan the content of the class most effectively. This is the same process we might consider in other curriculum areas. But in art, the end product often becomes the objective (e.g., making a card for Mother's Day). When setting up the learning objectives for art classes, think about more than what your students will make; consider what they will learn from the artwork. Art should be more than a leisure activity designated for Friday afternoons.

Be sure to consider the purpose for each art lesson. Art is not always about spontaneous expression. "Do whatever you want" seldom works, especially as children grow older. You need to set learning themes, objectives, and goals. Overemphasis on traditional holiday motifs in art classes may discourage students' creativity. There is nothing wrong with making a pretty picture, having a relaxing time, or making a greeting card, but probably that is not what the larger meaning of art should be.

For developing learning objectives, it may be helpful to think about the elements and principles of art. The language of visual arts has its own meaning system, and the symbols of this language are the elements of art—*line, shape, color, value, space, form,* and *texture.* These elements are the visual building box that the artist puts together to create a work of art. No matter what materials are used, an artwork will contain these visual elements. In art, the rules for organizing the elements of art are called the principles of art. These include *rhythm, balance, proportion, emphasis, variety, harmony,* and *unity.* When students learn to manipulate certain elements and understand the principles of art, they will gradually create artwork that expresses more complex, sophisticated thoughts.

While art lessons include a wide variety of activities, you need to plan a sequential arrangement of activities that provide continuity along with student ongoing development, appropriate for the age level of the student. In *Educating Artistic Vision,* Elliot Eisner (1997) cautions, "the curriculum that is provided to students or developed by them in art should not be a random array of novel explorations that simply lead to superficial dilettantism" (p. 161). During the elementary school years, the students' growth is in a state of flux as they undergo enormous physical, social, and emotional changes. Some of these changes may reveal themselves in specific areas of art, such as drawing, painting, sculpting, and other art activities, and also in the selections and manipulations of materials they select.

It is often observed that in early childhood, children may draw random circles or scribbles, followed by making pictures and designs and symbols. In the middle years of elementary school, students may be interested in making their artwork realistic, easily recognized by others. Gradually, they will begin to develop their ideas for representing an image that is more abstract, something more elaborate.

While teaching art, be sure to match your objectives with what's appropriate for the ages of your students. Doing this includes developing your own teaching techniques to help broaden their focus in art, allowing for gender differences and social, cultural, and ethnic diversity. It is important to respect and uphold certain behaviors, attitudes, expectations and values of culture, society, and tradition without sacrificing distinct concepts of individuality in the process of artwork. You need to recognize various approaches in learning styles and individual differences in students' artwork.

Here are some questions to consider for each art experience:

- What do you want students to learn from particular art activities?
- What aspects of art have students already learned?
- How can this learning be used to enhance the next series of art activities?
- How can students' abilities and knowledge acquired during an art lesson continue to develop?

Alternatively, you may be interested in integrating art with other subjects, instead of teaching it as a separate subject. This integrative method of instruction breaks down the subject barriers and empowers educators to use the influential role of art in a multidisciplinary approach. But, you should also note that focused art activities can provide special experiences and skills for student growth. Art is not just a tool, but a subject worthy of study, possessing unique opportunities for different ways of learning.

2. Working with Art Materials and Tools

Materials and tools are key to art classes. There are two important things to remember: understanding the limitations and exploring the possibilities of materials.

Students should explore the features of the different materials and tools useful in visual arts. For example, when a student is making a diorama and gluing stones, he could consider using a glue gun instead of a glue stick. When a student is painting a huge area and using a thin brush, she could be advised to consider a thicker brush.

Different materials can stimulate the students' imaginations. Exploring a different means of expression using a particular material or a combination of materials brings out students' problem-solving skills. Students can manipulate materials, then they can realize an idea by cutting, reshaping or adding, combining other materials, then turning the work into something different. This is a vital aspect of creativity. For example, how can a student turn a wooden board, spring coils, beads, sticks, and Styrofoam balls into an axle of a car? The process of selecting and manipulating materials is important for any artist. For young people, this process is particularly significant since they need opportunities to experiment and to discover the possibilities offered by these materials.

Having a resource table for displaying art materials would be useful. You will want to provide many different types of materials with sufficient quantities on the table which students can access during their artwork time. Arrange materials attractively, and invite students to use them: "Choose another interesting thing from the serving table," or "There are a number of very interesting and colorful materials you can use." Making suggestions is difficult in art because you do not wish to inhibit students' creativity and free expression, but you can add the phrases "... if you want," or "... but, you don't have to." Let students make their own decisions.

Sometimes, you may need to choose and control appropriate types of materials used for certain project goals. Often, you can make the lesson successful by

Imagination is fed by perception and perception by sensibility and sensibility by artistic cultivation. With refined sensibility, the scope of perception is enlarged. With enlarged perception, the resources that feed our imaginative life are increased.
—Elliot Eisner

intentionally limiting materials, so that students can focus on the central theme of the lesson. Elliot Eisner addresses this matter:

> *It is significant, I believe, that the practice of providing a limited palette to children when they are first learning to paint has not been common in the classroom. Indeed, many teachers go to the other extreme: the child has available to him a wider range of color than he can cope with adequately. This range of color has apparently been provided in the name of free expression and is considered a vehicle for maximizing the child's creative freedom. When such a range of color is combined with the use of large, nonresilient brushes and an upright easel, on which is tacked a sheet of thin newsprint, one can only wonder how much freedom is in fact provided in such a context.* (p. 160)

3. Translating Visual Language into Words

Teaching art can be an extraordinarily rich, collaborative experience, a continuous process of two-way communication to expand student experiences. By working together with them, you will be able to recognize each student's talent, and conduct a conversation that encourages the growth of visual awareness and skills. Through the creation of artwork, students can develop aesthetic understanding, coordination, concentration and self-confidence. A teacher is responsible for supporting students' creative processes by providing constant feedback to help develop their artwork. Of course, while unpredictable outcomes happen during the creative process, you can see these as valuable insights for learning, as they represent the unique nature of the process of art.

Assessing students' artwork requires communication between teachers and students. It is important to observe the student and consider the process he or she is using as the artwork unfolds. Try to understand each child's potential, as you do not expect the same product from all students.

As you observe students at work from the beginning of a project and, of course, throughout the school year, be sure to assess how much effort students put into their artwork. You can also look at the content of the art, commenting on certain interesting elements and principles demonstrated and by so doing, translate a visual language into words. You may also want to look at how diligently they have tried to respond to the use of materials, skills and information you have suggested and demonstrated.

Several classroom close-ups and related activities are outlined in the following section.

Painting and Sketching

Throughout the world, throughout time, artists have observed the world around them, representing and interpreting the world in a range of drawing and paint media. When young artists are given the opportunities to closely observe a tree, a plant, a flower, a piece of fruit and create a visual image of that item, they come to understand how art can provide opportunities to express and communicate their response to nature using pencil, pen, crayon, chalk, pastel marker or paint.

Students can be given opportunities to go outside the classroom, to focus their attention on a specific item and create a series of drawings of the object. Some students might be frustrated by their inability to draw accurately, but they can be

Participatory involvement with the many forms of art does enable us, at the very least, to *see* more in our experience, to *hear* more on normally unheard frequencies, to *become conscious* of what daily routines, habits, and conventions have obscured.
—Maxine Greene

assured that their representations are personal and valid. These studies can be used as a resource for creating a prepared, polished work of art. Alternatively, students might be given a palette with single color of paint to spontaneously create a painting of what they see. To help students explore different ways to "paint a tree," they can use different media, use real or fantasy colors, create the image in different sizes, work quickly to capture the image, work slowly to inspect details, pay attention to a part of the object, or interpret the image from memory. Young artists also should be encouraged to examine a tree from different points of view—up close, far away or from a different angle.

A Magical Tree Grows

Jen's Grade 3 lesson coincided with science classes during which the students were being taught the wonders of plant life. While looking through the window, she brought the students' attention to the trees outside. Some were shedding their leaves on the ground. She then took the students outside and had them touch and make rubbings of the trunks of different trees. The emphasis was on noticing the differences of texture, color and form. They then sat on the ground and began making pencil sketches of a tree. Sketching was a warm-up activity, enabling each student to concentrate on a "real" tree.

Observing Images: Later, back inside the classroom, Jen held up several picture books, by both photographers and painters, showing different types of trees. The students observed the unique tree shapes with their branches and leaves. When she showed a picture of trees depicted in the autumn, a student exclaimed, "Those trees are like fire!" They noticed that trunks, branches and leaves are rarely brown and green, but rather a multitude of colors. The teacher also showed a picture of a leaf. "Doesn't the design look like the outline of the shape of the tree?" She questioned them about different types of trees and leaves, identifying the uniqueness of trees and the relationship between the overall shape of each tree and its leaves.

Painting from the Ground Up: Jen's next step continued to arouse the students' curiosity. She held up a thick brush and a large piece of paper on a painting board. There was no artist's palette. On the painting table, there were a few yogurt cups filled with liquid tempera—white, red, yellow and blue, but no brown and no green—and a can of water. She sat down on the floor and encouraged them to mix colors to create all the colors of the rainbow. She then used a deep blue/gray and painted a small spot on a piece of white paper and said, "This is the seed of my tree that will be planted inside the soil." She made a line to symbolize the ground. "It will gradually sprout, then grow into a thin young tree, then finally grow into a tall mature tree with branches, buds and leaves."

As Jen continued her brush strokes, always starting from the base of the tree, she added some thin branches to the right and left of the trunk and then some smaller branches coming out of them. The small tree in the picture gradually began to grow, as she extended its height and showed the spreading of its branches. The students were fascinated as they watched the tiny tree grow taller and wider. She asked about the color of the background for the tree picture. One student mentioned a blue background. Jen didn't apply the blue color directly, but mixed different colors together into a muted shade of blue. Another student then interrupted with a request for an orange sunset, while the other asked for some magical background scenery.

The students were eager to begin their own trees. Unlike their sketches, their paintings required paying attention to the way a tree grows. The background was a place for enjoying the mixing of magical colors, while some represented the sky with clouds or a sun. The whole point of this lesson was to avoid using brown and green, the colors students always associate with trees, but to expand their experience and their observation skills. This empowered them to try different color combinations. Of course, it was fine if they mixed green and brown on their own, but she encouraged them to use other colors. Jen mentioned at one point: "Look at your paintings! You're color scientists!"

Making Self-portraits

Portraits are representations of people but this form of art depicts more than what a person looks like. Using visual images, an artist can interpret and communicate the identity of a person that they see from day to day, or may have never met at all (e.g., celebrities, historical figures, fictional characters). An artist can choose to draw or paint the subject's facial expression, posture and gesture, clothing, background environment, accessories and so on. Portraiture allows students to look closely. It is important to start at the head and observe all features. By looking through a tube or a frame, students can inspect the shape of eyes, ears, lips, cheeks and other features. By experimenting with portrait-making in a variety of media, such as chalk pastel, oil pastel, liquid tempera, construction paper, montage, and collage, students can discover ways of communicating ideas through color, shape, symbol and expression. Many students might be intimidated about not being able to represent a person accurately in their artwork. Projects that allow students to take an open-ended approach through color, materials, representation and exaggeration help them to create portraits that may convey new meaning about the individuals featured.

Studying the image of the self provides an excellent approach to the topic of identity. Who am I? What do I look like? What is similar and different about me in relation to my family or peers? (eyes, hair color, size, and gender). Painting self-portraits with the use of a mirror is a useful exercise, an experience in self-expression that can help students learn proportions as well. A new way to create self-portraits is to choose a household object and make a drawing or painting of the object as a self-portrait.

Many famous artists have left their legacy by painting their own portraits, making these an important subject in the world of art.

Self-portraits in Different Media

The fourth-grade students were seated in a corner of Paola's art room. After her usual cheerful discussion with them, she began her art class. "The first thing you are going to do is to sketch the way you think you look, without looking in a mirror." Learning to make a self-portrait arouses students' curiosity about their own faces. A good theme with which to develop artistic expression, it is one of the most popular themes taught in elementary school art classes. Paola brought the students' attention to some facial features by pointing out the eyes, lids,

Materials used: Liquid tempera (white, red, yellow, blue), brushes, paper, painting boards, pencils, water cans, sponge

The Impressionist painter Paul Cézanne indeed astonished Paris with his apples as he sought to see them with new eyes. He played with form and content, and enticed the eye of the viewer to look again. Cézanne painted what he saw in a way he saw it. He painted slowly. In the end, he shared his interpretive reality with the viewer by means of carefully painted canvasses, and often featured apples as part of the setting under re-view. Apples in comparison with other fruit are more varied in kind and they do not spoil quickly. Both are attributes that served Cézanne's artistic purpose well. For him, painting was slow, intensive, and prolonged work. As he followed the contours of each object with his brushstrokes, Cézanne searched meticulously to find just the "right" color. Each still-life apple canvas holds a multi-perspectival view that conveys to the viewer the same apples looked at from different angles. They are flooded with different light. These paintings seem to penetrate the innermost structure of things, only to reconstruct them using geometric shapes by juxtaposing, and by superimposing planes to express depth. Apples as phenomenon. With a revolutionary spirit, Cézanne abandoned the convention of the single vantage point and sought to present reality from different angles, a discovery that would later lead to Cubism. Drawing and color became inseparable.
—*Christine van Halen-Faber*

lashes, eyebrows, then she asked the students to touch some of their own features, the nose, mouth, teeth, ears, hair, neck and shoulders, before they began to sketch with a piece of charcoal.

Good art instruction helps to form a solid foundation in eliciting imagination, as well as building up and improving students' skills and knowledge. Students will enjoy a fulfilling experience as they are being introduced to a fascinating world of discovery.
—M.H.

Sketching: After ten minutes passed, the students had almost completed their rough sketches. Paola began to explain an important rule for drawing heads and faces, the rule of proportion: how to use specific measurements to balance the facial features properly. She used a ruler in front of her face to show that the eyes are in the middle of the oval and that the nose ends in the space between eyes and the chin, and so on. When the students were convinced that it was correct, she drew an oval shape and proceeded to mark the features on it. The students tried to measure their heads with their own fingers to find the correct place for the middle line, also measuring the distance between each eye on each side of the face line. Paola continued drawing the pupils inside the eyes, explaining the structure of the eyeball, then she added the eyelids.

Then, the students went to do their own self-portraits. This time, they each had a mirror in front of them and were encouraged to look at themselves and check their facial measurements with a small ruler. They were also shown how to sketch the neck and shoulders, measuring the distance from the end of the shoulder, and up to the neck and head. They kept looking in the mirror as they continued.

At the conclusion of the lesson, the students compared the progress they had made between the first and second self-portraits by discussing how much their portraits had improved. Paola recognized the fact that the students were at a critical stage in their cognitive development, a time when they need more direction and have the confidence to create more realistic artwork. This experience helped to build up their self-esteem and allay their fear of failure.

Painting with Liquid Tempera: One week after her first self-portrait lesson, Paola began the second. As in the first lesson, the students were reminded to consider the importance of proper proportion. After drawing a quick pencil sketch of a face, she had them look at each other, and had them notice the way shadows fall on a face to give it a three-dimensional quality.

Paola demonstrated how different shades of pink can be achieved by blending them in different ways. She didn't paint the whole area of the face with the same color because she intended to put interesting shadows on the face using soft brush strokes. She used more red to make the dark or shaded areas of the skin, while yellow or white was used for brighter parts. Then, the students went to work while encouraged to keep looking at themselves in the mirror.

The result was quite different from that of a real face. Paola didn't have the students try to make realistic representations. Changing colors allowed them to focus on dimensions, planes, and the uneven texture of the skin of the face. It was more important than trying to achieve the exact color of the facial features.

Sculpting out of Clay: Another week later, Paola gave the class a third self-portrait lesson. She mentioned that clay was one of the best media for exploring shape and form. First, she showed the students several examples of sculpted heads. Then, she told them to feel every part of their own faces and feel what protruded and what went in. As she sat with a wooden board on her knees, Paola began to demonstrate the shape of a head. She made sure that the students looked at each other's head and observed the shape three dimensionally, especially the thickness between the forehead and the back of the head. The students then went off to work on their own heads, always exhorted to strive for proper proportions by looking at each other's heads.

Before the lesson ended, Paola summed up all the work done during the previous three lessons, including making proper measurements, mixing colors to obtain tints and shades of various colors, and determining proportions for the 3-D structure and the round volume of the head. Her comments to the students seemed to inspire and encourage them to do their best. Paola remarked: "Students at this stage need some external stimulus to help them see. I hope I do that for them!'"

Materials used: Paper, charcoals, painting boards, mirrors, sticks, liquid tempera (red, yellow, white), brushes, water cans, sponges, pencils, erasers, clay

Creating a Puppet

Students enjoy making puppets that can be made to move by their own hidden hands. Puppet-making is a stimulating activity that can focus on the human shape. It links various forms of artwork, including designing, painting, modelling, and sewing, while at the same time students are learning to use different interesting types of materials.

Making puppets can be woven into thematic units explored in the classroom, story retellings, or scripted scenes as sources. The goal of making a puppet is to bring it to life. Many children can hide their identity behind a puppet and become someone or something else for a period of time. Paper bag, stick and sock or glove puppets are the simplest to construct. Puppet heads and hands can be built from clay, Plasticine, papier-mâché, or Styrofoam balls. Tongue depressors and popsicle sticks can be used and decorated as the puppet itself.

A small rectangular piece of scrap wood that has been sanded, a foam cup, a tin can, or a wooden spoon can be fashioned into a puppet. Features can be added with paints, crayons, markers, and even small wood scraps or trims. Students can also be challenged to make life-size puppets using large sheets of paper or cardboard to convey their own physical self or a story character they have read about. A classroom close-up describing the making of puppets out of papier-mâché is shared below.

From Newspaper Strips to Ribbons and Beads

Working with Papier-mâché: Jim showed his Grade 5 students a container filled with papier-mâché that he had prepared before the class had started. Jim had prepared the material by cutting several pages of newspapers into small pieces, mixing them with water in an electric blender, removing some excess water, then adding glue to the mixture. With both his hands he formed a round bumpy object out of papier-mâché and showed it to the students. This would soon be a head. The inquisitive students watched as he began to make the round form of a head, by adding small pieces of paper and applying them smoothly all over it.

Jim continued by forming the upper part of the puppet body, attaching the head to the neck, made from a toilet-paper tube. Then, he put his fingers in the tube and tilted it to make the puppet bow. The students laughed when they saw how the puppet could move. With excitement for this new project, they created their own puppet heads and left them to dry.

Designing Puppet Costumes: For the second lesson, the students' first task was to cut a paper pattern for each puppet's costume. They put one hand on the paper to measure the size. Jim cautioned them to make the pattern large enough to allow a space for movement inside the costume and also for each seam. When the pattern was made, they chose a piece of cloth from a box that contained various pieces of fabrics. After carefully measuring and cutting the clothes, they sewed the costume with needle and thread. By the end of this lesson, the students had painted the faces of their puppets.

Finishing the Puppets: Two more weekly lessons were given to complete the puppets. The students pasted the costumes around the neck of the puppets. They also glued hair made from yarn to the heads. Some of the students became so involved with their puppets that they gave them names and instantly created a short story about them. The final step was to decorate the puppets with ribbons, beads and other jewels and ornaments. Completing the puppets was an amazing feat. Only a few weeks had passed since the puppets were born out of pieces of newspaper and glue.

The puppet project required the students to overcome a number of problems. They had to use various skills and knowledge. Many supplies and materials for making puppets were sent by the students' parents. The students had learned to measure, sew, design and decorate. They were fascinated to learn the art of puppet-making and enjoyed bringing their masterpieces to life. Now, they were ready to create a puppet show.

Designing a Dream House

Assemblage is a three-dimensional collage technique which allows children to build a range of objects. *Construction* and *sculpture* are similar terms referring to three-dimensional art that may or may not resemble real-life forms. By constructing an artwork, students become aware that objects are composed of parts and pieces. They also develop problem-solving strategies to create support, balance and form.

Students might work alone, with a partner, or in groups to decorate and construct models of a room, home, or park, or they can design settings for a story or theme they've studied. They can display constructions within cardboard boxes or create large-scale models of towns, communities, fantasy worlds, seascapes, or spacescapes.

Non-representational projects can help students explore materials freely. A collection of three-dimensional recyclable items can be glued to a sturdy cardboard to create a junk collage. Young artists can also enjoy the freedom of creating a fantasy creature sculpture using found objects such as small boxes, cardboard tubes, egg containers, cartons, and straws. A basic animal shape can be made by gluing items together and then decorating the creature. A group sculpture can be created by collecting a variety of cardboard boxes and gluing them together. Once assembled, the sculpture can be painted or added to, using a variety of art materials.

A classroom close-up on making dream homes, even a model community, follows on the next page.

Materials used: Papier-mâché, paper, pencils, markers, needles, fabrics, ribbons, used jewellery, toilet role tubes, yarn, beads, etc.

Involvement with the arts proves one of the best ways in which children can come to know the greatest achievements of which human beings are capable; it is also an excellent avenue for them to contribute to their own culture.
—*Howard Gardner*

Model Homes

Laura enjoys instructing Grade 7 students on how to build a model of their own "dream house." This could be any type of house, at any place—at the seashore, in a cave, in a tree, or perhaps even in outer space. Each house could have its own specifications, suited to its distinctive regional environment and climate.

In one specific instance, Laura showed the class several pictures of different houses, built with different architectural designs, using various construction materials (e.g., brick, stone, cement, wood, metal). She aroused the students' curiosity by encouraging them to discuss their ideas relating to the geographical, cultural, social, and historical background in different regions of the world and the effects that the environment had on society.

Designing the Structure: To begin their houses, the students needed to think about the basic parts of their houses—shapes of rooms, floors, doors, windows, stairs, and walls. In order to select suitable types of construction materials, they planned to use pieces of corrugated cardboard, milk cartons, plastic boxes, glass jars, egg trays, pieces of wood, metal, fabrics, and more. Laura suggested they should first concentrate on the structure of the rooms, then fill in the small details afterwards. Excitement escalated as each student discussed ideas with the teacher and classmates.

Constructing a 3-D Model: As their construction progressed, Laura continued to offer suggestions for the shapes of the rooms. Some rooms could be square, triangular, round, or perhaps a combination of these. Laura instructed the students to consider the length and width of the floors. Some rooms could be made of three-dimensional designs, instead of a rectangular-box style. Some houses needed a staircase, or even an elevator. For the exterior design, she introduced some ideas that would complement the scenery. These included a balcony, sun-deck, fence, gate, garage, garden, trees, shrubs—even a swimming pool.

Making a Town: After the students had completed their houses, Laura introduced another exciting idea, asking them to build "The Grade Seven Town." Excitement continued to gather momentum as the students divided themselves into groups—each responsible for building one section of the town. For public use, the plans for the town's infrastructure required paved sidewalks, streets, parks, trees, and gardens. The students worked together assiduously. This support group was helpful in solving problems as they shared ideas and information. By the time this project ended, the students were proud of their achievement. Laura had opened the door to their creativity, giving them the opportunity to participate in a meaningful community-minded group activity.

Materials used: Paper, pencils, glue, cardboards, boxes, liquid tempera, brushes, markers, pens, wire, fabrics, sticks, egg trays, pieces of wood, metal, etc.

Exploring Patterns and Shapes

Patterns surround us. Young people learn about the world of patterns through math exploration, spelling conventions, story structures and observations of the world around them. They can see patterns in photographs, in building structures, and in the natural world. In art, patterning suggests rhythm, motion, or movement. As young artists explore patterning made with line, shape, colors or symbols, they come to understand the concepts of regularity and repetition.

Young children can explore patterns through simple printmaking strategies by using materials such as sponges, cookie cutters, lids, bottle tops or fruits and vegetables. Students need to be encouraged to identify a pattern and repeat it on their papers. Can they repeat the pattern horizontally, vertically, or diagonally by dipping their items in paint and making a pattern? Pattern pictures can be made by cutting shapes out of wallpaper, fabric scraps or gift wrap glued onto a paper in a repetitive sequence. Older students can learn about patterns using basic geometric shapes. Once a shape is decided upon (e.g., a star, a heart, a triangle), they can use construction paper to make versions of the shape in small, medium, and large sizes. A further challenge could be to use two or three colors for their creation. Students should plan, manipulate and rearrange the shapes on a page before gluing to create a successful pattern design. By exploring the geometry concept of flips, slides, and turns, the students will also come to understand how patterns can be created in different ways.

Paying close attention to aesthetic designs and shapes in our natural environment can open up opportunities to discover unexpected beauty, explore shapes, and transform shapes into different geometric forms. In the classroom close-up below, students learned about design in nature over several weeks and felt proud of their results.

Pattern and Color in Design

Sketching Patterns in Fruits and Vegetables: George began by asking his Grade 8 students to find different patterns in slices of fruits and vegetables and transforming them into two-dimensional designs. On a table in a large basket was a bowl filled with apples, onions, cucumbers, zucchinis, celery, lemons, eggplants, kiwis, mushrooms, carrots, pineapples, and more. He first selected a green pepper and cut it with a knife—vertically, horizontally, and diagonally—then placed the slices on the table. These introduced interesting patterns that the students could use for their work.

The students began to sketch their own designs by slicing different vegetables and fruits and placing them in interesting arrangements. They were encouraged to make designs that were not too complex. Students at this level often show dissatisfaction with their drawing thereby diminishing their self-confidence, but have a great sense of visual curiosity. George was able to guide their exploration for discovery in objects in nature.

Applying Color Theory: One week later, George decided to teach the students how to use color theory and apply this to two-dimensional designs. He explained how certain color combinations could produce interesting effects for designs. For example, colors can provide perceptions of light or dark, warm or cool. Using a color wheel, he demonstrated how different colors could affect each other—complementary colors (e.g., red and green), also monochromatic colors (e.g., different tones of one color). He then discussed the principles of art, especially rhythm and balance.

Humans invented each of the arts as a fundamental way to represent aspects of reality; to try to make sense of the world, manage life better, and share these perceptions with others. The arts therefore enrich the curriculum by extending awareness and comprehension while affirming the inter-connectedness of all forms of knowing. This is why an education without the arts is an incomplete education.
—*Charles Fowler*

Materials used: Vegetables, fruits, acrylic colors, pencils, color wheel, paper, etc.

A Variety of Art Activities

The following section provides a variety of art activities. It is important to consider a balance and a sequence for the art lessons you choose to introduce. Some activities are more appropriate for particular age groups, while others are open to students in any grade.

Mobiles: Mobiles are three-dimensional art forms that are suspended and move by using wire, string, yarn, and ribbon. Any attached shapes and objects are free to dance in the air. Alexander Calder is known for his mobile expressions. If available, photographs, slides, or videos can be shown to students in an art class, allowing them to see how wires can be used to make various shapes. Balance is the essential aspect in creating mobiles. Students can create mobiles using geometric shapes, animal shapes, or objects around a theme. The changing sequence of lines, planes and colors that emerges helps students explore three-dimensional movement.

Stabiles: This activity allows students to create a fixed form of sculpture with a variety of materials. Unlike a mobile, the parts that are assembled in a stabile should not move. Encourage students to use the materials in any way they wish to create a unique design. The problems of balance and weight will be experienced as stabiles are created. Not only do students learn to solve puzzles, but they also increase their aesthetic awareness as they try to create something appealing. Assembling Styrofoam pieces to sticks or wires is a basic activity for making stabiles. Students can put together and take apart shapes many times during the activity until they are satisfied with their creation.

Collage: *Collage*, a term that comes from the French verb "coller" meaning to paste, stick or glue, is a technique of picture making that helps students understand the principles of composition. Virtually any material can be used for creating collage. The inventive nature of this process allows young artists to play freely with shape, color and texture of materials. As students arrange patterns and textures, they explore the elements of design, including form, color and line, and the principles of design, including balance, unity, variety, contrast, movement and emphasis. As students explore collage techniques, they should be encouraged to plan, rearrange, and overlap shapes, and to play with the materials before fixing them in a final composition. There is no one way that a collage should look, so children are free to explore and create.

Gesture Drawings: Gesture drawings are quick drawings of a figure before it moves or changes shape. The nature of this activity loosens children up before a more concentrated session in drawing the body. Gesture drawing helps students to observe proportions and suggest the structure of the body in action or at rest. The goal is to draw not what the figure looks like, but what it is doing. Students should be encouraged to use loose, circular drawing forms just to get the essence of the shape and proportion, not the detail.

Relief Printmaking: This method of printmaking invites students to create an image that is raised from a background. The raised area is inked and applied to paper or another surface. Materials, such as cardboard, fabric, string, and textured paper, can be layered and glued to build up surface. Once students have

Given the value we accord artistry in our work, we might even say that the major goal of education is the preparation of artists, people who can think artistically about what they do, who can use their imagination, who can experience their work as it unfolds, who can exploit the unexpected, and who can make judgments about its direction on the basis of feeling as well as rule . . . At a time when standardization is bleeding our schools and classrooms of their distinctive vitalities, the need for the arts and for artistry in what we do has never been more important.
—Elliot Eisner

completed the image, the surface is inked smoothly using a roller or paintbrush. Paper is placed over the relief surface. A gentle rubbing over the relief transfers the image to the paper.

Paper Sculpture: Working with a range of paper materials can be very appealing to young artists. Different shapes, sizes and weights of papers should be offered to help students understand the versatility and flexibility of this medium. By creating paper sculptures, students can cut, fold, roll, rip, join, tear, paste or staple paper of all different shapes. As a focus, students can be limited to create a sculpture or paper montage just using paper strips. The strips can be suspended as a mobile, joined together to make a free-standing sculpture, or glued to a page to create a paper collage.

Murals: Since murals are intended to cover large spaces on a wall, they are appealing art projects to be created by groups. A variety of media, including pastel and construction paper, can be used to create a mural around a theme or topic. These projects help children understand the need to plan and cooperate to create a finished product. The simplest type of mural is one in which individual students each add an item to the mural.

Color Mixing: When young painters experiment with mixing colors, they develop an understanding of their own ability to create and control materials. As children mix two, three, or more colors, they can become color designers and make discoveries about the color palette. They also discover how much water needs to be added to create an effect. Students can be challenged to create abstract paintings with a limited color palette. To begin, offer students two primary colors only to create a painting that includes a variety of geometric shapes. Another mixing-color activity is to offer children all three primary colors—red, blue and yellow—and invite them to fill the page with stripes only. Students can also be given the opportunity to experiment with tints and shades using a single color, white, and black to create new colors.

Modelling: Modelling is a sculpture technique that is particularly appropriate for elementary age students as they rearrange material through manipulation. Sometimes the young sculptor adds material; sometimes he or she carves away to create a final creation. Plasticine, clay, play dough, salt and flour mixtures are suitable for making three-dimensional pieces. Many young people enjoy rolling, punching, slapping, pounding, pinching, stacking, adding and subtracting material to experiment with the medium they are working with. Creating Plasticine illustrations of a story they have heard or read is one way for students to experiment with modelling techniques.

Masks: Masks can be made from a variety of inexpensive materials: paper bags and plates, papier-mâché formed over blown-up balloons, moulds, or crumpled newspaper. Though masks can be made for decorative purposes, mask-making in the classroom should have a functional goal, such as representing a story character, creating a visual image of a culture being researched, or being used in drama presentations. Whatever material is used to create masks, students have an opportunity to explore design principles of color, shape, line and texture.

Art can play a meaningful role in the development of children. The focus of teaching is the developing, changing, dynamic child who becomes increasingly aware of himself and his environment. Art education can provide the opportunity for increasing the capacity for action, experience, redefinition, and stability that is needed in a society filled with changes, tensions, and uncertainties.
—*Viktor Lowenfeld and W. Lambert Brittain*

A Mirror into the Self

The goal of a visual arts curriculum is to develop students' creativity and enrich their ability to communicate with others through visual images. As young people learn to express themselves in visual ways, they experiment and explore to see what they can create with the media and materials that are available to them. When children create art, they are given the opportunity to make sense of their world as well as to communicate ideas, experiences, and feelings with others. No matter what medium they are engaged in, the art expression can provide young artists with a mirror in which they find themselves. This mirror can reflect their thinking, feeling, and imagined selves.

We have the responsibility to help children to find their ways of expressing ideas and feelings. We can then increase both the possibility of form and the competency of form by stimulating the imagination and supporting children's problem-solving situations. The art process should be given full value and worth as a significant contributor to the education of the whole child. You, as a teacher, can guide and facilitate this important process.

Art as Thinking and Problem Solving
— Paola Cohen

When asked to give a definition of art, a child once said, "I think, and then I draw a line around my think."

Art activities, if properly set up, require thinking and problem solving. "What on earth is there to think about and solve," you may ask, "when a child bashes around a piece of clay, or splashes paint on paper?" The answer—a lot.

The key is to design projects where each child has to be challenged and given suitable tasks that require thinking and problem solving at their appropriate developmental stage. Activities have to be designed where children have to think about what they are doing to be successful.

An example will help understand what I mean. Let's take Billy in Grade 4 who has been given the task of building the longest and thinnest possible suspension bridge out of clay. First of all, if Billy does not know what a suspension bridge is, he will have to find out. For this there is research, pictures and recall. When he has a clear idea of what he wants to make, other problems have to be solved and dealt with. How thin can I roll the clay before it breaks? How thin can I make the pylons and how close together should they be to hold the horizontal strips for the bridge? What other structures can I use to give strength to a pole? Is a triangular shape stronger and more stable than a rectangle? Not only problems of conceptual representation have to be explored, evaluated and integrated in their design, but also ones of elasticity and flexibility of clay, stress, weight, balance, gravity, buttressing, structural stability, and other mechanical, physical and architectural concepts.

Similarly, Sara, while doing a painting, even an abstract one where colors are placed next to or over each other, is using her mind as well as her senses to problem-solve, to form concepts and to articulate expression. She needs to have control over form, space and shape; to make choices and selection of colors; to coordinate mind and hand; to be aware of differences and similarities; to evaluate her work, and to learn that ideas and emotions that are not physically present can be symbolized.

What is the process that Billy and Sara go through to achieve success in their task? First, they need to perceive and observe the problem to be resolved. In other words, "How do I change this lump of clay into a bridge?" To that question Billy brings an assemblage of past experiences to help in the attack—what he has seen, what he has done with clay or similar media in the past. He thus formulates a strategy and applies it to the problem that needs change. He then predicts what the outcome of his actions will be. "What will happen if I make the pylons thin and the cross pieces thick?" Conjecture and prediction, together with planning a strategy, will allow him to be more or less successful in achieving his aim. Once that is done, Billy can observe his actions and the way that the clay reacts. He is then ready for the resolution, evaluation and assessment of what he has done. At this point he may need to modify his actions and ideas to achieve his aim. This process continues until Billy is satisfied with his bridge. These are the same steps as in problem solving! Yes, there is a lot of thinking while working with clay!

Visual arts help children acquire the tools that make analysis and synthesis of visual qualities possible. Seen this way, art for the young child is a way of learning, not something to be learned.

If thinking and problem solving are to be important elements in an art activity, three components have to be present in the task. The activity must inherently have challenges that stimulate the mind. It must be presented appropriately, so that each child feels free to solve the problem in his or her own way—where there is no right or wrong solution, and the project is open-ended. Lastly, it must be developmentally appropriate. The latter has to be delicately balanced because, although the child must have the skills to be successful in the task, she must also be stimulated enough so that new skills are acquired while doing the activity.

The Importance of Child Art as a Foundation for Teaching and Learning
—*Marni Binder*

"Big Head, Little Body"

It was a typical day in my Grade 1/2 classroom. The room was buzzing with activity. Groups of children were engaged in drawing and writing stories. Some were constructing with a variety of building materials. The paint centre was energized with talk and giggles. Tyler, a Grade 1 student, was painting a self-portrait in blue. He had written across the bottom of his painting: "Big Head, Little Body." While later talking with Tyler, I discovered that he loved the color blue—hence his delightful hairpin portrait painted totally in blue. At first, when I saw the writing, I assumed that he was reflecting the picture itself. Tyler proceeded to tell me that the reason for this title was that his older brother always told him he had a big head and a little body.

Children use spontaneous drawing as a language to articulate, express, and communicate their deepest and most complex thoughts.
—*Bob Steele*

Child art has been a dominant influence and passion in my practice for many years.

The stages children go through when developing pictorial representation are equally as important as the stages of writing or reading. From scribble to early representations to more complex visuals, children are opening up spaces of thought and revealing the world of their experiences. The visual narratives create a language of meaning that often transcends the text.

The artwork I have explored as a primary teacher explicitly shows children representing objects of their experience. The significance of self-direction, problem-solving, creating something new, and engaging experience in a different way has ultimately enriched my understanding of how children struggle to make sense and relate to their world.

Drawing as a Language to Use and Interpret

I have often heard educators reflect on their own issues when dealing with child art. Many feel that in this climate of accountability, it is difficult to justify painting and drawing as regular practice in the classroom. There are those who feel they do not have the skill to present artistic encounters in authentic ways. Some feel too overloaded to spend the time to learn another language of understanding, but taking the time can reveal much about children's development.

Artistic Connections

I recall a parent-teacher interview with a Tamil family who had concerns with their daughter's English language acquisition. She was in Grade 1. During the three months prior to the interview, this child had made tremendous gains in oral language and was experimenting with print. I pulled out her paintings and drawings to show her parents. From the visual images, it was evident that this child was able to organize and represent her thoughts. Color and detail revealed an understanding of the world around her. Some of her drawings reflected retellings of stories read in class.

I read the pictorial representations for the parents and explained stages of development and how examining the images enabled me to understand the potential for English language acquisition. It was clear she had a solid foundation in her first language. It had been my experience that there was a connection between a refined and detailed drawing or painting, and the likelihood of a solid language foundation, in English or another language.

Implications for classroom practice are outlined below.

1. *Reading the pictorial world of the child reveals multiple ways of knowing.*
Multiple ways of knowing uncover the connections children make to other areas of their learning. Utilizing drawing and painting as an alternative form of learning generates the multiple possibilities of interpreting what the learner understands. Internalization of knowledge often unfolds naturally in drawings and paintings. Discovery of a child's interests also emerges when reading the content and context of pictorial representations. Providing opportunities for a child to draw, with textually recorded learning in a particular area, for example, social studies, builds a repertoire of tools for understanding, not just for the child but also for the teacher.

2. First read the images, then the text.

One should read the visual depictions with the same attention and intensity as the text and recognize that the text goes through several phases in accompanying the drawing or painting: text as separate, text as an aside, text as complement, and text as extension. The pictorial representation will often reveal more depth of narrative and detail than a written story. In the initial stages of literacy acquisition, drawing or painting a story provides an alternative for children to represent their real and imaginary worlds. The visual stories frequently reveal how and what a child thinks. When children have numerous opportunities for freedom of expression, the teacher is given multiple perspectives into their world. Reading the images first honors the importance of voice in visual form.

3. Meaning making is at the heart of all learning.

Making meaning is at the core of our existence. For primary children, playing, painting, drawing, talking, and writing are the rites of passage through which they connect their inner and outer understanding of the world. Through active engagement in their learning, children explore the patterns of the past and present experiences, and pose future questions. Learning in the classroom cannot be done through isolating subjects, or just through memorization and skills. To learn something implies a process of internalization. Through this process, meaning making becomes the path of discovery and connection between the lived experience of the real world and the classroom. One derivative for the word "learn" is the Old English word meaning footprint. Like a footprint that leaves its personal signature, so does the child through his or her artwork. When looking at child art, each image should be valued as a particular child's signature. The visual footprint presented communicates personal meaning.

4. Multiple literacies provide new possibilities.

Making meaning, which is at the core of quality literacy practices, is not a one-dimensional endeavor. The ability to read and write is only one part of acquiring the capabilities to decipher the layers of past and present influences. Young children do not always possess the refined abilities to use reading and writing to express the multitude of thoughts embodied in their everyday lives. Multiple literacies offer paths to explore alternative forms of expression and understanding. Visual literacy has been a prevailing influence in my practice and, in my experience, one of the most stimulating and accessible for a classroom teacher. Visual literacy is commonly defined as the ability to read visual symbols and interpret visual images. I view visual literacy as a form of graphic thought, reflecting a child's understanding of the world beyond the printed word. This symbolic form of representation promotes the child's ability to be visually literate and make the connections between visual forms of thought and print.

5. Identity reveals the sociocultural significance of past, present, and future experiences and helps build community.

Past and present experiences comprise how one identifies with the world. Cultural and historical influences impart a unique signature that reflects personal interpretations and interrelationships. Child art reveals the crucial components of a student's world—family, friends, traditions, and community. Children come to the classroom with an abundance of knowledge and understanding. These lived experiences need to be honored and can present themselves as a focus for curriculum development. Through drawing and painting, these experiences present the teacher with the tools to frame the potentialities of learning.

I once asked a Grade 2 class why art was important. These two responses crystallize the significance of child art in teaching and learning. One child said: "If there were no art, we wouldn't be able to express ourselves." I asked him what this meant. He replied, "It means we wouldn't be able to show people how we feel." Another child replied, "When we are looking and doing art, we can tell people what we see and think."

Child art is an individual means of expressing a personal story or experience, regardless of the interpretation by adults of the form. Pictorial representations open conversational channels at the personal and interpersonal levels, breathing interactive life into the tableaux of a child's meaning making. Stepping into the inner landscapes of children has intensified my own awareness and uncovered the interconnecting threads of meaning making that are revealed. Learning is transformed into an expression of lived experience and the sharing of lived worlds between teachers and students.

100 Years of Student Art

—Masayuki Hachiya

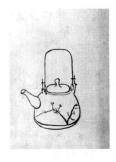

1908

1910

1914

Fifteen thousand pieces of student artwork . . . Masayoshi Tsuchiya and his colleagues at Tokyo Gakugei University in Japan have undertaken a research project involving an analysis of 15,000 pieces of Grade 6 student pictorial work. These have been preserved and accumulated annually by Bakuro Elementary School in Toyama, Japan, since 1908, a time when the society stood at the dawn of schooling. The idea for collecting student artwork was based on the initial school policy that was intended to connect to students who had graduated from the school.

This art collection provides an authentic picture of Japanese art education, portraying the changes in trends in the student artwork and teacher instruction in 100 years. This project makes it possible to examine the school art curricula, Ministry-approved art textbooks used in the school, art educational trends, and reviews of major research in children's artwork. It reveals a vivid record of the changes that gradually took place in Japan's regional, social and economical conditions during all those years. The report of this study provides information about the introduction of Japan's art education and its ensuing historical changes, as well as the cultural, anthropological, pedagogical, social, and ethnographical orientations.

The research examines the changes as the student artwork emerged from copying. Sketching human figures and scenery appeared gradually in the 1920s. Copying work still remained during those years, but the students used the original images from art books and arranged them in their own ways. In the 1950s, the students began creating narrative paintings and prints. This new movement contributed to a release of skills or techniques for representation, often altering the standards that adults had demanded in art. The student pictorial work seems to tell a history of the change from the classical excellence begun from copying.

1918

Teaching methods in Japanese art education have continued to develop. Today, students are not encouraged to copy from books as students in the past were. Recent students have been allowed much freedom, especially in terms of selecting motifs. It is probably true that these student pieces reflected teacher expectations of what adults wanted students to accomplish in art education. In the early years, art demanded skills of depiction, including perspective, composition, shading, and coloring, but after the Second World War, a child-centred approach has become pedagogically accepted.

Year by year, the art samples are accumulating at Bakuro Elementary School. The preservation of this historical artwork connects people in the community, raising their pride, telling the story of their artistic spirit, and articulating how confident and persistent they were in believing in art education for their children.

1924   **1929**   **1939**   **1949**

1956   **1959**   **1963**   **1968**

1971   **1977**   **1980**   **1984**

1988   **1993**   **1998**   **2001**

Building Blocks for Programing: Visual Arts

☐ **Drawing and Painting**
- ☐ Portraits
- ☐ Still lifes
- ☐ Narrative painting
- ☐ Murals
- ☐ Cartoons/Caricatures
- ☐ _____

☐ **Printmaking**
- ☐ Relief printmaking
- ☐ _____

☐ **Sculpting/Modelling**
- ☐ Construction (3-D)
- ☐ Dioramas
- ☐ Mobiles/Stabiles
- ☐ _____

☐ **Designing**
- ☐ Creating a puppet
- ☐ Pattern making
- ☐ Puppet costumes
- ☐ Collages
- ☐ Poster making
- ☐ Charts and diagrams
- ☐ _____

☐ **Craft**
- ☐ Bookmaking
- ☐ Calligraphy
- ☐ Mask making
- ☐ Folk art
- ☐ Ceramic/Pottery
- ☐ _____

☐ **Photography**
- ☐ _____

3 Joining in the Singing

Meaning Making and Music Education

By Lee Willingham

Lee Willingham is an instructor of music in the Preservice Teacher Education program at OISE/UT. He is the principal of the Music Additional Qualifications Course and founder of the Bell'Arte Singers. As well, he is co-editor of Canadian Music Educator Journal.

One way that I can be connected with my inner self is through listening to or performing music. A piece of music or the sound of a singing voice can bring me to a contemplative state and help release and relieve the mind and soul.

We live in a precarious world. If we can replace the great disconnect that we often feel with a musical human expression of hope, then we are teaching the most important thing that children can experience. We need not look very far to realize that singing and dancing prevail, even in tragic times. Our classrooms can be places where each student senses a personal possibility to express optimism and hope for a better world. What greater expression for such a voice than music.

In his book *Education and the Soul*, Jack Miller relates a wonderful story about a tribe in Africa that connects each child to a song. When the mother wants to conceive a child with her mate, she goes and sits under a tree until she can hear the song of the child she hopes to conceive. Once she hears the song she comes back to the village and shares with her husband. They sing the song while they make love, hoping the child hears them. When the baby starts to grow in the womb, the mother, along with other women in the village, sings the song to the baby. Throughout labor and during birth the baby is greeted by this song. Most of the village learns the song so that it can be sung to the child whenever he or she becomes hurt or is in danger (p. 134). I think this profound story can speak to us on many levels, both professionally and personally.

What we do in our music classrooms is more vital today than ever before. Music fortifies the spirit, gives order to the mind, and ultimately helps us make sense of life in the midst of chaos. Music connects students to themselves and to the world around them. We must continue to play, sing, and dance, for it has been said that the stresses and anger in the world today are a result of an unsung song or an undanced dance.

The purpose of an effective school music program is to develop musical understanding, or musical literacy, in the thinking, feeling, and active lives of our students at home, at play, and all through their lives.

Musical literacy is the ability to make meaning with sound. It is the ability to simultaneously *think* and *act* in a musical context in order to personally express and understand and enjoy what the music is about. It means knowing enough about music to function with a certain amount of independence, and knowing enough to value music in one's own life. (The ability to read standard musical notation does not in itself make one musically literate.)

Listening, Creating, Performing

Children learn best while engaged in active, concrete, and authentic experiences. In a musical world, all experiences involve one or more of these activities:

Listening
Creating
Performing

As listeners, we experience music in a thinking-acting mode through making meaning with how-the-music-goes and what-the-music-says. As creators, we "think-act" by composing or improvising new music, or by arranging music in a new way or style. As performers, we "think-act" by making music audible through singing or playing. This music might be music stored in our minds or music we are re-creating from the printed score.

In the classroom close-up below, three learners apply their musical understanding in a collaborative process.

A Cycle for Composing

In Grade 5, Alisha, Anwar and Andrew are composing a short piece of music, using "found" percussion sounds (a homemade shaker made of a vitamin bottle and dried seeds, and a plastic tub and wooden spoon) and a small musical instrument with wooden tone bars called a xylophone. In their conversation, they work towards a class performance of their new piece of music.

Alisha: I like using the pentatonic scale for our melody. It just sounds better on the xylophone than using all of the notes in the do-re-mi scale.

Anwar: I agree, but don't play each note in order like a scale. Mix them up more so they have some surprises in them.

Andrew: OK. I think Anwar should play the xylophone, and Alisha and I need to fix the percussion pattern a little more. I don't think we are keeping a steady pulse all of the time. I'll patsch the beat on my knees and you play the shaker the way you were before.

Alisha: Let's try it again . . .

The three students continue revising their work through listening to what they have done so far, adding new ideas to create a more interesting and complex work, and rehearsing it repeatedly until they feel that it expresses what they want. When the class listens to their performance, the cycle will be complete.

Alisha, Anwar, and Andrew were engaged in a complex form of meaning making as they worked out the details of their composition. They *listened* and *responded*. They *created* through experimentation and editing their work. They *prepared* for a *performance* where they would make evident their listening and creative work, demonstrating evidence of musical literacy.

All of these musical events are processes of *thinking in action*. Quality musical experiences require full cognitive engagement and address the development and growth of an intricate interconnection of brain, motor, sensory, and emotional skills. In other words, music learning and music making are, like the other arts, a holistic, whole person enterprise. Music addresses the body, mind, and spirit.

Providing a school with a quality music program may seem like a complex undertaking, but music has many facets and dimensions.

Music *listening, creating,* and *performing* are the means through which all musical experiences occur. By moving beyond a simplistic involvement with music, classrooms become learning laboratories in which students function as real musicians and not simply as consumers of knowledge. In order to do this, they must be problem solvers. They must be curious about how music works and must see the connections to real life. They do this by becoming *literate* in the structural and expressive elements of music.

Teaching *in* and *through* music supposes that the curiosity of how music works will translate into the wider world of learning and living. The music teacher who has created an authentic problem-solving learning environment is likely to be addressing important questions about how the world works, far beyond the musical processes.

The creative potential of the student is not limited to the walls of the music classroom. However, the music classroom foments the possibility of rich and profound experiences that cannot be duplicated elsewhere. Counter to the homogenizing influence of media and pop culture, we can make a sincere attempt to plumb the depths of the human spirit through the evocation of the musical voices of our children. It is an effort worth the investment, and an endeavor worth celebrating.

The Rehearsal Imperative

Since music is a performance art, it is necessary to rehearse. Some ensembles may rehearse within the school day. However, most schools have extracurricular ensembles, both choral and instrumental, who, under the supervision of a teacher, rehearse before and after school, and during lunch hours. These programs are vital to the students' sense of belonging to a musical community, to the public presentation of concerts and to participation in festivals.

It is a given that a school with a healthy music program has rehearsals outside of the normal school day. Teachers who are generous in volunteering for these responsibilities must be acknowledged and commended for providing these important opportunities for student growth and deepening musical experiences.

The Teaching Setting

Music teachers may not always have control over the physical space in which they teach. Sometimes music must be taught in someone else's classroom or in a corner of a gymnasium. While these conditions are not ideal, teaching through problem solving, where students are learning to conceive, plan and carry out instructions, can be adapted to just about any teaching setting.

Some music teachers travel with carts from room to room. In such cases, classroom teachers should reset their furniture before the music teacher arrives, moving desks out of the way and resetting the chairs in a circle with plenty of room for music making.

Ideally, there is a room dedicated to music instruction. Since music is experienced in a "sound" environment, it is important that, as much as possible, the learning process be free from external interference; also, the music learning processes should not encroach on the disciplines that require silence in order to function best.

A music classroom should reflect what will take place therein. If the principal aim of the music room is to rehearse the choir or band, then the setup of chairs will look quite formal. However, where singing games and movement are encouraged, the room will need to be flexible with wide open space. Instruments can be stored and brought to the centre when needed, or can be placed in a permanent location that is easily accessible to class members.

Technology, while it can never replace the expressivity of the human spirit, can support music teaching. A music classroom should have a high-quality sound system for playing recorded music, with capabilities for playing compact discs and cassette tapes. MIDI (musical instrument digital interface) stations with headsets can be set up in various locations so that students can work on their compositions and productions when they have discretionary time.

Teaching for Musical Understanding

Before children ever walk through the doors of their school, they have had multiple exposures to music and have experienced music in many different ways. As infants, they naturally "babble"; as toddlers, they invent little songs or tunes, as four- and five-year-olds they make up songs to accompany their play and learn to sing familiar songs. All children *move* while they sing and play. In pre-Kindergarten programs, children play classroom instruments, explore sounds, play singing games, and respond to music of various types, times, and cultures. Experiencing music playfully and joyfully is part of preschool life.

When children enter elementary school, there is no reason why the joyful and playful qualities of music need to cease. General classroom music should be designed to enhance and stimulate a child's natural musical intelligence: that which comes out of a preschool life of musical experiences.

Teachers need to know what their students understand about music and about how it functions in their lives. It has been pointed out that children often know more about music than they are able to articulate in standard language. We can learn from what students do naturally. As we did with Alisha, Anwar, and Andrew, we can listen to children as they work with peers in solving a musical problem, paying attention to their descriptions of how the music goes and their discussions of what is important in the music. As teachers, we can begin to identify our students' musical inventory.

A Constructivist Approach

Students learn *in* and *through* music, through the acquisition of musical concepts, which are based on understanding the elements and principles of music. These concepts are understood through active, concrete, and authentic experiences which are constantly expanding and changing. The development of these concepts must begin with what the student already knows, and must occur in the context of quality music works through processes of *listening*, *creating*, and *performing*.

When teachers approach teaching and learning in and through music from this perspective, they are providing the conditions for learning whereby students ultimately construct their own understanding in order to make personal meaning from the learning experience. This *constructivist* approach suggests that the best learning situations are those in which students are asked to take the initiative in their learning through the solving of musical problems.

Compelling evidence supports the hypothesis that musical arts may provide a positive, significant, and lasting benefit to learners. There is no single evidence, but the diversity and depth of supporting material is overwhelming. If this were a court case, the ruling would be that music is valuable beyond reasonable doubt.
—*Eric Jensen*

Musical Problem Solving

To some degree, all musical enterprises involve problem solving. Solving problems requires the use of what is already known and provides opportunities for the construction of new understandings and the clarification of existing understandings. The teacher asks the students to provide a satisfactory musical solution, whether it be in the processes of listening, creating, or performing. (The antithesis of problem-solving learning is the dictatorial "maestro" standing in front of the ensemble, where the power and authority for learning reside within the ensemble director. Sensitive ensemble conductors will stop the group when a problem is encountered and ask a "fix it" type of question. The students are then empowered with the responsibility to contribute to the musical solution.)

Elements of Music

Music is sound moving through time and space. In some way, even "chaos" music is organized to express, in order for the listener to derive meaning. There are some basic structural elements of music that serve as a starting point for teachers to construct musical problem-solving experiences. The expressive and structural elements of music are outlined below:

- Rhythm, long and short
- Pulse or beat, which is a steady, reoccurring event resembling the heart beat—it is what we dance or march to.
- Tempo, which is the speed with which the pulse goes . . . fast and slow
- Patterns, which group rhythmic events to create metres and accents (from which we get time signatures, syncopations, and often the "hooks" that we remember in musical works—think of the opening pattern of Beethoven's Fifth Symphony.)
- Pitch, high and low
- Melody, where pitches rise and fall to create a shape or *contour*
- Harmony, where melody is supported by other musical pitches
- Dynamics, loud and soft. Expressivity in music is created through contrast and gradual intensity changes. Getting increasingly louder is a *crescendo* and increasingly softer is a *diminuendo*. *Forte* is loud (Italian for "strong"), and *piano* is soft.
- Timbre or tone color, or sound source, or quality of the sound itself. What makes a drum sound like a drum, a voice sound like a voice, a guitar a guitar, and so on?
- Texture, thick and thin . . . the combining of more than one musical sound, such as melody and accompaniment, or more than one melody together, or a simple *monophonic* melody
- Form, same and different, dependent upon repetition and contrast. Like a story, music may have a beginning, a middle and an end.

As students begin to make sense of these structural elements, they are building their conceptual understanding of music. These concepts are necessary for and interrelated to the music they hear, create, and perform. They serve as the conceptual grounding for all kinds of music classes. This is what music teachers need to use in their everyday lessons to help unlock the meaning in music for their students.

Rhythmic Problem Solving

While many theorists advocate starting the classroom music experience with singing, I have found that teachers without a singing background can use rhythmic exploration as an effective portal into music activities. The *echo clapping* activity is a simple way to engage all students in listening, then re-creating and performing the pattern in the manner they heard it.

> *Teacher:* Clap Clap ClapClap Clap
> *Class:* Clap Clap ClapClap Clap

The teacher changes the pattern, and the students continue to respond in the manner they hear the teacher's pattern. The teacher adds more complex patterns, makes them longer, changes the pulse, and the students respond, either individually or as a group. The echo clapping activity is a great springboard into many other kinds of problem-solving procedures. Consider these options:

- Call and Response: One student or the teacher claps or taps a pattern, and a student answers with a different one. The pattern repeats until all have experienced either a call or a response.
- Question and Answer: The activity is similar to Call and Response, but more like a dialogue between two students or the teacher and a student.
- Canon: Starting points of patterns are staggered to created a *round* effect.
- Rhythmic Layering: Students combine individual patterns or create interlocking patterns that fit together over a steady pulse.
- Adding to the Pattern: One student starts the pattern, and the next adds something to it until everyone is participating with their own piece of the rhythmic puzzle. The result is a rhythmic class *ostinato* that can be looped to continue over and over. It is rich in rhythmic interest, dynamic contrasts, timbral varieties, and textural qualities. The class's rhythmic sound can be used as a background for solo improvisations, ceremonial processions, or just a fun way to do something together with sound.
- *Ostinato:* This is a repeated pattern to which other patterns or sounds can be added. (Ostinati can be rhythmic, melodic, or both.) Students can be given an ostinato upon which to create their own musical ideas, or they can be challenged to create an ostinato for a song they already know.
- Exploration of Elements: While engaging in rhythmic exploration, the teacher invites the students to also consider the *timbral effects* of how the various sources sound together and alone, the *dynamics* and *contrasts* by changing the loudness of the parts, the *texture* of putting the various rhythms together, and of course, the *form* of rhythmic exploration. The problem-solving activity is rich as it both develops and enlarges the musical literacy of each participant through experimentation, trial and error, conceptualization, and revising/editing.

Singing

Children naturally express themselves through singing. Listen to them use songs in their playground time. The voice is their own personal musical instrument and they have used it expressively from the earliest years. Children need frequent opportunities to continue their singing as they mature physically, socially, and mentally.

A child's singing voice is clear, open and free. It must not sound heavy or forced. Correct posture and a lack of physical tension most often result in the desired effects. Children must be encouraged to explore their singing voice without fear of judgment from others. The singing classroom is a safe place for all students, a place where the teacher also sings.

Our classrooms are places where real people make real music together. The music that students make while becoming musically literate is not a consumable product that demands perfection, and occasionally, the sounds that the teacher or students make might be considered amateur, or even primitive. Hooray for those sounds! We honor the gifts of musical expression that we and our students bring to the classroom. And, as in the acquisition of reading skills, we honor attempts and approximations that enable students to get a feel for singing, to develop pitch memory, and to fine-tune the small muscle systems involved in music making.

So, let us always establish the scaffolding in our singing classrooms that supports the invitation for all to participate, and honors the contributions that all make. Only then, can we move along the path to a deeper experience that music begs to offer.

The do-re-mi Scale

Knowledge of the scale is essential. Students learn it quickly and use the accompanying hand signs to establish a sense of home key, or *tonal centre*. Lots of fun exercises can be used with this scale and students can learn to solve simple musical problems with this basic knowledge. Consider the following sequence:

Teacher sings: "Good morning girls and boys."
So so so so so mi (only *so* and *mi*)
Class echoes: "Good morning, Ms. McKinley."
Teacher sings: "Who knows what day it is?"
Class responds: "I know what day it is. Today is Thursday, October 16, 2004."

(This exercise is called *singing the calendar*. It is used in many classrooms as an opening focus exercise. As the class sings, a student is chosen to change the calendar to the appropriate day. A singing exercise establishes the daily class routine.)

Teacher sings: "Who had breakfast?"
Class responds: "I had breakfast." (if indeed they did!)
Teacher sings: "Who had milk for breakfast?"
Class responds: "I had milk for breakfast."
Teacher might continue: "Who is wearing running shoes?"
Class responds accordingly.

This exercise, using only two notes, involves students in listening, thinking in action, and responding accurately. It also allows the teacher to observe who is able to match pitch and get the response correct within the rhythmic and tonal framework, and who is having some difficulty. The teacher then adds the note *la* to the pattern, so that it looks like this:

Who is wearing blue jeans?
So so mi la so mi

In our consumer culture, music has shifted from being a human participatory endeavor to a *product* that one buys at the store. The music product, due to digital mastering and special effects, is "perfect" in technical quality. Rarely do we hear mistakes or wrong notes in commercially available music. Even in live recorded broadcasts, the CBC makes a rehearsal recording to overdub any of the live portions that might be weak or not "perfect."

Individual students are then invited to lead the response. They are encouraged to be respectful in their singing questions, and to try not to centre out individuals. (Not: "Who has red hair, a pink sweater and blue shoes?")

The reader may have already noted that the intervals *so*, *la*, and *mi* are the basis for universal playground patterns. Songs such as "Rain, Rain, Go Away," and "Ring Around the Rosie" are based on these intervals, as are the derisive finger-wagging sounds children make when they sing "nah, nah, nah, nah, nah."

Echo Singing

The teacher models the singing tone for the class in a clear, light tone. For Kindergarten and Grade 1, the teacher might sing only on one pitch . . . not too high, not too low. She might sing, "Hello everyone." The class responds, "Hello Ms. (teacher's name)" on the same pitch. The teacher continues to sing either questions to elicit singing answers or a call that is echoed (e.g., Teacher sings "one and one are two," and class echoes back exactly what she sings).

Gradually, another pitch is added. It is best to use *so* and *mi* as the first two pitches. By Grades 2 and 3, students are easily mastering *so*, *mi*, and *la*.

Echo singing can be used for learning the daily calendar, for taking attendance, for finding out who did what last night, for remembering numbers and tables, lists, the alphabet, and anything else that normally is done with language.

Rote Singing

Teachers should learn the songs from memory with correct pitches and rhythms before introducing them to their classes. The teacher should establish clearly the starting note and the home note (*do*), ask the students to keep a steady beat by patching on their knees (palms down) and sing the entire song. The teacher then sings the song line by line and asks the students to echo her. This activity continues until the class can sing the entire song without teacher prompting.

When songs are taught by rote, students learn "by ear" without the use of music notation. This is the most common way to learn music all over the world. Most cultures do not rely on the printed page to store music, but the memory, and music is passed down from generation to generation in the *aural tradition*.

When learning by rote, it is very important to keep students engaged and focused, and this is best done by asking them to problem-solve. For example, students keep a steady beat by patching on their knees, but clap on the very last note or word. Or, they clap each time the word "frog" is sung. Or, the teacher might say "Do as I do," and she moves her hand up and down to represent the *contour* of the melody.

The teacher also asks clarification questions during and after the learning of the song. She might ask, "How many times did we sing the word 'frog'?" or "What was the name of the woman in this song?"

This process follows the principle that sound comes before the written symbol. Children learn to speak a language before they read it. It is important that children develop confidence and accuracy in singing prior to mastering the written notation.

Reading Songs

Once students are able to enjoy singing with confidence, they also learn new songs by reading standard musical notation. The musical symbol system is introduced bit by bit, and students easily learn rhythmically notated patterns and eventually the systems of lines and spaces. The song is presented on large chart paper or on

The arts are, and have always been, essential for developing and sustaining mind, as are other forms of representation, including language. And this development of mind is *intrinsically* rewarding, absorbing, exciting.
—*Keith Swanwick*

an overhead projector screen. The teacher then invites the students to first say the rhythm patterns. Then, the students sing the melody pitches to tonic solfa names: *do-re-mi* and so on. They are invited to clap the rhythms and sing the pitches. Finally, students sing the text with the accurate rhythms and pitches.

If you are wondering, "Where does problem solving fit in this activity?" let me reassure you that the teacher creates and provides opportunities for students to make decisions about their work. She might ask, "What would you change to create excitement? Should the music go faster or slower, be softer, or sound more like a celebration?" So, the students are manipulating the elements of music in order to express specific concepts, moods, and expressions.

In the same manner that students discover meaning in reading by reading aloud and by making attempts at new words or sentence combinations, students also benefit by reading and singing music aloud. They discover how-music-goes through decoding a logical and fairly simple symbol system. Please note that the ability to read music is a desirable skill that should be neither neglected nor overemphasized. Once students have acquired the ability to read, they can be independent music learners for the rest of their lives.

Singing Games

Singing games offer opportunity for bringing a child's joy of play into the learning environment. Singing games involve movement (more about that later) and some routines that are played out in the song. A singing game might simply be an *action song* where there are motions to accompany the singing (e.g., rocking a baby in a lullaby). Or, it might involve a complex set of directions using partners, leaders, circles, hand motions, or any combination of these actions. Some songs use number games and others depend on lists of items to keep track of. For example, songs such as "I bought me a cat," or "When I first came to this land," require the singer to add items and related sounds and/or actions to the song. Tonal memory singing games require the student to hear silently the pitch while leaving it out of the song. This strategy can be applied to any song.

Playing singing games has many benefits. Games provide an internal motivation that creates a natural exploration of the elements of music. The teacher asks, "What did we manipulate to create this particular mood?" Games aid in repetition and teach rhythm through the movement in the song. Teachers have also found that singing games are excellent activities for learning disabled students. For example, the students can walk in time to the music or go around the circle to the beat.

Improvising in Sound

Improvising occurs when students spontaneously perform original music live and in real time. Improvising occurs *during performance*; it is not pre-formed or pre-composed. It is thinking out loud in music. Improvising can take on many forms, some more structured than others. For example, in rhythmic problem solving, asking a student to "add something to this pattern" is a form of improvising.

Students may also improvise "answers" to given rhythmic or melodic phrases. They may improvise simple rhythmic variations and simple melodic embellishments on familiar melodies.

Improvising can be used in providing sound effects to a story or poem, or atmospheric effects, for example, in a Halloween play. Students may also be asked to improvise freely for a period of time (say, four bars) within a structured piece.

Improvisation is an important part of musical literacy and is a rich form of problem solving in the teaching/learning process. There are infinite possibilities, both in practice and in performance. There are also many world music traditions where improvisation is embedded within performance practice. In North America, jazz is the most commonly improvised musical form. However, improvisation is common to virtually every musical tradition, including classical music.

Exploring Music through Movement and Dance

Because children use their bodies and minds to understand their world, movement is a natural and ideal way for them to explore music. In fact, music serves to heighten a child's desire to move. Almost all child-based curriculum approaches make extensive use of movement with music (e.g., Orff-Schulwerk, Dalcroze and Kodaly). Many of the world's cultures consider music and movement as synonymous, and in some languages, the same word is used for both.

All of the structural and expressive elements of music (see page 45) can be expressed through movement. Movement can be categorized into several types. *Fundamental* movements are walking, skipping or running, or clapping and finger snapping. These can be *locomotor* (moving from one space to another) or *axial* (movement that is performed in-place). Creative movements are *interpretive* and may be rhythmic or not. Many *singing games* and *dances* contain movement that the children learn as they learn the song. It is part of the song itself. *Hand jives* and other patterned rhythms are sequential movements that fit the song's rhythmic structure or form.

Movement and dance need to be frequent experiences at every grade level. It is hard to imagine children singing and developing a musical understanding without the connection to the kinesthetic. Neurobiologists have discovered that without the development of the motor-cerebellar-vestibular system (the parts of the brain that are directly stimulated through movement and dance), we observe problems in attentional deficits, reading, emotions, memory skills, reflex skills, lack of classroom discipline, and writing.

Using Instruments to Create Music

At the beginning of this chapter, we listened in on three students creating a musical composition using instruments. Musical instruments are an exciting and colorful aspect of classroom music. They can range from body sounds and inexpensive "rhythm toys" to full orchestral and band programs. Instruments amplify the expressivity of the human spirit and are the best way to explore the musical element of timbre: how music sounds. All students should have the opportunity to create, improvise, and perform using an instrument.

Body percussion includes clapping, stamping, patsching, clicking with tongue, or combinations of these. *Non-pitched percussion* includes hand drums, wood blocks, finger cymbals and more. *Pitched percussion* may include drums that can be tuned to a pitch (roto-toms, tympani) or barred instruments such as xylophones and metallophones.

Many schools have a collection of *Orff instruments* (part of the Orff-Schulwerk programs) and these can be used routinely to introduce composition, improvisation, or basic accompaniments to singing and movement. Orff instruments include non-pitched percussion and barred instruments, such as glockenspiel, xylophones and metallophones in a variety of sizes.

The piano is a fixture in many music rooms. It is used to accompany singing, but also provides a focal point for demonstrating the spatial qualities of music (pitch: high and low; intervals: distance between notes; dynamics: loud and soft). The piano is also a place where students can explore sounds and sound colors (timbre), and for those studying privately, perform their work for others in the class. There are many well-designed electronic keyboards on the market and several have excellent samples of real piano sounds.

For many of us, the recorder was our introduction to playing a wind instrument. Plastic recorders can be purchased very inexpensively so that students may have their own. The recorder is an excellent way to develop small sequential motor skills (lifting fingers independently and controlling the wind supply with a variety of articulations), as well as introducing written notation. Students may play as full-class ensembles or as smaller consorts in twos or threes, or may provide accompaniment to the class singing. The recorder has a rich and interesting history and is the forerunner to the modern flute.

Autoharps, ukuleles, handbells, and guitars are sometimes used in the music classroom, as well.

The traditional ensembles of bands and orchestras are often introduced to schools in Grades 4, 5, and 6. Schools that have approached these performance ensembles inclusively (i.e., all in the grade participate, rather than auditioning for special musical abilities, or withdrawal of a smaller number within the class) with qualified and competent instructors have found this to be a tremendous resource within their school community. Parents proudly support such ensembles, and the self-esteem and confidence of the participants are enriched. However, budget cuts have reduced such programs in recent years.

Our imaginations have been enlarged by the Blue Box percussion ensembles, such as Stomp. These groups use found objects and recycled materials to create exciting and interesting music. Drums can be made from sono-tubes cut from different lengths using cellophane packing tape for heads, and may be decorated colorfully. Bottled water containers make excellent drums as do plastic tubs of all sorts. Shakers can be made of anything that will contain rice, seeds, or stones. Pieces of metal can sound like cow-bells. The coil from a spiral ring notebook can be played to imitate a Latin American *guiro* or a washboard. There are also natural links between recycled music and learning about the need for careful management of our garbage and refuse.

Students may wish to explore the instruments of the orchestra as a listening activity or the many different instruments found in the musics of the world. Teachers are encouraged to discover what instruments might be found within the family members of the students. Perhaps members of extended families or parents may be accomplished musicians. Invite them as guests to perform and demonstrate the music traditions of their own lives.

Celebrating World Music and Polycentricity

Today's social realities in North America increasingly make multicultural education a must. When a classroom includes Caribbean, South and East Asian, African, Native and Anglo North American children, many of them recent arrivals, the music program must find ways to reach them through an understanding of and relationship to their cultural backgrounds. The mandatory "trip around the world" concert that features "Kumbaya," "My Paddle's Clean and Bright," and the Walt Disney "Siamese Cat Song" does more harm than good.

Teachers may not feel they have been given adequate training or resources to provide world music opportunities as part of the problem-solving learning processes for their students. However, there is much information available on the World Wide Web, as well as authentic recordings of every conceivable musical style and practice. Chances are, there are resources right in the school community that can assist in providing student learning experiences.

The festival days of various cultures provide natural opportunities to incorporate songs, dances, costumes, and special guests as part of the school music performances. For example, consider a Festival of Lights concert that incorporates Diwali, Chanukah, and Christmas music, all dealing with the theme of light.

Seasonal festivities are natural occasions for songs that represent world traditions. Celebrate the harvest in September, Thanksgiving in October (or November in the United States), the winter solstice in December, and so on. A musical exploration of Halloween or All Saints Day is an interesting one, and takes the students far beyond the commercial superficiality of the typical night of trick or treating. Find out how these seasonal events are recognized in the cultures represented in the school.

I used the word "polycentricity" in the title of this heading because it is a natural process to incorporate musical practices of many different cultures, beliefs, and personal experiences in a holistic and integrated manner. I have attended many music concerts in schools, and the following scenario, although only a composite picture, is worth examining. It offers a hypothetical summary of the music experiences that students can have in a polycentric musical environment.

Carrie, Seema, and Carlo, three Grade 6 students, performed with their classmates in a school music concert. Along with their classmates, they opened the concert with their own arrangement of the baroque piece known as "Pachelbel's Canon," processing from the back of the gym singing while a small ensemble played tuned and non-tuned instruments. They moved to Orff instruments and joined the full-grade ensemble in an arrangement of the medieval melody "Greensleeves," followed by a Calypso rendition of "Turn the World Around." They participated in a recorder consort, and after opening with a movement from a fifteenth-century French suite, played an arrangement of "Yesterday," a Lennon/McCartney tune. The whole class joined in a choral version of "Al Slosha N'verim," an Israeli song in Hebrew, and then supported by the instruments, the choirs sang the American-African spiritual, "The Water Is Wide."

By the end of the evening, the three students had played more than eight different instruments, had sung songs in six different languages, and performed music composed by master composers as well as by student composers and

I have been pretty lucky with my music program. Four years ago, I applied for the Itinerant Vocal Music program that my school board provides. It's a five-year program where an itinerant music teacher comes into the classroom and teaches the classroom teacher how to teach music. The students are able to see the teacher as a student, which helps build community. My itinerant teacher Mike Thomas, who is a member of the professional choir the Elmer Iseler Singers, is a big burly guy who drives his motorcycle to school, comes into class with his leathers on, carrying his helmet. Every student in my inner-city class connects with him and they are always excited about music class. The boys are continually asking if they can see his motorcycle. One day this year, two of the boys were given the opportunity to help him carry some materials to put in his saddle bags and they loved it. The bonus is that they learn music and sing so well that the hair stands up on my neck. I cannot imagine my music program without him.
—Tom McKeown

teacher arrangers. They also danced the dances of several cultures and covered music from a 700-year historical span and a 15 000 km (25,000 mile) geographical one.

When a school music program contains strong teaching/learning experiences in rhythm, singing and singing games, improvising, movement and dance, and instruments and a receptivity to world music, it is virtually a foregone conclusion that the musical listening, creating, and performing experiences of the students will reflect the polycentricity of the supporting community.

Using Digital Technology

Music and computers are now part of many school programs. The software available ranges from theory instruction (such as *Music Ace*) to powerful compositional and production tools (*Cubase, Sibelius, Finale*). Most school boards have purchased licences for such software, affording system-wide use for educational purposes at no cost to the school. The cost of MIDI setups is now quite affordable, and recent research has shown that systematic instruction with primary and junior age students, using electronic keyboards and computers, has tremendous academic and social benefits.

Keyboard (piano) labs are found in many schools. The traditional piano skills are developed, but these instruments also serve as compositional, improvisational, and collaborative tools for student musical growth.

At the outset of this chapter I stated that listening is one of the three main music enterprises that engage one in becoming musically literate. The technology of the digital record, or compact disc, has made classroom and individual listening much more accessible.

In addition, digital recording enables students to hear and edit their own creative work. CDs can be created for just pennies per disc and each student can have their own copy of a school performance or of their own musical collaboration with peers. Most schools now have CD-writing capability.

Technology has made the process of creating, analyzing, editing, revising, and public presentation much more accessible to younger composers and performers. Teachers are encouraged to make use of the freeware found on the World Wide Web, as well as licensed software available to them.

An Invitation to Make Meaning

We are all invited to join in the music.

School music programs are important because the development of musical understanding results in complex forms of meaning making. These various concepts or meanings are windows through which our students perceive and comprehend the world. To be fully human is, to some degree, to be able to partake in listening, creating, and performing experiences with our whole selves—body, mind, and spirit.

Students become musicians, problem solvers, investigators, and ultimately connoisseurs of quality not just in music, but in life!

The Music Program at Joyce Public School
—With notes from Cheryl Paige

Located in Toronto's northwest quadrant, Joyce Public School has 370 students attending Kindergarten through Grade 5. Students are received from the community and from two childcare centres. More than 66 percent of the school population comes from homes where English is not the first language. A unique feature of Joyce is its technology emphasis and rich information and communications technology (ICT) endowment. This endowment was first conferred in 2001 and is now used in up to half of the school's teaching and learning hours.

At Joyce Public School, reading and language are top priorities, as are information technology literacy and the arts. It is the unique music program and its use of technology as the principal mode of delivery that interests this inquiry.

Research informs us that countries whose students are achieving at the top in university and high school in math and science all introduce music training in the early years. At Joyce, we decided to give this opportunity to our students.

Everyone at Joyce Public School does music. With this whole school approach to integrating music into all facets of the curriculum, teachers find authentic ways to use music to enhance student learning. Strategies range from the integration of songs and movement to sophisticated teaching/learning processes using music technology. Although the teachers are in different stages along the continuum of expertise and experience with music and have different teaching styles, they all use music in some form within their classroom programs.

All students receive two classes of music instruction with the music teacher in the Music Lab each week. Computer technology and music software are integrated in the Music Lab, allowing students to see the actual music and the virtual keyboard and then work on the notes on the staff. They learn how to read the notes, play games that reinforce the lesson, and create their own music. Students from Grades 1–5 learn *MusicAce I* and *II* and *Cubase V*, theory and composing programs. The students learn about various instruments and listen to their sounds on the computer. Primary students learn that the voice and body can be instruments too. Orff and Kodaly methods are used with early primary students. Students create, reproduce, write, and read rhythms of increasing complexity.

Music and the Literacy Link

- Students learn music using visual cues. They learn the location of each note, where the pitches are, and what the range of the keyboard is. Then they go to the actual keyboard to work with the notes. These skills translate to learning to read—looking at the words, how the syllables are broken down, and what the syllable structures are.
- By exploring how a song is created, our students can see relationships with the English language. For example: (a) a sentence has a form (beginning, middle, and end), as does music; (b) in music, a rest means to pause like the comma in language; (c) there are phrases in both music and English composition; (d) a few sentences become a paragraph similar to musical form and phrases, e.g., ABACA as in a rondo. Our students learn the correlation between word and rhythm structures or the melodic structure of a song.
- Our Grade 5 students have explored the blues. They listened for the pattern as in poetry. They explored the traditional call/response pattern (say one line, repeat it, third line rhymes with the first two) and followed it to create their own blues lyrics. The individual lyrics were melded into a group song, then into a class song. This opportunity for authentic editing and revising for

an authentic audience had a positive effect on the quality of the students' writing.

- Students added their own words and melody to a blues rhythm track. They recorded the song and sent it to their partner school, Crook School in Durham, England. The English students created a drama portion for the song on video and sent it back to Joyce. In this unit, the music-literacy connection with other subjects was strong. Students have studied the blues in literature, found blues music, and explored a poetic form with a definite pattern. As an extension, the teacher had the students put feelings to colors.
- Grade 5 students memorize poetry. Connecting song lyrics with poetry helps them develop vocabulary. The teachers create a poetry café where students can work alone or with a partner to present their poems in creative and imaginative ways, e.g., devising poems for two voices, creating their own musical accompaniment, or performing to an audiotape of popular music.
- When fine-motor skills are still developing, moving creatively to music enhances higher level thinking and processing better than pen-and-paper responses. Students create tableaux to music to make meaning as a response to reading literature.

Music and Mathematics

- Patterning: Music is mathematical in structure. For example, patterning in music is the form of the composition (A section, B section, and chorus). Students can deconstruct a familiar song like "Old MacDonald Had a Farm" to see the words and sentences and relate them to the music pattern.
- Fractions: The structure of music is formed by beats. Within the beats there are different notes that create patterns. Students related the notes to fractions, for example, quarter notes divided into two eighth notes were used to show equivalent fractions and this was compared to dividing a pizza. With this approach the students learned the concept of fractions more quickly. They related fractions to the notes they knew in the music they had studied for three years.
- Measurement: Students can fill identical bottles with liquid, measure the heights, and hit the bottles to make a sound and create a scale. Doing this helps them relate volume to tones and pitches and see the actual amounts of liquid.
- Graphing: Our students plot their rhythmic patterns on a music graph.
- Integrated Unit: This Grade 5 unit was created and implemented by Joyce teachers to integrate math and music seamlessly by addressing both math and music expectations. Students learn how sound is used and how the beat is divided, and relate this understanding to equivalent fractions. They create rhythmic, melodic patterns and then compose. The teachers created worksheets of geometric patterns that connect mathematical patterns with the patterns in music.

Music and Science

- Building their own instruments can help students understand sound and measurement. They can see how a plucked string vibrates and how air blown into a pipe makes a sound.
- Music can be used to demonstrate the wave theory. A tuning fork touched to a tray of water helps students see what sound waves can do as they radiate from the source.

- Music can be used to demonstrate particle theory. The slower- or faster-paced music models how particles react.
- Music is the prime way to study the science of acoustics. Students can experiment with sound by performing music in various places within the school and describing the characteristics.
- Acoustics can also be studied digitally, with sound enhancement devices such as reverb, digital delay, distortion, and many other applications.
- Students use songs, such as rap or blues, to memorize and remember information and data, for example, the different layers of rock or multiplication tables.

Music and Core French

- Music helps teachers capture the intensity and dynamics of French and make learning it interesting. The French language involves a lot of patterns than can become familiar and are reinforced with singing. Songs reinforce and teach vocabulary, e.g., body parts, by contextualizing key terms within simple sentences and catchy tunes so students are not learning phrases in isolation. This helps with both accent and pronunciation.
- Students can rewrite a song, using it as a model and changing the vocabulary and content.
- Listening to French or French-Canadian popular and folk music helps students gain an appreciation of the culture.

Cheryl Paige is the principal of Joyce Public School, Toronto.

....

The San Francisco School's Approach to Music
—With notes from Doug Goodkin

A parent once commented that The San Francisco School is like a small town in the big city. The school certainly resembles a quiet village tucked in a corner of a bustling metropolis. Just over the fence, folks are rushing hither and yon, the pace of life leaving little time for reflection. On our side, children climb trees and play in the sand.

Every week is filled with art and music, exuberant play and focused learning, carefully orchestrated discovery and deepening understanding. Students keep a continuous eight-year journal of personal milestones, make friends for life, and celebrate the cultural diversity of the world.

The music program is based on the philosophy and practices of Orff Schulwerk, a dynamic approach to music education developed by the German composer Carl Orff. This approach is characterized by active involvement in music-making through the body, voice, movement, and work on specially designed Orff instruments. It recognizes the many doors through which a child can enter the musical world and provides opportunities for aural, visual, and kinesthetic learners to feel successful in music via a multidimensional approach. The nurturing of the whole musician who can hear, feel, understand, and physically express music contributes to the child's ability to synthesize the intellect, senses, emotions, and physical body in ways that have important implications in their total educational experience. The social dimensions of group music-making are also a central quality of the music program.

The Music Classes: Each elementary class has music two 45-minute class meetings each week, in groups ranging from 10 to 18 children. These classes develop both skill and understanding in the basic elements of music via experiences in body percussion, speech, singing, movement, folk dance, games, drama, and the playing of pitched and non-pitched percussion instruments. Within any one class, the activities might be mixed, perhaps beginning with a circle dance, playing a game, working with a poem, adding instruments, creating movement and gesture that act out the text. Each of the media is a strand within itself with its own sequence of development. Rather than spend two months on singing alone, two months on folk dance, and so on, the strands develop side-by-side, with the teachers keeping track of each to form the overall design of the year.

Singing Time: In addition to the small-group classes, the entire elementary school gathers for a 20-minute singing time. This time is devoted exclusively to singing, with emphasis on developing a varied repertoire of songs from the American folk and popular tradition, as well as songs from cultures around the world. It is also the time for guest performers, ranging from the children themselves sharing a song or dance to professional artists presenting a program.

Elementary Chorus: Third, fourth and fifth grade students sing in the Elementary Chorus every Monday and Tuesday for 20 minutes. This class is a formal chorus rehearsal, with the hope of further extending singing and aural skills, with special emphasis on part-singing and reading scores. Students are placed in First Soprano, Second Soprano, and Alto sections. The material reflects the program by offering a varied repertoire of singing traditions.

After-School Music Opportunities: Elementary school students can study beginning violin, clarinet, flute, saxophone, and trumpet in small-group lessons through the Extended Day Program. Students with at least one year's experience on their instruments can join the After School Band.

Curriculum Integration: Music is inherently a subject that both requires and helps develop academic skills. Though teaching music as an independent subject with its own special skills and knowledge is a priority, conscious integration with other curriculum areas is practised widely. Some examples include extensive work with rhymes, poetry and song as a springboard for musical improvisation and experience (language arts); exploring the mathematical structures of music (math); using songs to teach history, geography and culture study (social studies); understanding acoustics (science); developing grace, coordination and dexterity through movement and instrumental play (physical education); and experimenting with graphic notation (art). The height of such integration is often realized in the school's traditional celebrations.

Celebrations: The music program is directly linked to the all-school celebrations through music, dance and drama. Festive gatherings that include decoration, costume, food, games, plays, songs, dances, and music occur throughout the school calendar. A spring concert and a professionally recorded CD set of the children's music-making from that year are two ways we share the students' accomplishments.

Doug Goodkin is a music teacher at The San Francisco School. He is also the author of recommended resources on music. Content for this article also comes from http://www.sfschool.org.

Building Blocks for Programming: Music

☐ **Listening**
  - ☐ Listening for patterns
  - ☐ Using visual cues to learn music
  - ☐ Connecting song lyrics with poetry
  - ☐ Appreciating popular and folk music
  - ☐ _____

☐ **Creating**
  - ☐ Composing, using found percussion sound
  - ☐ Using instruments to create music
    - ☐ Orff instruments
    - ☐ Recorders
    - ☐ Percussion ensembles from found objects
  - ☐ Rewriting songs
  - ☐ Rhythmic problem solving
  - ☐ _____

☐ **Performing**
  - ☐ Instrumental
    - ☐ Rehearsed instrumental performance
  - ☐ Singing
    - ☐ Echo and rote singing
    - ☐ Reading songs
    - ☐ Singing games
    - ☐ Rehearsed choral performing

☐ **Celebrations and Festive Gatherings**
  - ☐ _____

☐ **Music, Movement and Dance**
  - ☐ _____

☐ **Using Digital Technology**
  - ☐ _____

4 Learning "in Role"

Drama in Education

By Larry Swartz

Larry Swartz is an instructor in the Preservice Elementary program at OISE/UT where he also serves as principal of the drama continuing education courses. He has been a classroom teacher and language arts and drama consultant for the Peel District School Board. He is the author of the books The New Dramathemes *and* Classroom Events Through Poetry *and co-author of several language arts series. Larry shares his enthusiasm for literacy learning, children's literature and drama at conferences throughout North America.*

Opening the Curtains

As part of a drama course for teachers, I was teaching a demonstration lesson with a group of 25 students, ages 9 through 12, in a large gymnasium on a hot July morning. We had been exploring the novel *The Music of Dolphins* by Karen Hesse, a story about the rescue of a young girl who apparently had been living all her life with the dolphins. The students were working in role as expert doctors discussing the girl's education, socialization, and fate. I was working in role as the director of the institute where the girl had been living. After improvising a meeting to discuss the girl's progress after being in an institute for one week, the students were anxious to meet her first-hand. It had been agreed in the drama that they would, as doctors and teachers, visit with the girl to observe her behaviors. I invited some teachers in the course, who had been observing the lesson, to prepare the girl's bedroom in the institute and they spontaneously arranged some standing bulletin boards, mats, a chair, and some gym equipment to create a room for our drama. I led the children over to the area to inspect the girl. On a signal, one of the children acting as my assistant, opened the "curtains" to the room and we looked through the "one-way mirror" to watch the girl. As the imaginary drapes were slowly drawn the students remained silent, stood on their tiptoes and pushed their heads forward to stare into the room. One boy said: "I see her curled up in the bed. She seems scared. I don't think she wants to be here and we should all think about what we are doing." There were no curtains. There was no girl. There were, however, belief and commitment for this boy and the group who were caught in the "as if" world of drama we created together.

Out of This World

The following summer, I was working in a gym once again, with a group of five- and six-year-old youngsters. We had received a "Message from the Moon" (from the story by Tim Wynne-Jones and Ian Wallace) and were role-playing the scientists who met to solve the problem of helping the moon that was falling apart. We decided that we needed to visit the moon, but first we'd need a rocket ship. "What kind of ship should we build?", I asked in character as a scientist. "I think we should use everything we can find to build it." For ten minutes the children worked to build a vehicle that would take us into space using mats, chairs, benches, ropes, pails, building blocks, and other toys they had been playing with earlier in the morning. Once the spaceship was built, the children and I arranged ourselves in preparation for take off. On a signal we counted down to "Blast Off!" When we shouted out "Zero," one boy shouted, "Let's do it again!" and so we repeated the activity counting slowly, and on "Blast Off!" the children lay back in the spaceship. Through narration I took the children on a trip through space until we "landed" on the moon and were greeted by the grateful moon people. For these children working inside a story, extending their world of play, and making a play about visiting a place that can only be realized through imagination, the drama was, as the Australian educator John McLeod wrote several years ago, "real pretending."

Creating Drama from the Inside and the Outside

Drama is experiential, active learning. Through drama, all students—including those with exceptionalities—can improvise action and dialogue using a set of teaching strategies that guide them to imagine, explore, enact, communicate, and reflect upon ideas, concepts, and feelings at their own level of development. In drama, teachers lead children to create action and dialogue, using a range of drama conventions to structure the process. For art lessons, students can choose from a palette of crayon, paintbrush, marker, chalk, clay or any number of media to express ideas. For music, we use voice or instrument to create sound and music. In drama, students use voice, body, and space to make others believe in an idea, message, or mood as they take on "pretend" roles to generate creative problem solutions. We create drama both from inside and outside ourselves. As Johnston puts it in an article within *The Arts as Meaning Makers*, "To create drama, a person must concentrate, sense, perceive, imagine, think, and use the physical body and speech to communicate all these inner processes" (p. 213).

In drama, we can be anybody, at any place, at any time. We can live in a world of dolphins, meet with moon people, talk to Miss Muffet, create a medieval community struggling to save itself from a mean king, become an explorer to a new planet (or become the citizens of that planet), step inside the skin of a soldier who has been to war, invent a dance of the creatures of the undersea world, write a letter to the mayor expressing our views about the polluted factory in the village, make decisions about whether to immigrate to a new land, or imagine that we have discovered a bottle on the beach that says "Do Not Open." We can tell stories of slavery, draw pictures of memories, or demonstrate a day in the life of an adolescent who is about to leave home. We can interview Harry Potter, sail with Christopher Columbus, or sit on the bus as witnesses to Rosa Parks's historical moment.

Drama is process-centred learning, learning that is taken into the personal realm. In drama, children respond intellectually, physically, and emotionally to a variety of imagined situations calling forth actions and reactions that may have been unexplored and unexamined. For Jonothan Neelands (2000) drama is "the direct experience that is shared when people imagine and behave as if they were other than themselves in some other place at another time" (p. 4). Judith Ackroyd (2000) wants drama "that enables children to make choices, decisions, and to make sense of the worlds they encounter, yet be mindful of the literacy learning to be delivered" (p. 4). David Booth (1994) informs us that the primary aim of drama "should be to help children extract new meanings from their experiences and to communicate those meanings in the form of efficient, coherent responses. In this sense drama is both a subject matter and an approach to teaching of inherent value, particularly to the school curriculum" (p. 49).

Entering the World of Drama

A teacher's understanding of the world of drama and comfort with introducing drama practice seems to be dependent not only on early drama experiences but on the professional development explored through teacher training programs, workshops, texts, or documents provided. The children, of course, will come closer to an understanding of the drama world through the activities and opportunities a teacher chooses to provide. Some teachers start small by scattering games and activities into their program, while others choose to develop lessons on a theme or issue over several days. The time will depend on the relationships a teacher can see between drama and other curriculum goals. The classroom can provide sufficient space for the drama lesson. I remember an occasion when David Booth, who was about to work with a group of children, was asked by a teacher, "What kind of space you want for the drama?" "The only space I need," David said, "is the space between their ears."

Games and Drama Activities

These provide an effective gateway into drama since they help participants become aware of themselves, both as individuals and as members of a group. In the drama program, a spectrum of games can be introduced to encourage participation and social interaction. Through games, young people can learn social rules, release tension, respond to and follow directions, develop listening skills, and increase concentration. Different games stress different developmental activities—movement, imagination, brainstorming, trust and verbal communication. Games help build an atmosphere that is non-threatening, non-competitive, and fun. Through experiencing games and dramatic activities, students become willing to join in and work with others, take risks, and respond verbally and non-verbally to directions, narration, recorded music and sounds, and become aware of the interpretations and ideas of others.

As students develop a sense of acceptance and significance within the larger group they show more willingness to risk participation in open-ended games that invite them to respond creatively and spontaneously. One such learning strategy is called This Is a Scarf.

See how the author John Mazurek puts such drama games in the context of TRIBES learning strategies on page 81.

This Is a Scarf

—John Mazurek

The teacher demonstrates the procedure while the class stands in a circle. I like to open up a large square scarf made of thin fabric and say, "This is a scarf, but it's not really a scarf . . ." I manipulate the fabric into a flat shape of another object and announce, "It's a pizza!" The scarf is then passed to the next person in the circle. Each person is challenged, in turn, to follow the script of the previous person, then transform the scarf into something else (e.g., "This a pizza, but it's not really a pizza. It's a sari.") The class is encouraged to demonstrate attention and open-minded acceptance of each interpretation that is offered. Everyone confronts the difficulty of deferring thoughts of their own ideas and impending presentation in order to focus on what others are saying and showing. The post-activity reflection and appreciation discussions highlight and celebrate these aspects of performance as much as the imaginative variety of what has been shared.

Three Ball Pass

—John Mazurek

One of the activities I choose to introduce during the early stages of the year is Three Ball Pass. The students are arranged in a circle. I offer a small, soft rubber or foam ball and toss it to a student, calling out his or her name. He or she then repeats the process: another student's name is called, the class echoes the name, and the ball is tossed from the first student to the second. Students fold their hands in front of themselves after they have had a turn so they will not be called upon and receive the ball a second time. Once every student has had a turn, the ball is returned to the teacher. To promote a degree of challenge, everyone is encouraged to choose and toss to someone who is not an immediate neighbor in the circle. Additional rounds can be added to the first, as everyone's familiarity with the game and the names increases. As the class becomes more adept at the game, a second ball might be added for the rapid toss, then a third. To promote fun, I sometimes introduce a surprise object (a rubber chicken) instead of a ball. Circle games such as this one ensure that each student hears his or her name affirmed by the entire group, and gives each individual a "safe" way to learn the names of everyone in the class.

Storytelling

This activity increases students' mastery of language, showing them how words can be manipulated to make meaning. It develops the ability to turn narration into dialogue and dialogue into narration. Storytelling can provide the initial starting point for the drama; it can reveal an unexplained idea in a familiar story; it can focus details; it can serve as a review of what has already taken place; or it can be a way to build an understanding of role. Students can tell stories in a circle, with a partner, through mime and tableau, chorally, or as narration for mime. They can improvise from the story, change the story, or find new stories within the story. Storytelling also provides a meaningful context for students communicating with an audience. As students tell stories that explain what has gone on before or that present another point of view, they are enhancing the communication skills that are essential to all their drama work.

Storytelling is an important form of talk in terms of human intellectual and emotional development. When students come to school they already know a great deal about making stories and responding to them. This knowledge forms the foundation of the storytelling work along with methodologies that encourage the students to collaborate, discuss, and support one another in the storytelling process.

I believe that we need to provide opportunities for students to engage in language learning opportunities in which they have a certain amount of power and control. We need to structure various dramatic contexts in which students have opportunities to talk and write about something of significance.
—Kathleen Gould Lundy

62

Inside and Outside and All Around the Story

—Bob Barton

What follows is an outline of a storytelling project with junior aged children at Bowmore Road Public School sponsored by the Drama and Dance Department of the Toronto District School Board.

Thinking about Stories: In the initial session, I involved the students by having them think about what stories are and why people tell them. I encouraged the children to think about different kinds of stories and the ingredients that are important in them (e.g., characters, dialogue, settings, the element of surprise).

Sometimes a simple activity can release a torrent of stories. For example, I often ask the students to sit in a circle, to tell their name and how they got it, and to explain what they think it means. Some students know a great deal about their names. I have a hunch that other students go home to further research information about their names and learn stories surrounding their own naming as well as that of other family members. To promote personal narratives, I have asked students to sketch a map of their neighborhoods and to place an "X" somewhere on the map where something happened to them. Perhaps there was a fire on their street or a fall from a bike might have resulted in a chipped tooth. Since I was going to explore folk tales for a period of time with this Grade 6 class, I asked the students to share their earliest memories of folk tales. Several students recalled stories that they heard told by parents or grandparents, while others remembered reading folk tales in school. To conclude the session, I told the students the story *The Storm Wife*. My storytelling allowed us to discuss how important body language, gesture, and facial expressions are to communicate our stories and served as a model for the storytelling that I would be inviting the children to explore during future visits.

Heeding the Imagination: For many students, storytelling means going to the library to find a folk tale to memorize. For my second visit I wanted to help the students understand that learning a story is not about memorizing but is a highly creative process. It has a lot to do with paying attention to what your imagination is telling you. I told the story *The Wax Children* and as a follow-up I encouraged the students to tell me what had happened in their heads. The simple question "Did anyone see pictures in your mind?" was enough to spark a lively description of characters, landscapes, and events. And there's more. Stories trigger questions in our minds (e.g., How did the rest of the community react to the presence of the wax children? How might the wax children be taken care of?). Stories also beget stories and many listeners will suddenly recall a personal memory which becomes part of their story listening experience. On this occasion, comparisons to familiar stories were mentioned, aspects of story structures were referred to, and students identified powerfully with the dilemmas of the story characters. This is the process that a storyteller must engage in when learning a story. The elements that the students identified are all essential to the development of the tale. It's so much more than words.

At the conclusion of our "tell me the story of your listening" session, I asked the students to work in pairs and draw the story in quick sketches. This activity provided an opportunity for the students to retell the story visually and to rehearse it in a discussion with a partner. Once the story was sketched, I invited the students to retell the story in their own words by taking turns back and forth with story segments.

Understanding Character: An important part of storytelling is getting inside characters' heads in order to understand their motives and feelings. Drama can play a significant role in helping students to look at a character close-up. The drama convention of teacher-in-role is an effective strategy to use in order to have the students work together to solve problems, ask questions, give opinions, and tell stories in role.

For this session I began the drama work in role by explaining, "I am going to pretend to be a character from the story. The character is going to talk about a problem. Your job is to listen carefully to what the character says and to observe the character's behavior." In role, I enacted the scene as Frau Goethal, the sorceress in the story "Rapunzel."

We next worked out of role. I introduced another drama convention called Role on the Wall (see page 78) to have the students record observations about the character of Frau Goethel, whom they had just met. I drew an outline of the character on the board. Inside the character outline I recorded the information and observations the students gleaned from the role taken (e.g., she seems to be vengeful). On the outside of the figure, I recorded the questions that the students wanted to ask the character in order to better understand her dilemma (e.g., Why do you think you are better than your neighbors?).

I chose to go back into the role to have the students interrogate the character. The big idea here is to stimulate the students to examine the difficult decisions that story characters must make. All stories are about decisions and having some idea of how decisions are reached (sometimes carelessly; often with great difficulty). These decisions can open up possibilities for the teller to interpret story incidents with greater insight. For example, in the interview Frau Goethel argued powerfully that she was acting for the good of Rapunzel, not out of meanness.

Going Back into the Story: To tell a story effectively, I believe that students need every opportunity to have their vision of the tale expanded. I do this by taking them back into the story to explore memory metaphor and personal connection. By means of *tableau* work, *soundscaping* (see page 78), *movement*, *improvisation*, and *retelling* we can investigate every nook and cranny of the story so that the landscape, events, and characters are as familiar as the backs of their hands.

In this final session I asked the students to develop an image of the story "Rapunzel" that was strong in their minds and write a two- or three-sentence description. After sharing these, I then had the students prepare a brief plot summary of the story and write descriptive passages of three or four sentences to elaborate key scenes in their outline.

Exploring Presentation: Presenting the stories to others was carried out in varied ways. Some students were keen to tell the whole class; others were not. In order for students to explore aspects of storytelling presentation, such as eye contact, tone of voice, pacing, clarity, modulation, gesture, and body language, I integrated pair work and small-group work so that the students could consider, experiment, and rehearse with effective ways to tell a story to others.

Role-playing

Role-playing is at the heart of the drama curriculum. Through exploring drama, students develop an understanding of themselves and others and can learn about the lives of people in different times, places, and cultures. Pretending to be someone else involves an act of the imagination that is of central importance in the development of the ability to understand others. As students live through experiences of others, they learn to understand a variety of points of view and motives, and to empathize with others. They also learn to clarify their own point of view and to develop their ability to think carefully. When students role-play in groups they are encouraged to interact with others and adjust their in-role responses to the cues of others. In doing so, students learn to work with and respect the ideas of others.

It is the business of drama to open up for scrutiny what we think we know and examine how it is we know it.
—Kathleen Gallagher

Exploring Alternative Perspectives through Role-playing

—Catherine Combs

As part of the Grade 6 social studies curriculum, the students in my class were studying the lives of Aboriginal Canadians. In order to help them become more aware of contemporary issues related to the lives of Aboriginal youth, I selected the novel *My Name Is Seepeetza*, by Shirley Sterling, as a source for drama exploration. The book informed the students significantly about the culture. In particular, the life of Seepeetza helped us examine the history of the forced departure of Aboriginal children to Indian residential schools. I recognized that my students could experience what it might have been like to attend one of these schools through the imagined context that drama can offer. Through role-playing, discussion, and contemplation of the dilemma, students connected to the learning in a deep, intense way. They became empathetic to one Aboriginal child's experience, and questioned why these children were forced to leave their homes. Through their experience of the drama, the students were led to new insights.

Fostering Personal Reflection: Since my students were studying school life of Aboriginal children in the 1950s and 1960s, I wanted them to first draw upon their own experiences of school. I began the drama structure by having the students recall happy and sad moments that students can have at school. These were shared with each other in pairs, and a few were shared with the whole class. The students then froze in a pose for a school picture. They held in their minds and showed through facial expression and body language whatever moments were most predominant in their minds. In beginning the drama structure with personal reflections, I felt that the students could begin to make connections to the Aboriginal children's experiences of school. A context had been set to introduce the source, an excerpt from the novel, which I read aloud to the students.

Interpreting Text: Next, my students brainstormed questions that they would like answered based on the text. They also made a list of who might answer these questions. I then divided the class into small groups and gave each one another text excerpt representing a scene in the day in the life of Seepeetza. For this activity, the students were asked to interpret the text through reading, movement, tableaux and mime to represent the events and conversations that

Seepeetza would have at school. Once improvisations were rehearsed, each group presented their work and the class had the opportunity to witness each of the scenes to better understand a variety of perspectives.

Writing-in-Role: I felt that the students were identifying with Seepeetza, the Aboriginal girl whose experience we were studying. I had wanted them to "live" for a few moments the life of another child and since Seepeetza was the same age as my students, they had little problem identifying with her. I knew that I had to give them time for reflection so that their understanding of her world would deepen. I decided to have the students write in role with the following instructions: "Imagine that you are Seepeetza. You have run away from residential school and you have only one piece of paper and stamp to write a letter. Who would you write to? What information would you convey in this letter? What feelings would you share? How might you explain your decision to run away?"

Their writing-in-role turned out authentic and thoughtful, and the students really felt the pain and sorrow of Seepeetza. One girl wrote: "I hate the school and I want to move so badly because of the way they treat us. I don't like the food and the way we get disciplined. And most of all, I cannot talk, hug, kiss or hold my sisters and that makes me feel sad. And when I am feeling not so good there is no one there for me to talk to." Another wrote: "We only get to go home in the summer. Think about it—sleeping in your school! We all want to get out of school and live with our Moms and Dads." My students felt deep in their hearts the suffering of Seepeetza.

A few other students even went beyond the sad feelings of being separated from one's family. They saw the effects of having one's identity stripped away. "I'm writing for you guys to understand how I'm doing here. I can no longer stand this school. . . . I hate this stupid law. It isn't fair." Another girl wrote: "I hate school, it's the worst. I hate that they changed my name to Martha Stone. I felt mad and sad. It wasn't a nice feeling." And finally, one boy, fairly new to Canada, wrote in his writing-in-role letter: "At school, we're just a bunch of robots that are commanded to do something. When we grow up, we'll need people to order us around." To help the students better understand the internal struggles of Seepeetza, I used the convention of Voices in the Head (see page 78) which allows group members to articulate the thoughts of a character. As I tapped each student on the shoulder, they could speak aloud an improvised thought, or one adapted from their writing-in-role.

Deepening the Drama: At this point in the drama, I felt that the children had "stepped into another's shoes" and were empathetic, but they were only connecting with the personal situation of Seepeetza. I wrote in my journal about the experience: "The drama isn't going deep enough. I need it to go to another level—but how do I push the children in that direction? How can I deepen the drama?"

It was my turn for reflection. I realized that what was missing was a connection to the universal. The children felt Seepeetza's personal sorrow, but they didn't see her pain in relationship to all those who have suffered racism. I decided that the best way to lead them to a deeper understanding of the situation would be to give them another perspective in a group role-play situation. And I would offer this different perspective by working in role as a government official from the Ministry of Indian Affairs.

The role-play started off with the students asking questions only about Seepeetza. In order to steer them to the bigger question of the general treatment of Native peoples, I, in role, refused to answer any personal questions about Seepeetza, claiming that I could talk only about what was in the best interest of Native peoples as a whole. The children then started seeing the treatment of the other children as part of a bigger picture of racism. One girl spoke with passion: "We should make our own decisions. If we [as Native people] respect them [as white people], they should respect us!" Another claimed, while pointing to her chest, "You're taking away what is inside of us, and that's not right. Just because we're different doesn't mean we need to change!" The students were so engaged, so connected with the situation that they quickly lost the masks they most often wear at school. Two of the toughest boys—with the usual slouch and complete look of boredom—took on female roles and remained totally authentic and impassioned in role.

Reflecting on the Drama Structure: After the group role-play ended, we reflected on the whole structure through Corridor of Voices (see page 77) and discussion. Learning continued as the students made links to instances of racism around the world. They even thought about what they could personally do. One girl said: "If I make fun of someone who is different in the schoolyard, that's the same as what the government did to the Native peoples—not accepting people for who they are and trying to change them."

Later, the classroom teacher had the students write about what they learned, allowing them to reflect further. One boy, who is designated learning disabled, wrote, "I learned that the chidren [children] once had a drem [dream] now thay [they] have nothing but a mamaer [memory]." He completely understood that these children lost more than just their childhood. Another young man offered that the Aboriginal children "had to change their beliefs and throw their dignity away. When they grow up they were confused and felt that they did not belong." A few others thought about what we did in the drama and connected to their lives at present. They wrote that they would try and not judge people by how they look.

In order for the students to complete the writing-in-role task, they had to reflect on what we had done in the drama structure. Dorothy Heathcote contends that "for students it is not only the experience arising out of the action which enables them to learn . . . without reflection there is no learning from the experience. When students live through an experience on the inside, they gain the double effect of knowing internally and reflecting on the product of their knowing." Within the structure of the drama, a teacher must build in times for reflection. Edmiston claims that "the teacher can thus structure the drama so that the students will have opportunities to reflect in ways which would not arise if the students were left to themselves as they are in spontaneous dramatic play." I realize how important it was for me to allow the students this opportunity for reflection. Connections were made. Insights were experienced. New attitudes were being constructed.

Improvisation

This spontaneous activity encourages students to be responsible for giving direction to a drama using the information and ideas they receive from others. To experience what drama is, students need to spend time in role, improvising. Improvisational situations may be initiated and developed from suggestions by the teacher, from peers, or from the source they are exploring. Improvisation demands that the students face the challenge of the situation and negotiate directly with the group members and the teacher, using language appropriate to the situation, and responding to and building on the ideas of others involved in the drama. Working in groups, each participant has the responsibility of giving to and taking from others, solving problems, and making decisions. Improvisation invites students to respond to a dramatic situation through verbal and non-verbal means and since there are no correct answers in improvisation work, students have the opportunity to explore, take risks, and be creative.

Improvising from Picture Books: Three Moments in Drama

— *Christine Jackson*

In drama, teachers are always working for "the moment." We plan on our feet, shaping for significance—reframing and focusing the thoughts, feelings, and questions of the group so that the power of a moment can be fully registered. Here are a few such moments—moments whereby the richness of the drama source, the sensitivity of the group, the selective use of conventions, and the innate power of drama converged to touch our hearts and minds.

A Music Box: I am working with a Grade 5/6 class, new to drama and new to group work. It is only the third week of the school year. I have read a very brief passage from a picture book, *Trupp* by Janell Cannon. We are weaving a story together, constructing the life of a woman who is homeless. Drawing on clues from the story, the class has determined that she is kind, cautious but courageous, and wants to be needed. These insights and inferences are discussed and debated, and then a representation of the character is drawn on chart paper, upon which these character attributes are recorded. The students are divided into small groups to weave a bit of story about her life, based on a treasured object from her cart—a sea shell, a photograph of a soldier, a string of pearls, a tarnished key, a broken music box. Suddenly, the shared focus and sensitive consideration of the group begin to fragment. Disgruntlement and argument ensue. I realize that I have not provided enough structure for these students who are unaccustomed to working in such an open-ended medium. I am just about to stop and redirect the exploration when a strain of music cuts through the din and disquiet. Everyone stops. A student whispers," Ah—it's Bernice's music box." Capitalizing on this accidental opportunity, I add—"Yes, her new friend, Trupp, fixed it for her." We all listen: a long drawn-out, deep listening. We read the metaphor. The mending of something broken. We feel the tenderness. We linger in the moment.

Then, somewhat abruptly, the groups return to the story-building exercise and the same disgruntlement ensues. Perhaps I should have harnessed the power of that moment and turned to a reflective writing activity. Was this a missed moment, or was the moment complete unto itself?

A Clap of Thunder: I am working with a Grade 2/3 class. I have read to them the story *Barefoot*, by Pamela Duncan Edwards. In this wonderful book, the story of a slave's escape is told from the perspective of the forest creatures, who work together to guide the slave to safety. So far in our drama exploration, we have created contrasting tableaux depicting life in the master's house and life in the slaves' quarters. We are now gathered as slaves meeting secretly under cover of night. In role, I announce that I have planned my escape and will be leaving in the morning. The students (in role) entreat me to stay, warn of the dangers of the bounty hunters who will surely find and punish me. We speak in hushed tones, feeling the imminent danger of the guard dog and night watchman—a very real tension pervades our imaginary circumstances. With a sudden fury, a clap of thunder shakes the very foundation of the building and we all spontaneously duck, burying our heads in our arms. We stay like that for a long moment, feeling the fear, connecting in some small, but significant way to that time and that place. Slowly we re-emerge to face one another. A student whispers: "Go. Allow courage to grow over your fear and go, now. They won't chase you in the storm." In turn, each student gives me a word of advice or a small gift for my satchel. "Follow the north star."

A piece of bread.

"Travel at night."

A jug of water.

"Find Canada."

A warm hug.

A Cloud: It is my first classroom visit as a consultant and it just happens to be a JK/SK/1. I have come to do a demonstration class and I arrive with a new picture book, *Cloudland* by John Burningham, and much eager, earnest, anxious energy. The children are adorable and engage with the imaginative world of the story from the very first page. We create chants—magic words that allow us as cloud child to rescue Albert, a young boy who has fallen off a cliff. We float him safely to a magical, beautiful land in the clouds. We retell the events of the story, making statues of our favorite Cloudland games—cloudball, stormmaking, cloudraces, dipping our paintbrushes in rainbows. We have a merry time. Except for one little boy who does not show the slightest trace of interest. He has found a spot on the floor where he is engaged in what looks like yoga—complicated postures—twists, rolls and lifts.

We are now gathered on a cloud, which we have formed by fluffing together all of our little clouds. I am in role as Albert and the students are in role as my cloud friends. I explain that I have been enjoying myself in Cloudland but that I am missing my rock collection, my friends, and my Mom and Dad. I want to go home. A moment of quiet consideration ensues. The children sit with the realization of Albert's loss—here in the weightless world of the clouds, we feel the weight of Albert's heavy heart. And so the problem solving begins. The children create new chants—magical words to safely guide Albert home. They summon the winds to steer Albert in the right direction. Out of thin air and soft clouds, they carve a winding staircase that leads to Albert's doorstep. All of this transpires, while one little boy continues with his pretzel pose. He is ever present in my teacher mind.

It feels like the drama is ending. I, as Albert, have arrived at the front door to my house. Suddenly, the little boy untwists from his inverted pretzel pose and cries, "WAIT!" He comes over and hands me an imaginary box.

"What's this?"

"A present. Open it up."

I pretend to carefully open the precious package. I hold the precious something in my hands, and look to the child for guidance.

"It's a cloud with a string," he answers. "Hang it above your bed. If you miss us, tug on the string three times, say the magic words, and we will come for you."

A special drama moment, bringing powerful closure to our adventure. An unanticipated moment. A learning moment for me, about the inner workings of drama. A reminder of the unseen, unheard dramas that are shaping beneath the surface of our work. A reminder that drama can facilitate the intersection of private and public worlds, creating moments of resonance.

Interpretation

Oral interpretation of text allows students to manipulate a text and trains their eyes and ears in exploring the rhythms of language. Reading aloud lets students demonstrate their reading comprehension as they make print come alive through their voices. Reading aloud in the drama class may involve the teacher reading to the class, the class reading to the teacher, a student reading with a group, a student reading with a partner or a group reading to a group.

Drama provides a number of contexts for students to read aloud: reading scripts or dialogues with a partner or a group, choral dramatization, singing, reading narration as others move in response, reading text that has been written specifically for the drama, reading research information that will affect the drama. Working with peers to read aloud stories, poems, or scripts on a particular theme or topic allows students to take part in a creative activity that involves experimentation with voice, sound, gesture and movement. Because of these variations, no two oral interpretations of a single poem are alike. When students interpret scripts or prepare choral dramatizations, story theatre or Readers theatre presentations, they are involved in a process that enhances rehearsal, revision, and presentation skills. Moreover, when they work with others to read aloud together, their problem-solving skills are likely to be enriched as they make decisions about the best way to present a text.

In the end there is nothing left but who we are and what we see, feel and do about it. That is art.
—*Jane Alexander*

Exploring Script

— *Carmen Alvarez*

In my Grade 5 class, we had been exploring the theme of bullying by reading picture books, poems, and novels to help the students come closer to an understanding of bullying behavior and to have them consider *I Met a Bully on the Hill* by Martha Brooks and Maureen Hunter and ways of handling put-downs and bullying. An excerpt from the script served as a worthy source for exploration.

Reading Aloud: After the students read the script independently, we discussed what information we knew about Raymond the bully and J.J., a new student to the school who was caught in Raymond's web. Raymond threatened J.J., saying that the hill belonged to him and that if J.J. wanted to use it she'd have to pay rent. To begin the interpretation of the script, it was read aloud. I read the part of Raymond, the students read the part of J.J., and then we repeated the activity, reversing roles.

Students then worked in pairs to read the script aloud. Each student had a chance to assume Raymond's part so that the script was read twice. On the first rehearsal, the students were instructed to portray the bully as a calm, quiet character while J.J. was told to demonstrate her anger. When the activity was repeated, Raymond was instructed to show his anger while J.J. was calm and quiet. In this way, the students came to understand how voice, gesture, and intent can change the meaning behind the words of a script.

Improvising the Scene: To deepen the understanding of the scene, the activity was repeated. This time the script was not read aloud, but pairs improvised the situation. To begin, J.J. moved away from Raymond and on a signal quietly approached him. Each pair was invited to continue the dialogue for a moment or two following Raymond's threat. As a follow-up to the activity, I interviewed each J.J. by asking questions to find out how she felt: "Why do you think Raymond is targeting you? Did you feel that you did anything to deserve this treatment? Are you going to tell anybody about what happened? Why didn't you just leave the hill and walk home another way? What do you think is going to happen the next time you meet Raymond?"

Providing a Forum: Using the convention of Forum theatre (see page 77), the scene was improvised using two volunteers from the classroom. The class offered suggestions on how the characters might move and offered dialogue for each of the characters. This technique helped the students to explore a variety of attitudes to an event and rehearse ways of handling a bully.

Working in small groups, the students brainstormed plans for J.J. to handle the bully on the hill should they meet again.

Creating a Corridor of Voices: As a final activity, the class created a Corridor of Voices (see page 77) representing the thoughts of J.J. as she approached Raymond the following day. One of the students volunteered to assume the role of J.J. This convention allows students to make public some of the conflicts and dilemmas that a character in a drama might experience. The class was divided into two groups, each facing the other. As J.J. strolled up the "hill," she listened to the Corridor of Voices that served as her conscience and helped give her courage to confront the bully. When J.J. reached the end of the corridor, she met Raymond. A short improvisation which dealt with J.J. making a decision about handing money over to Raymond followed.

After the improvisation, students discussed how J.J. handled the situation and brainstormed a list of ways to deal with a situation like the one conveyed in this script. Students then worked with a partner to prepare a short script that would continue the excerpt they had been exploring. Students wrote the conversation that might have taken place between Raymond and J.J. thus creating a new dialogue that might occur between a bully and target.

Playmaking

In playmaking, improvisation is extended into a sequence of lessons organized around creating a more formal, structured piece of work—a play. Playmaking enables students to learn about dramatic structure and to experience the satisfaction of having carried a relatively ambitious project through to a conclusion. The source for the extended improvisation may be a strand from the curriculum, a story, or suggestions from the students. It is important that the teacher focus the drama by defining the situation and the task. Presentation before an audience is not necessarily the goal of this model of work. If the class chooses to present their work, the teacher needs to allow time for development before polishing is begun.

Confronting Issues through Drama

—Sheena Robertson

September 2001 found me in an unusual place with my students. Working with a Grade 7/8 class, I had the opportunity to teach many students for a third or fourth year. We were accustomed to one another, able to work together and collaborate easily, and happy to debate and explore ideas and philosophies, and to tackle challenging issues when they emerged from literature or day-to-day events. The years of doing intensive drama work together had created a strong bond among us, and the students were highly versed in both the practice and theory of drama. The challenge to me, as a teacher, was to design programming that would not be repetitive, would address the learning needs of my new adolescents, and would also engage and include two student teachers who would apprentice in our classroom throughout the year.

The summer of 2001 had been a particularly difficult one in the Regent Park community. A number of young Black men had been shot and killed then, and there was a palpable tension between the police and the Black community. Sydney Hemmans, a young man known and respected by many of my students, had been shot six times in the chest, and left to bleed to death on the street. The media coverage of the Regent Park neighborhood seemed to be particularly negative and focused only on the dangers and violence connected to the area, and not on any of the many positive initiatives and qualities of this diverse multicultural community. All of us arrived at school that first week full of sorrow, and feeling a little overwhelmed by how to cope with the negative things swirling around us.

Gathering Research: In collaboration with the visiting student teachers, we decided to begin the year with a media literacy unit, utilizing drama, photography, and video skills to draw a more well-rounded picture of the vibrant community where the students lived. We began by gathering research about the past and present of Regent Park, interviewing parents and community advocates, and exploring the students' points of view that included both positive and negative perspectives. The teacher candidates worked individually with each student in the classroom to take digital photographs, stressing that they wanted images that explored how each student saw "The Park." There was no right or wrong idea here, just information and image gathering. The photographs included images of street people, garbage, and drug dealers, but there were also many images of people from different cultures interacting positively, children playing, basketball tournaments, amazing graffiti art, and proof of advocacy initiatives.

We had just started to gather steam with our explorations when larger tragic events overcame us.

Finding a Common Voice: September 11, 2001, is a day that profoundly affected the world stage, my own world, and the world of the students I worked with every day. How something so awful could have happened initially seemed unbelievable to all of us in Room 218, but that sense of horror was tempered by politics and points of view outside that of mainstream western media. There were many conflicting voices in our class. Many of my students came from Muslim backgrounds and from parts of the world where politics plays out very differently than it usually does here. Their viewpoints were greatly influenced by their home situations, their experiences prior to coming to Canada (often as refugees), and by discussions they were overhearing at mosque, at home, or within the community.

In the end it was my students, who knew me so well, who led me in the direction we needed to go to confront the issues and the sadness we felt. They asked to talk. "Please, Miss Sheena, can we just talk about this. It needs to be our 'hot topic' today!" A bit lost, I followed their lead, and did what we had always done as a group. We started to collaborate, to explore how we felt and what we should do *together*, and we used writing, and art, and drama to do it. One of the key tools I have always used is journal conversations between myself and my students. Journal entries give me insight into what students are thinking, which guides me in my teaching. We wrote and created art pieces first, and then I took their ideas and questions and we talked from there. At times when our talk seemed too raw, we would work in role, to help us step back a little. Slowly, gradually, we started to unravel how we were all feeling and move towards action. During one particularly emotion-filled talk, one of my quietest girls burst out with, "Why do good people let such bad things happen in this world? What do *you* do so things like this won't happen?" The last part was not an accusation; it was an honest question from a student who knew me well, and authentically wanted to know what an adult in her world did to try to make the world a better place. There was an overwhelming silence, and all those eyes fixed on me again.

I took a deep breath and answered from my heart. "Sometimes I feel like I'm not doing enough, but I became a teacher. I'm here with you having this discussion, and I'm asking you to think, and debate, and question so you can answer that for yourself. I became a teacher because in looking for my place in the world, I started to believe that you have to think globally and act locally, and that's what I try and do." Heads slowly nodded. Ideas started to percolate. "What if we stop talking, and start *doing* something? We can't control the world, or New York, or the Americans, or even Regent Park, but we can do something here in our class, in our school! Yah, it's not like our school is the most peaceful place around. What if we got kids here talking about these issues . . . Imagine if every classroom in every school in the world did *something*, had these kinds of discussions. Would that stop bad things from happening, do you think? What can we actually do though? Who's going to listen to us? Well, the little kids would, they think we're kind of cool." The students in Room 203 had started to find their way, and so had I.

Acting Locally: So off we went on a year-long journey to *act locally* in whatever way we could. The kids identified harassment as a major issue within the school and linked that to the things they saw happening in the world at large. The first step we took was to utilize our earlier research on the stereotyping of Regent Park, and identify what was true and false about it. Then we explored how harassment, if unchecked, could grow and lead to much more violent behavior by the time you were a teenager with greater freedom in the community. We defined harassment very broadly and then explored how frequently it happens—on a daily, hourly, indeed, a moment-to-moment basis. The students felt strongly that it didn't just happen out of the blue, that it was a choice, and that you were contributing if you stood and watched, or just laughed, or didn't step forward and tell someone to stop—a tremendously difficult thing to do when you're 13—indeed, when you're 30! All of these issues were explored through scene study, and research was presented in a docudrama format, almost as if we were watching video clips of actual scenes occurring in the school.

Creating Forums for Problem Solving: Next, we created a choral speaking performance for the entire school. This piece was written collaboratively by the students, and the presentation was done in a hip hop style, which engaged the audience and invited them to participate, while at the same time defining harassment and giving specific examples and solutions. Once the entire school had seen our presentation, we went into every primary and junior class and did Forum theatre workshops with the younger students. This idea came from three of the boys who had been in my class for four years. They were debating how best to get younger kids thinking and problem-solving, and came to me with a proposal to take real-life situations, run the scene, and then freeze it at the point of conflict. They felt that if they facilitated it properly, they could get the younger students to step into the drama, and find more positive resolutions. These workshops were tremendously successful, and we then followed up with ongoing announcements, posters around the school, and a buddy system which linked younger students to an older buddy to whom they could come to facilitate positive solutions to schoolyard and hallway conflicts. Our classroom was a busy place, with many small people coming through, sometimes at inopportune moments, but the positive effects on my students and on the tone of the school were well worth the occasional inconvenience.

A Celebration of Community: The culmination of this work came in early June, when CBC Radio approached us. In response to the ongoing killings involving Black youth, CBC was organizing a Forum concerning the issue. Through the grapevine, they had heard about the work we had been doing, and they wanted to record our choral speaking piece and use it to promote the Forum. In addition, they wanted representatives from our class to participate. We took part in both ways, and were thrilled to do so. My students were the only people of their age who spoke on the radio, and they spoke with great pride and poise about who they were, about the positive things they were doing in their community, about their hugely multicultural class, and how even in the aftermath of September 11, they never targeted or blamed one another, but instead decided to do something *together*. They also knew that in a year which had started with so much negative media focus on Regent Park, they had created a tiny slice of something entirely positive for the world to see.

Theatre for Young Audiences

Attending a live performance can be a significant experience for students as they learn about the excitement and possibilities of the composite art. The basic aim of any theatrical performance is entertainment, but good theatre, while entertaining the audience, needs to satisfy deeper cognitive, emotional, and social needs. In today's rapidly changing, often troubled society, theatre for young people, when well written and well produced, can intrinsically inform, stimulate feelings, offer hope and truth, and enable young audiences to gain understanding and insights into situations they may or may not have experienced. When children are exposed to theatre, they can learn to develop their responses and learn about the responses of others. The more young people are given opportunities to see live performances, the more their insights are honed, the more their appreciation can grow, so that as they mature, they can become their own best critics of the art form.

The world of theatre for young people is complicated and fragile. Productions are often required to address a specific age group. Plays also need to be cost appropriate, whether students are taken to the theatre or plays are brought to the schools. Also, when selecting a performance, teachers often consider curriculum expectations and activities that the experience can foster in the classroom—usually with the support of a teacher's guide—for classroom activities as a response to the themes of the play. For companies that tour schools, the productions must be economical, easy to transport and assemble, and good enough to produce magic in the dimness of a crowded gym or auditorium with often poor acoustics. For companies that produce plays, the bums-in-seats mentality predominates. It is worrisome when plays are presented only for their familiarity of title and commercial appeal geared to luring audiences into the theatre.

Nothing But the Best Will Do

—Jim Giles

I am commited to organizing an arts series within the school and take the initiative to integrate curriculum events before or after students take part in a performance by a visiting theatre or music group. I believe that to make the theatre-going experience richer for students, it is important to set time aside in the classroom to reflect on the experience or to offer opportunities for students to be involved in presentations themselves, perhaps hitchhiking on the content or techniques they've experienced while watching theatre.

Hitchhiking on Performance Experiences: For example, after seeing *Faustwork*, a theatrical presentation featuring masks and mime, I tapped into the enthusiasm of my Grade 2 students by having them create simple decorative half-masks using foam and cloth and bright colored paper. These masks were used for presentations of familiar tales, like "Little Red Hen" and "Chicken Little." Working in small groups, the children were motivated to read and reread a scripted version of a tale. The students rehearsed to become familiar with the plot and assigned themselves speaking parts to enact the script. I then arranged for the children in my class to prepare their Readers Theatre presentations for two Kindergarten classes in school. The experience allowed the children to practise their read-aloud skills, to revise their work for presentation and to develop social growth as they worked with others. For the students with limited language ability, the safety of the masks gave them confidence to speak in the drama presentation.

Responding to Theatre: I am fortunate to be able to attend a number of productions, and to witness the range of stories, presentation styles, production values, and acting talent that give me a perspective on the quality of a piece. I am naturally responding to plays as a lifetime theatre-goer. I can admire the square white cloth used in the play *The Happy Prince* by Oscar Wilde, adapted by Leslie

Arden, to show the snow that settled in the street and then delight when it is reversed to show a shining silver fabric to convey that the snow has turned to ice. I can laugh out loud and be moved when two brothers argue in an invented language ("No leeba me here") in *Dib and Dob and the Journey Home* by David Craig and Robert Morgan. I can have my consciousness and compassion raised about those who live on the streets when watching *Danny, the King of the Basement*, also by David Craig. Of course, I can be frustrated by productions with substandard acting or ones that misuse special effects that I feel only serve to compensate for the tediousness of a convoluted narrative. My lens is framed by my age, experience, values, and previous theatre-going experiences. If I try to see these productions from a child's point of view, I cannot grasp their delights and understandings, even though they may be similar to my own. Their lenses are framed by their own stage of development, their knowledge, values, narrative, fantasy, wonder, and life events that they are bringing to the theatre-watching experience.

Structuring and Grouping for Drama

Drama needs to involve as many children in the experience as possible. It is best if all the children take part in experimenting with the flow of thinking, the flow of language and the flow of movement at the same time. Sometimes the class may work as a single unit, each individual functioning as part of the whole. At times, students might work separately without interacting with others. This provides an opportunity for deepening concentration and allows for the privacy of individual exploration. Distractions can be minimized, too. Within a drama structure, students may work in pairs or in small groups engaging in social interaction, supporting one another, stimulating each other's thinking and negotiating to build and perhaps share the work. Sometimes the children will work as one large group, learning to compromise, cooperate and communicate as they gain an understanding of power struggles, conflicts and the need to combine the thoughts of several individuals. Some events require the students to simply observe or discuss. They should be participating not just as an audience, but as individuals who want to learn or gather information from a situation. In any lesson, some participants demand immediate and continuous involvement and need to be challenged into deeper achievement; others must be encouraged to participate and be persuaded to think in terms of the good of the whole group.

In a drama structure, there may be several sides to an issue being explored. By switching roles, students can explore the perceptions of the characters. By seeing different students play the same role, they can examine the facets of a character and the dilemma he or she encounters.

Common Drama Conventions

In their book *Structuring Drama Work*, Jonothan Neelands and Tony Goode have offered teachers an outline of many conventions that are available to teachers and students in order to structure drama activity. The authors define conventions as being "indicators of the way in which *time*, *space* and *presence* can interact and be imaginatively shaped to create different kinds of meanings in theatre" (1990/2000). The following are examples of conventions that teachers can select from in order to establish appropriateness between the needs of the group, the content chosen for the drama, and the opportunities for learning.

What makes drama—in the hands of strong and responsive teachers—particularly able to raise the stakes in learning enterprises is its capacity to both teach content in a meaningful and imagined context and to feature relationships between co-creators of the drama, in both the imagined and real classroom context.
—*Kathleen Gallagher*

Collective Drawing: The class or small groups make a collective image to represent a place or people in the drama. The image then becomes a concrete reference for ideas that are being discussed or are half-perceived.

Corridor of Voices: The class forms two facing lines, thus forming an alley, or corridor. The teacher or a student in role represents a protagonist from the drama. As the character walks slowly down the alley, the students, serving as the character's conscience, represent his or her thoughts about making a decision. The voices can offer advice, warnings, or quotes from earlier in the drama. As the character reaches the end of the corridor, he or she decides what course of action to take.

Creating an Environment: Students use available materials and furniture to define a space where a drama is happening as accurately as possible. An office, a bedroom, a garden, a factory, and a jail cell are examples of sets that can be designed to physically represent where events have taken place or are talked about in the drama.

A Day in the Life: This strategy is useful, particularly when a character is faced with a problem she or he must solve. Played in pairs or in small groups, it helps students recognize the roles we assume in various situations. This convention allows the class to organize improvisations around a central dilemma; however, by assigning different times of the day for each group to prepare a scene, the teacher can enable the class to show the day in the life of one character prior to making an important decision.

Documentaries: Preparing a documentary allows students to examine a theme, issue, or story from different viewpoints using a variety of drama conventions. As they work in groups to plan and prepare a documentary film, students come to understand the power of using the media to inform or persuade audiences about a topic or issue. When dealing with historical or news events, students have an opportunity to gather, interpret, and deliver information at both a personal and societal level.

Forum Theatre: A situation is enacted by a small group while others observe. Both the actors and the observers are invited to stop the action whenever they feel it is losing direction, or help is need to develop the scene to make it more authentic. Suggestions can be offered for changing dialogue, gesture, voice, or space to give meaning to the experience. Observers may step in and take over any roles or add to them. In Forum theatre, a scene is chosen to illuminate a topic or experience that is drawn from the drama.

Hot Seating: In drama, Hot Seating can be used for *any* in-role characters, including historical figures. When a person takes the hot seat, that person is interviewed by classmates or group members who want to discover more about the character—how she or he feels about events, people, and places. Assuming the hot seat allows students to solidify their perceptions of a character.

Objects of Character: This convention helps students to flesh out a character by assembling a variety of objects or personal belongings that serve as clues about the owner. These items can be "discovered" as a way of introducing a character in the drama. Once the group meets this person in role, the behavior may confirm or contradict the group's interpretation.

Overheard Conversations: This strategy allow students to work both in the role of the participant and spectator. Usually, these conversations are not meant to be heard (e.g., spies plan a secret mission; a group of factory workers plan a strike). One strategy for eavesdropping on the conversations is to have groups freeze on a signal. Groups are brought to life one at a time to continue their improvisation. In this way, students are able to listen in on conversations by various characters in the drama.

Role on the Wall: A central role that is to be explored in drama is represented in picture form, diagram, or outline on a chart, which is put on the wall. Students reflect on the thoughts and qualities that may be significant to this character. Words or statements that describe the character's behaviors, personality, or feelings are added to the Role on the Wall image. Information about the role can be added as the drama is introduced and progresses. This role can be adopted by one or more students in the improvisation.

Consider the following options for recording information on the Role on the Wall diagram.

- What are the external and inner characteristics of this character?
- What are the different views that others—community, family members, the character himself—might have?
- What is known or not known about this character's life?

Voices in the Head: This strategy is useful in helping students reflect on the many facets that a character in a drama must face in making a choice. Individuals represent the possible conflicting thoughts of the character at the moment a decision is made. The "voices" become the character's conscience that gives the person advice, forcing him or her to make an important choice. Voices in the Head helps the students to become more aware of the complexity of a problem and allows them to influence the imminent action. As students call out their thoughts (often prompted by a signal from the teacher), the action of the drama is slowed down, adding tension to the moment.

Soundscaping: Soundscaping gives the students the opportunity to create an environment using their voices, the sounds of hands or feet, and if available, musical instruments. The sounds that students create, which can be realistic or stylized, can tell a story, create a mood, or establish a sense of place.

Tableau: Working alone, with a partner, or in small groups, students create a still image using their bodies to crystallize a moment or an idea in the drama. By creating a frozen picture with others, students are required to discuss, negotiate, and make a decision upon images that will communicate or express their ideas. (Tableaux can be shared by one group watching another, or, the large group can be an audience as the work is presented. As these images are interpreted, students should be encouraged to brainstorm many messages that may be conveyed.)

Ten Ways to Build Drama from a Source

Print can be the starting point for dramatic improvisation, and dramatic work can lead to a greater understanding of print. Drama becomes the medium for the exploration of the ideas, relationships, and the language of the print source. The situation from a story or poem can serve as a beginning point for drama and may deepen and enrich the learning experience. We need to consider the source carefully for dramatic possibilities: for issues, concepts, or problems to be solved that might absorb the students' attention. We then need to consider the conventions we will choose to extend ideas and themes from the source and structure drama work.

1. Raise Questions

Questions can stimulate the students, helping the students to go beyond what they already know. Questions are used both inside and outside the drama, both in role and out of role, to give purpose, direction and shape to the learning activities. Students can work as a large group, or in small groups to brainstorm questions inspired by a text that can be answered through further drama exploration. Questions can be discussed orally or written down. Questions can also be used by the teacher to deepen belief and commitment and help students to reflect on the work and on their personal views.

2. Explore Time

The group considers scenes that take place in the present and then brainstorms events that might have taken place in the near or distant past to explain or give background information to a conflict. Alternatively, the class can consider events that might take place in the near or distant future to predict how an issue will develop or be resolved.

3. Select a Role to Play

When a teacher works in role, she or he adopts a set of attitudes to work with the students. While acting is not required, the teacher must alter his or her status in the classroom to help students explore issues or examine possible directions that a drama may take. Depending on the role that the teacher takes, she or he can extend the drama, focus attention, challenge the class, suggest alternatives, support contributions, slow the action and clarify information in order to enhance the commitment, the language, and the thoughts and feelings of students as they work in a fictional context.

4. Build a Community

A source may offer the group the dilemmas of a single character or of a group of characters. Drama is about exploring different points of view and a community can be invented where students choose to create and become different characters who live in the community, work together, or are involved in a common mission.

5. Interview Characters

Characters are interviewed by reporters in order to question their motives, values, and beliefs or to elicit more facts about a given situation. This can be done in pairs, in small groups, or with the whole class. Interviews can be conducted in role by the teacher.

6. Tell Stories

Storytelling can provide the initial starting point for the drama. It can reveal an unexplained idea in a familiar story, it can focus details, it can serve as a review of what has already taken place, or it can be a way to build an understanding of character and situation. In drama, stories can be told in and out of role to express concerns, ideas, and feelings about a situation. Stories can be told alone or with others, can be written or created visually, can be enacted through voice and movement. Students can enact a story to represent what they have experienced; elaborate the story, building on its key events or issues; or invent a story, creating new stories from old ones.

7. Conduct a Meeting

The group gathers together within the drama to hear new information, plan action, make collective decisions, and suggest strategies to solve problems that have arisen. The teacher can lead the meeting by assuming a role, or a committee can chair the proceedings without the presence of the teacher.

8. Create Still Images/Tableaux

Working alone, with a partner, or in small groups, students create a still image, or series of images using their bodies to crystallize a moment or an idea in the drama. By creating a frozen picture(s) with others, students are required to discuss, negotiate, and make a decision about images that will communicate or represent their ideas to depict a story or theme.

9. Read Text Aloud

Texts—including excerpts of texts—can be offered to groups to be read aloud. Groups can work together to prepare a reading that experiments with pace, pause, emphasis, voice, and gesture. Members of the group can make decisions about assigning parts that could be read aloud as solos, with others or in unison. When students interpret texts, they not only enhance their skills of reading aloud, but through rehearsal, come to explore strategies for presenting text. The construction of the read-aloud can be shared with others to give information or give form to situations or issues presented in the drama.

10. Write in Role

Letters, diary entries, journals, or messages from a single character or a number of characters can be used to introduce the drama by creating tension or giving information. Writing samples can provide evidence or reveal insights about a character's motivation. Writing-in-role can also help students to engage in expressive and reflective aspects of drama, drawing on their own life meanings and experiences. Drama also provides opportunities for collective writing, in which groups collaborate on a mutual enterprise—cooperating in collecting data, organizing information, revising and editing—to be used in the subsequent drama work.

A Way to Understand the World

Drama is an art form through which students can develop awareness, heighten perception, manipulate language, increase cognition, explore emotions, and improve their abilities to interact with others. By taking on a role, students can rehearse alternatives in life and consider their consequences. It is a way of learning—a positive and fulfilling way.

Drama encourages—indeed, requires—students to speak and act more spontaneously than they do in the formal student-teacher relationship. Drama also provides the means by which students receive oral feedback from the group. It can offer opportunities to develop and practise language by reporting, informing, questioning, sharing ideas, explaining, defending, negotiating and mediating. Drama offers the teacher the opportunity to present students with alternatives to their everyday models of thinking, behaving and communicating. Role playing, improvising, and experiencing drama activities allow students to learn new uses of language, thought, and feeling from new situations. It is in this way that drama extends students' understanding of their own world and the world of others.

> One cannot educate vision. One can only make sure there are plenty of good glasses with which to see things.
> —Jane Alexander

....

Connecting Drama, Play and Collaborative Learning through TRIBES
—*John Mazurek*

Three Ball Pass and This Is a Scarf, on pages 61 and 62, are two TRIBES games.

Like many teachers wanting to build a community in their classrooms, I often seek practical advice to improve the prominence of drama and, more generally, the quality of novelty and interaction in my classroom. In particular, *Tribes: A New Way of Learning and Being Together* by Jeanne Gibbs is a resource and a program that has provided a significant framework to build social growth and a caring environment and helped me to meet significant expectations for a healthy drama program and a healthy classroom. By following the approach advocated by this book, my students and I have found frequent and manageable opportunities to connect play and laughter with reflection and learning.

TRIBES is not a comprehensive drama program, nor a curricular program in any conventional sense, but rather it is a process that strategically uses events and experiences, including games, activities and simulations, to promote students' psychological, social and academic growth. The TRIBES text, which provides a comprehensive outline of the TRIBES program, contains, among other things, more than 100 cooperative learning games and activities, some unique to TRIBES and others adapted from a variety of sources in the dramatic arts, physical education and other disciplines. It involves learning and facilitating a sequence of three group (community building) development stages, four positive group "agreements" (foundational social norms), and other specific collaborative skills. Students also learn to reflect on their learning and interaction and to show appreciation to others for their contributions.

Accordingly, I try to plan cooperative games and levels of group interaction that are appropriate to the psychological and social development of my students, given their ages and personal histories throughout the school year. Like most teachers, I recognize the importance of beginning September with events that build each individual's sense of belonging, fitting in and feeling listened to. Through games and drama activities I can build basic social skills and promote positive attitudes of working together.

Many of the games and activities within TRIBES learning strategies can also be used effectively on their own as energizers whenever the group needs a change of routine or a positive shift in mood. A game will be fun and effective only if the students already have a good grasp of the social skills that it requires. Through TRIBES I have acquired more options for meeting my students' needs to learn through talk, movement, role-playing, and through laughter, spontaneity and play. Also, I am more confident that compelling opportunities like the ones offered in TRIBES can be found within the wide range of resources that offer drama games which can help teachers to develop positive attitudes, social competencies, and thence a foundation for powerful inquiring learning.

Building Blocks for Programming: Drama

☐ **Games/Exercises/Mime/Tableaux**

    ❏ _____

☐ **Storytelling**

    ❏ Partner and group retelling
    ❏ Jigsaw stories
    ❏ Story responses
    ❏ Telling in role as a character
    ❏ Retelling through tableaux, movement, sound
    ❏ Presenting stories (Readers Theatre, story theatre)
    ❏ _____

☐ **Role Playing**

    ❏ Interviews
    ❏ Writing in role
    ❏ Reflecting—Corridor of Voices, discussion, writing
    ❏ _____

☐ **Improvisation**

    ❏ Meetings
    ❏ Story building
    ❏ Decision-making in role
    ❏ Problem-solving in role
    ❏ Playmaking
    ❏ _____

☐ **Interpretation**

    ❏ Choral speaking
    ❏ Scripts
    ❏ Monologues
    ❏ _____

☐ **Theatre**

    ❏ Exploring theatre history
    ❏ Forum theatre
    ❏ Responding to theatre
    ❏ Audio and video plays
    ❏ _____

5 Moving in the Circle

Dance Education

By Andy Anderson

Andy Anderson is associate professor, Elementary (Physical and Health Education) at the Ontario Institute for Studies in Education, University of Toronto. His primary focus is on preparing prospective teachers to think about health and physical education as an integral part of life in school and beyond. Andy unites his passion for health, wellness, and education in his research and writing by focusing on depictions of health-inspired school improvement.

Dance Examiner: What does it feel like when you're dancing?
Billy: I don't know. Sort of feels good.
Once I get going I forget everything. Sort of disappear. Sort of disappear.
I feel a change in me whole body. There is this fire in my body. It's just there.
Fire.
Like a bird.
Like electricity. Yeah, electricity.

—*Billy Elliot*

Dance, like poetry, is a way for ideas and images, feelings, and emotions to be expressed so that whole new strings of ideas and interpretations can emerge. Dance allows children to know themselves in other ways, through the body's capacity to express thoughts and feelings, through the different forms of movement. It is important, therefore, to remember that dance forms, movements, and actions are not the content or subject of study; rather, it is the *dancer* who is the subject of study: the dancer's feelings, insights, and development of sensibilities expressed through movement forms.

There are many things we know and feel that are not expressible in written form. In other words, we know more than we can say. Fear, love, grief, and loneliness are often expressed in our hearts and communicated through our bodies before we can find the words. Dance is a medium through which we can begin to sort out and develop understandings that are first experienced by the dancer, then shared with others.

Dance as a Way of Conceptualizing

There is a tendency in school settings to focus almost exclusively on symbolic manipulation (letters, numbers, text). Learning, as a whole, is sometimes viewed as a disembodied, placeless activity. Use of computers, for example, is communication that is largely textual, transmitted and received as discrete signals or cues broadcast through a medium or channel, which often filters out or limits the cues or bandwidth of a particular channel. Audio-visual experiences widen the bandwidth, thus creating a higher degree of presence. Imagine what dance can do!

Poetry, music, art, and drama are important friends, often providing a trigger or cue to stimulate exploration—informing, challenging, intensifying each other. They incite curiosity, evoke and provoke, and refine thinking and feeling.

Through movement and language we can engage a profusion of worlds in which the child can live as pictures unfold of a "peacock's fiery tail . . ., cascading down a mountain . . ." Worlds of poetry allow words and images to tumble about the child; as these are translated into dance, a further sensory experience—the kinesthetic—is added, and this has the power to call forth more words and images. As Joyce Boorman writes, "Words and language belong to dance, and dance belongs to words and language, both belong to the child."

So, what is educationally important about dance?

- Dance can increase sensitivity, respect, and cooperation.
- It can bridge generations. Students can dance to become familiar with customs, festivals, celebrations, and traditions.
- Teachers can use dance to teach concepts—heavy, soft, fatigue, force, acceleration, gravity, force absorption, friction, levers.
- Students can experience the joy of movement and even express a sense of humor.
- Dancing can improve concentration, self-discipline, self-reliance, and self-esteem.
- Dance is a part of all life forms: leaves dance, flowers dance, people dance, eyes dance.
- Dance can contribute to a person's overall health and well-being—mental, emotional, spiritual, social and physical.
- Dance is a way of knowing and showing, a vehicle for conveying ideas, interpreting the world and our feelings, a way of thinking and communicating.
- Dance is an aesthetic experience. It can be awesome and spectacular, or gentle and reflective.
- Dance can become an important way to build a sense of community.

If you wonder about the distinction between creative movement and dance, consider these two suggestions for movement:

a) Boys and girls, I want you to show me how a cat moves.

b) Boys and girls, show me the shape of a cat's body, how it would walk along a window sill, if a dog came in the room, if a bowl of milk was placed on the floor, if a mouse ran out of its house . . .

The first example tends to elicit stereotypical movements. The second invites exploration of the movement possibilities of an idea rather than the idea itself. Dance is about trying to become.

General Teaching Principles

- Dance encompasses a variety of rhythm and movement activities, such as folk dance, jazz dance, social dance, aerobics, and rhythmics. Be sure to pick appropriate activities for each group of students.
- Almost everyone enjoys moving to music. Take advantage of this! Play music as students enter the class. Allow them to move spontaneously prior to the start of class, exploring space and equipment such as hoops, skipping ropes, scarves, and blankets. Show tunes from movies such as *The Lion King* and *The Little Mermaid* work well.

Movement is the most powerful and dangerous art medium known. This is because it is the speech of the basic instrument, the body, which is an instinctive, intuitive, inevitable mirror revealing man as he is.
—*Martha Graham*

Dance is not about something, dance *is* something.
—*Joyce Boorman*

Every child is a dancer. A child in a wheelchair can "wheel" forward, backward, and so on. The arms can support the body and swing back and forth. I have even seen adolescent boys swing from a seated position to a handstand, using the arm supports of the wheelchair like a gymnastic parallel bar. A group of wheelchair dancers can rock and roll with the best of them. Able children can use wheelchairs to join in the dance too. Integrated dance involves wheelchair and non-wheelchair performers blending their talents and imaginations. It is beautiful and fascinating to watch.

- Start each class with a warm-up, for example, walk to the music, skip, gallop, wiggle, stretch, bend, twist, curl to the beat. Invite students to be the leader. Rotate this role so everyone has a chance to be the teacher.
- Be very aware of your students' comfort level. Alter dances to be sensitive to their religious backgrounds, social maturity or physical ability. Most dances can be easily altered to include everyone. Partners are A and B, not male and female. Allow students to hold bandanas if they prefer not to hold hands.
- Be enthusiastic! Practise prior to class. Your enthusiasm and knowledge of the subject will greatly increase the students' enjoyment.
- Teach progression for set dances:
  a) Start in scatter formation and introduce basic steps.*
  b) Allow students a few moments to work on each step at their own pace.
  c) Play the music and practise the steps (assigned or that they design).
  d) Introduce the pattern of the dance—how many repetitions of each step, and so on.
  e) Set up the form for the dance, for example, in a circle with all holding hands.
  f) Let each group work through the dance at their own pace.
  g) Emphasize and practise transitions from one step to the next and the starting over of the dance.
  h) Add the music, cue them, and have fun!
  i) Work on style and precision last.
      After learning the steps, change the music. For example, the first few steps of the Virginia Reel are just as easily performed to the *Ghost Busters* theme. Add movements such as a moon walk, sports actions, and even martial arts moves.
- Cueing: Call cues ahead of the music to prepare the class, using a consistent cue each time. Consider using metaphors as cues, for example, stir the pot, hit the lonesome trail. Once students know the steps, let them dance without interruption or cues.
- Do not single out students. You can assist students by dancing near them and providing quiet cues.
- Never let an "extra" person sit out. They can dance alone or with the teacher. (If the word "dance" is problematic, rename it as creative movement. Every religion and ethnicity has movements that are rhythmic and expressive, accompanied by music that is always symbolic of deep meanings—explore them together.)
- Provide activities that allow students to be creative. For example, take out a section of a dance and include their steps.
- Integrate dance as often as possible: gymnastics, creative movement, basketball, soccer, drama, and language arts.

How to Encourage Dance

There are lots of ways to encourage dance whether it is structured, free, folk or just for fun. Here are the stages that enable the child to progress:

1. *Explore.* How might the body move to feel, express, interpret? Listen and move to the music. "Now, let's try to move as I count to 8. When I reach the number 8, change to a different movement pattern."
2. *Experience.* "Try it, try another way, try it the way your partner is moving, try to include at least two different levels."

In dance-in-education, the body is the instrument and movement is the medium that bridges inner knowledge and outer experience. The role of the teacher is to provide structures that move students comfortably into the realm of aesthetic and symbolic representation, using dance to give form to meaning.
—*Christine Jackson*

Worth Watching
- Scenes from movies such as *Billy Elliot* (Some language is not appropriate, but the right scenes can be pre-selected to communicate important messages about dance.)
- Television programs that feature synchronized swimming, precision skating teams, aerobic dance groups, ethnic dances

3. *Excite.* Make suggestions, invite ideas, and be innovative.
4. *Examine.* Reflect on what the students imagined and performed. Take time to understand how the children are processing the experiences. "How does it feel to curl up like a caterpillar? Tell me about the energy in your body when you tighten all your muscles? Tell me what pictures come to mind when your muscles are really relaxed."

Harnessing Creativity

—Jacqueline Karsemeyer

I began teaching dance in schools in the early 1970s under the auspices of Inner City Angels, whose mandate was to have artists introduce their medium to students. I worked with students in Kindergarten through high school, including many Special Education classes. I was in total awe of the creative expression that burst forth when students were invited to play with movement. Rudolf Laban, a seminal movement theorist, defines dance as stylized play, suggesting its accessibility to all.

Planning a dance lesson can follow the structure used for many classroom lesson plans: there is an introduction, a main statement (predetermined or generated by the collective), and a conclusion. In dance, the introduction includes warming up the body to reduce the risk of injury and to broaden the repertoire of movement beyond the pedestrian. The main statement consists of bodies and minds fully engaged in the creation of dances, or the learning of technique. The conclusion is the cooling down of the body, so as to continually develop long limber muscles. In the dance classes that I teach, the underlying assumption is that each student has the ability to do a dance, one that reflects their unique perspective of life, the expression of which inherently enriches the lives of others. As eloquently stated by legendary dancer/choreographer Martha Graham: "There is a vitality, a life-force, a quickening that is translated through you into action, and because there is only one of you in all time, this is unique."

The following is a sample lesson plan. I have purposefully avoided the inclusion of music in it. Music is a wonderful tool for teaching dance. The tendency, however, is to follow the music, placing it at the centre of the dance class. There is nothing wrong with this, but we must be aware of the boundaries of structure and mood that each musical selection introduces. There is no age limit to the activities outlined below.

Introduction—Kinesthetic Bubble: As a stretching exercise, students move in their imaginary bubbles, testing how far they can reach in all directions with different body parts. Have them move around the room being mindful of other bubbles. Use prompts such as "What part of your body can you reach the highest with? How far back can you reach with your toes?" Let students experiment with imitating the movements of others. Little ones respond well to concrete images: you can start them in tiny shapes and mimic blowing air into them until they are giant bubbles floating around; senior students usually need reminding to explore movement possibilities close to the ground.

Main Statement—Stop, Look, Listen: One person simply calls, "Stop, look, listen," introducing a movement and a sound that the whole group imitates. Use a drum or instruments to amplify the activity.

Variations can be done in a line formation as a follow-the-leader activity. More structure might be added by limiting number of turns allowed per person Comment: After having worked with versions of this activity for years, I went to California to study with Anna Halprin, of the San Francisco Dancer Workshop. Anna had focused extensively on harnessing collective creativity, particularly in high-energy environments, such as in Watts after the riots. When she did this exercise, there were no limits on how many times a person could call a change. Anna told us that groups can discover a movement that all members can feel at home doing—a common movement denominator. We could stay with the activity until we found ours. When we did, it was mythic the way the whole group clicked in recognition. There were drummers who joined in when we reached that point, and the work went to an entirely new level. It took our group of 60 people about three hours to reach this threshold. I have used this version of the activity with students who have serious control issues. They love it, and I love it, as it gives them control in a structured way. It also expands our movement repertoire by introducing movements beyond our personal patterns, outside of our comfort zone. It generates a shared vocabulary to begin building dances with.

Cool Down—Triangle Catalyst: Hit a triangle. Each person will move only as long as they hear the triangle. Start by moving your hand as long as you can hear the triangle sound. Enlarge to include other body parts, then the whole body. Use the triangle sound as a prompt to move slowly around or across the room, perhaps even into a line ready to leave through the door!

Drawing and Writing: When I first started teaching dance in schools, I got into a lot of trouble with teachers because when the students returned to the classroom, they would enter leaping, twirling, or in some other energetic way. The transition to sitting was too abrupt, and so our cool-downs needed to include slow, controlled movements. As my teaching matured, I discovered that I could also allow students to draw or write after dancing. This extended the cool-down and elicited meaningful reflections.

Sources for Dance

In all grades, students will have opportunities to draw upon a variety of sources, such as literature, poetry, music, and topics and themes from curriculum areas, in order to communicate interpretations through dance. Words, percussion, song, and equipment can provide stimuli for expressing ideas physically.

Words

Words and music can set children in motion—physically, spiritually, emotionally. Letting children experience words enables them to grasp the idea that dance is painting "word pictures" in space. Through dance, children have a chance to "taste words" with their bodies. Invite children to use their bodies to feel what these words mean. Before children begin to move, give them a moment to envision the action. From a list displayed on chart paper, invite students to compose actions that represent these words:

swirling, floating, twirling, whispering, trembling

Have a partner guess which word they are dancing.

It is movement that allows us to discover and make contact with other people, our surroundings and even ourselves.
—Heberta Wiertsma

Add words that signal *direction*—up, down, across, along, dripping, sliding side to side; *pace*—slowly, pulsing, darting, dashing, drifting, fading, lingering; *effort*—softly, quickly, drooping, dragging; *pathways*—straight, curved, meandering. With the class create a movement vocabulary and movement dictionary.

Dividing words into categories such as the following may be helpful:

- seeing words: flashing, bursting
- hearing words: beating, dripping
- touching words: piercing, crunching

Student can write poems and stories that contain dancing words. These contributions can be put on colored cards, later read to everyone, then displayed on the walls. Students can create a movement story based on something like a forest fire or rainstorm and fellow students can pick out which story they want to tell with their bodies.

Nonsense poems offer wonderful opportunities for fantasy dances. Favorite stories can be the setting for dances and movement games that bring characters, plots, and alternative endings to life.

Animal movements are always a great way to bring children out of their shell. Incorporate the movements into a game, link it to a story from class, then add music and watch what happens.

Percussion

Rhythm patterns can be created using percussion instruments such as a tambourine, drum, or sticks. Let the children gather together the instruments they think are needed in their story, for example, plastic wrap to make the sound of fire crackling. Invite students to gather "instruments" on which they can drum or beat. Options include shoes, soda cans, plastic jars, and plastic pails. Create a beat that is consistent and definite so students can identify a movement pattern, for example, slow walk, skip, or stomp. On emphasized beats, students change direction, levels, pathways. Students can dance in place and on the beat step, tap, or stomp—forward, backward, or sideways. Add hand gestures—circle, reach, or wave. In pairs and trios students can mirror and mimic their partner(s). Facial expressions add emphasis and laughter.

Song

Start each class with music that allows the children a chance to shake out the "sillies," relax and let the tension drain out of their bodies, or imagine what it is like to be floating like a feather over a field—of soft grass, of sleeping lions!

Invite students to act out a song. There are thousands of great folk songs and well-loved children's songs. These songs often tell stories about the building of a railway, life as voyageur, or pioneer harvest and more. Let children capture these moments through dance, music, and drama.

A Parachute

The parachute is a great way to introduce circle dances and directional elements of movement. It provides novelty and containment. Explore the parachute by playing games that involve inflating the parachute, exchanging places when the parachute becomes a cloud, making waves and bouncing balls.

Self-knowledge is a by-product of dance, and you dare to express more with your body and take more risks when you have a better sense of who you are.
—*Paul Rooyraker*

Try the Mexican Hat Dance, circle dribbling (where students hold the parachute with one hand and dribble a ball with the other while moving in a circle), ball circle (where students attempt to keep a ball rolling around the perimeter of the parachute as long as possible), and merry-go-round movements (where some children are up while others are down, as they move around in a circle).

Emotions

Through body movement, explore the gamut of emotions: loneliness, frustration, anxiety, helplessness, surprise. Show the students a picture of a child expressing a particular feeling or emotion. Invite students to create the story that led up to this moment.

Abstract Scientific Concepts

Long before children engage in the academic study of force, friction, acceleration, mass, volume, and space they are exposed to these concepts in the real world. Movement experience can help students make sense of many abstract concepts. Students can pretend to be cars that accelerate and decelerate according to signals provided by the teacher. They can ride scooter boards and navigate obstacle courses. They can also ride carpet samples pulled by classmates using skipping ropes. Students can use benches to explore centre of gravity and try stork standing—eyes open and closed—to learn more about balance and how the body uses vision (spotting) to coordinate balance.

Make abrupt beats with a drum, ask the students to use their bodies to make actions that they think would accompany this. Challenge them to make not a harsh sound, rather a harsh-looking movement. What feelings are associated with these actions? What are the movements like?—blunt, quick, striking action, fast and straight lines.

> Children move throughout their lives, encountering many experiences. Movement is the vehicle through which they obtain experiences, express feelings, receive inspiration and develop concepts. Through body movement children have life experiences and then respond to those experiences.
> —Janet Millar Grant

Three Facets of Dance

A dance curriculum is intended to help students develop an appreciation of the art form, as well as the ability to create works using the forms, elements, and techniques of dance. When dance is introduced into the curriculum, students are given opportunities to become aware of a number of dances relevant to the cultures of the world. As art, dance offers students a context for communicating with others and performing for an audience. As students develop skills in expressing ideas and emotions through the body, they can discover how dance can be both joyous and therapeutic.

Dance as Cultural Expression

There are thousands of dances that represent various ethno-cultural backgrounds that span thousands of years. Each has tradition, custom, and form. Each often is part of a larger story.

Gumboot dance, for example, was born out of the oppressive gold mines of South Africa. Forbidden to speak and in almost total darkness, the slave laborers developed their own language by slapping their gumboots and rattling their ankle chains. Over time, this type of dance has developed into a truly unique dance form that has captured an international audience. Unrivalled in its energy and

Worth Inviting
- Local dance clubs to perform at your school
- A choreographer involved in local theatre
- A physiotherapist who can speak about the benefits of dance, about foot care, and about appropriate shoes for physical activity

physicality, it celebrates the body as a musical instrument while highlighting South Africa's rich and complex culture.

Another example of dance as an expression of people's lives can be found closer to home. As part of their dance education, one of my classes became an audience for a member of a First Nations band who performed a Prairie dance for us.

Getting the Job Done

We listened to the music and watched the performer's movements and then joined in. We tried to follow and replicate his movements as he continued to dance. We were stiff, awkward, and self-conscious. When there was a break in the action I asked him to tell us why his people would perform this dance. He told me the story of how Prairie tribes were constantly on the move following the buffalo. At the end of the day they would make camp, which involved breaking down the grass to flatten an area suitable for teepees to be erected. The dance is a way to get the job done enjoyably while giving thanks to mother nature for providing a good place to rest. The arm motions represent the Prairie grasses blowing in the breeze and the foot stamping is the pounding down of the grass. Circling around the space is the creation of the large camp area for several families.

The dance now made sense, and when the drums and chanting resumed, we danced the dance with expression, fluidity, and ceremonial grace. We became less aware of foot patterns, time, timing, and pace—we were involved in the story. I remember envisioning the wide-open spaces, the smell of the earth, the sounds of horses in the background and the sense of others working in harmony with me. It was a marvellous experience.

In every community there are dancing storytellers. Traditional Greek dance, the storytelling gestures of East Indian dance, or the Hawaiian hula are wonderful celebrations of dance as a part of culture. We may want to look at dancing on Much Music to see what our culture says today.

Dance as Performance Art

Worth Attending with Your Class
- Local dance recitals
- Rehearsals for dance and theatre productions that involve choreographed movement—combat, dance, stage movement
- Arts festivals

Dance performances can be an important way for children to see story, appreciate the beauty and grace of movement, and understand more about the variety of ways to dance—ballet, tap, jazz, modern, character, line, hip hop, step, as well as folk and ethnic dances that represent the culture and history of people from all parts of the world.

Children love to dance as part of theatre and operetta performances. They also love to dance as an integral part of dance and cultural festivals. I am reminded of a spring dance festival that involved a number of schools in the area. Each dance group performed a dance of their choice. Throughout the day we were audience to more than 50 different dances from around the world and, in some instances, choreographed by local dancers and students themselves. The last dance was the ribbon dance that every dance group had learned for the festival. It was an amazing spectacle to see 200 children in mixed groups performing it and the newspaper pictures were outstanding.

Note: After a performance, children can write newspaper articles about the event, interview others in the class, or present arguments for increasing the opportunities everyone should have to be a dancer.

Dance as Therapy

Dance may be an important way for children who are experiencing sickness, grief, and fear to gain therapy. In hospitals therapists initiate games such as pat-a-cake and hide and seek to help create defence mechanisms, to locate and interpret concerns about the ill body parts, and to make contact with the social and physical environment in ways other than for medical purposes. As Goodill and Morningstar recorded it, an example of how dance can be used in therapy is described below.

A therapist introduced a mime game in which several girls gave the others imaginary gifts. This structure provided for the objectivity and concreteness so often helpful in separations, but gave room for the use of abstraction, symbol, and imagination. The girls sculpted the air, then "gave" one another get-well gifts, such as balloons, cards, sunny days, and rainbows. They gave the therapist make-up and jewellery. Their gift to the therapist was in keeping with their view of her as a grown woman, but may also be seen as a view of themselves as women. In this way, they used the mimed gifts as a statement of hope for their own futures.

Many Ways of Dancing

The following pages present an array of dances and creative movement activities that you might introduce your students to.

- Play Bean Bag Touch and Go. Spread bean bags throughout the gym or outdoor area. Begin by travelling around the area and on a designated beat or number, touch a bean bag. One, two, three, touch; four, five, six, touch. Vary the task. "Skip around the yellow bean bags with the left hand leading. Skip backwards around the blue bean bags. Move to the music and on the eighth beat make sure you can touch or jump over a bean bag." You can also use traffic cones, different kinds of balls, or scarves.
- Hoop it up! Repeat bean bag activities but use hula hoops. Now align six hoops side by side to create a hop scotch pathway. Students can step in each hoop or create rhythmic patterns—hoop 1—one touch, hoop 2—two touch, hoop 3—one touch, and so on. In pairs, the first student creates a pattern; the partner tries to replicate it.
- Look for the bamboo dance. For many around the world, the traditional Filipino dance "Tinikling" (teeh-NEEHK-lihng) is a favorite. The most popular and best known of the dances from the Philippines, it is honored as the national dance. This dance displays coordination, endurance, agility, and grace as the dancers step in and out of bamboo sticks. You might consider trying it in a gymnasium.

  Tinikling is very similar to jump rope, but instead of a spinning rope, two bamboo poles are used. Two people hold the poles, one pole in each hand. They hit the poles on the floor, then raise them, then hit the poles together. The performers in the middle hop over and outside the poles before they come together. The sticks are repeatedly being opened and closed by two performers during the dance. The performers with the sticks must follow a rhythm, but the rhythm isn't the same for all the other performers. The changes in speed, as well as the twists, turns, and steps, are what make the Tinikling an exciting dance to watch.

Movement is both expressive and practical. It contributes to, and mirrors, human growth and development.
—*Lynne Anne Blom and L. Tarin Chaplin*

The dance imitates the movement of the tikling birds as they walk between grass stems, run over tree branches, or dodge bamboo traps set by rice farmers. Dancers imitate the tikling bird's legendary grace and speed by skillfully maneuvering between large bamboo poles. (Further information can be found by going to Ask Jeeves and entering the search word: tinikling.)

- Capoeira is a collective art form that brings together dance, music, acrobatics, and martial arts. It was created four centuries ago by African slaves in Brazil in their struggle for freedom and survival. Capoeira has acquired enormous popularity among people of all ages and backgrounds in Brazil and throughout the world. Practised in a communal setting, within a circle of players, or "roda," and set to a hypnotic, pulsing rhythm, capoeira calls for intuition, skill, grace, and physical strength. (Read more by going to Ask Jeeves and entering the search word: capoeira.)

- Line dance formations are a great way to work on hip hop, step, boxercize, or country and western dance movements. They allow the instructor to provide a model, chunk the dance into segments, and build the routine progressively over several classes.

- Watch a cheerleading group perform. Select basic movements such as stepping forward and making letters of the alphabet—Y, M, C, A. Add arm circles, leaps, and cartwheels. Create a cheer using foot stomps, hand claps, hip hop and even push-ups. Think of interesting ways to work together, overlap, and combine.

- Make balls dance! Using basketballs, soccer balls, or bean bags, students can create fantastic routines. The Harlem Globetrotters have perfected this technique, but any class can create a movement sequence using these or other pieces of equipment. Rhythmical bouncing of basketballs can also form a routine that can be performed with music and chants.

- Skipping routines are decades old. Skipping rhymes are a way to time the turns, and add fun and creativity. There are examples of skipping techniques in many books and the Heart and Stroke Jump Rope for Heart materials offer a wide variety of tricks and suggestions for schoolyard skipping. Jump rope teams can create routines to music that add street dance, gymnastics, and ball handling. Imagination is the key ingredient.

- Wearing vintage clothing and hats, in particular, can change the mood, invite participation, and remove barriers to participation. With an old felt hat and a cane, a student can become a completely different character. Hallowe'en is lots of fun when students dress up in costume and learn the Monster Mash. (Drag one foot for 8 counts—the Hunchback; then walk stiff legged and arms outstretched for 8 more counts—the Frankenstein . . .)

- Combine brushes and basketball to make a routine. The performance group Stomp showed us how varied and exciting dance movements can be using simple everyday objects. What can your students do? Compose a routine with instruments from the kitchen, the garage.

- While seated or lying down, with or without musical accompaniment, have students use only their hands and arms to show flowers blossoming, the sun rising in the morning, clouds moving, and insects scurrying around looking for food. Now invite them to move through, around, and between desks and chairs to show how fish swim, how a fog rolls into a village.

- Lipsync. A number of different pop singers and groups have dance as an important part of their performances. Students love to imitate their favorite bands. Replicating their dance routines is lots of fun and students can extend this comfort with dance into other areas of creative and dance movement. Organize a lipsync concert, then be prepared to sign autographs afterwards.

- Some music gets your toes tapping and your fingers snapping. Either in their seats or on their feet, let children explore the various ways they can keep or create beat. Snap, clap, tap, slap. There are a number of street dances that use repeated rhythmical patterns that can be accompanied by chants, raps, and stories. A popular dance form, called Step, has its roots in Black slavery. To send messages, workers clapped out rhythms that signified language in code. What messages can we learn to send with our hands, feet, fingers, and eyes?

- Do the Hokey Pokey. Canada holds the world record for most people simultaneously dancing the Hokey Pokey, and the numbers recorded have been entered into the *Guinness Book of World Records*. Can your class host a Hokey Pokey day? Start with the Hokey Pokey and create variations. Challenge other classes to the world's fastest Hokey Pokey, the most languages used to sing the song, the whole school dancing at once.

- Create a school dance, chant, anthem or cheer. Start your day with the "Roberts Street Romp" or the "Winston Heights Wiggle."

- Make a ribbon routine. Tear off a long streamer of toilet paper (1 m) for each child and ask students to work in pairs. "Holding one end of the streamer, make larger circles from head to foot, around the body, as a figure 8, waving up and down as high as you can. Make wavy lines in the air, shadow your partner, then pretend you are throwing a baseball or hitting a tennis ball." Have students create a movement pattern that they can repeat four times. Arrange them in groups of four. Have each student present his or her pattern while the rest follow along. At the end of the fourth repetition the second person in the group begins his or her patterns, and so on. In total the group now has a ribbon routine. With the right music in the background, the class can produce an exciting display of rhythmic gymnastics.

- Use dance in science class. Students can show changes of state—solid, liquid, and gas. In groups of three, they can demonstrate condensation, sublimation, and the formation of fog. They can show how worms move. In groups of eight, they can replicate the movement of an amoeba. Groups of three to five can depict metamorphosis, osmosis, or the working of a semi-permeable membrane.

- Make mathematics concrete. In groups of three, students can show how the Pythagorean theorem works. They can explain the parts of a fraction using body actions and can also use their bodies to measure the perimeter of gymnastic mats (non-standard units of measurement). They can also work in groups of three to create an hourglass or sundial to show the passage of time.

- The social studies curriculum offers many opportunities for dance. Students can dance in a way that shows cooperation or offers a message of peace; perform a ritual; show customs, perhaps related to eating; present legends, such as the discovery of fire; mime the invention of the wheel, or dance out a historical event, such as getting new rights.

- Think of sports dances, such as the seventh inning stretch at baseball games.

Activities Related to Dance

Creating a Dance Garden: What would a Dance Garden look like? What kinds of shoes might be worn in such a garden? What plants or flowers would be displayed? What kind of music might you hear?

Preparing a Museum Exhibit: What would a museum exhibit devoted to dance have on display? There might be photographs taken by the children of each other dancing, poetry writing that inspired the movements, advertisements for a dance recital, interviews with dancers, or paintings by classical artists that depict dance. See Bruegel—children are shown playing 87 different street games, rolling hoops, making mudpies, walking on stilts, shooting marbles, blowing bubbles, doing acrobatics, and inflating pig bladders among them. Imagine all the different kinds of dance that could be displayed in a mural or collage.

Researching Hidden Meanings: What is the real story behind "Ring Around the Rosy," a favorite dance enjoyed by children in many parts of the world? (Hint: It has to do with the plague.) Do other nursery rhymes and folk tales have hidden meanings? (Yes, these include "Humpty Dumpty" and "The Musicians of Bremen Town.")

If we accept Gardner's theory that movement is a form of intelligence (bodily kinesthetic), then incorporated into the learning process, dance becomes a tool for learning which contributes to the distribution of intelligences enabling learners to do what they do best. Dance becomes a way of knowing and showing what learners know. Dance is a way to increase and intensify what children feel and try to make "sense" of. Dance heightens sense-ability—seeing, hearing, feeling, imagining. For the teacher, dance can be a way to learn more about what students make of the ideas and concepts presented in class. Most of all, dance should be a joyful event, a chance to experience the fire within, to experience the electricity of movement.

Building Blocks for Programming: Dance

☐ **Moving to Music**
- ☐ Creative dance
- ☐ Folk dance
- ☐ Jazz dance
- ☐ Social dance
- ☐ Contemporary dance
- ☐ Interpretive dance
- ☐ Aerobics and rhythmics
- ☐ _____

☐ **Dance Drama**
- ☐ Retelling a story through movement
- ☐ _____

☐ **Dance as Cultural Expression**
- ☐ _____

☐ **Dance as Performance Art**
- ☐ Wearing costumes, using props
- ☐ _____

☐ **Dance as Therapy**
- ☐ _____

☐ **Movement and Singing**
- ☐ School chants or cheers
- ☐ _____

6 Plugging in the Arts
Media and Arts Education

By Jennifer Rowsell

Jennifer Rowsell teaches literacy education in the Bachelor of Education program at the Ontario Institute for Studies in Education of the University of Toronto (OISE/UT). Her research focuses on applying New Literacy Studies and Multiliteracies in the classroom; multimodality in children's meaning making; and the role of new media in literacy education. She has co-written The Literacy Principal *with David Booth and has two forthcoming books on literacy and New Literacy Studies with Kate Pahl.*

What is sculpture? What is painting? Everyone clings to old-fashioned ideas and outworn definitions, as if it were not precisely the role of the artist to provide new ones.
—*Pablo Picasso*

Media compel children to think in a different way from linear, printed texts such as a science textbook or even a picture book. Media are often choreographed around lead characters or avatars who guide children through a site or a film and help them to interpret the story (e.g., *Dora the Explorer* or *Super Mario*). The level of interactivity in media allows students to enjoy music, dance, drama, and visual arts all at once, without being made aware of doing so. As educators we want to harness our language programs to this interest in print combined with electronic texts to build a bridge to literacy.

My daughter Madeleine, almost two years old, is exhibiting classic preliterate behavior. Some of the literacy events witnessed daily are pulling tabs, scratching and smelling surfaces, rubbing fur on animals in books, pretending a pull car is a steam engine (as in *Thomas the Tank Engine*) and dancing to Caillou. These acts are vestiges of literate behavior. By pulling on tabs in Maisy books, Madeleine knows that Maisy's horn will sound out "tooty-toot" or opening a card, it will read "Happy Birthday, Maisy." When Madeleine reads *The Runaway Bunny* with her mom, she cannot decipher the written text, yet she knows that the big bunny is mother bunny and that she is following her child until he realizes it is far better at home than out in the big world. It is precisely for this reason that publishers commission art from illustrators—for their aesthetic, for their unique depiction of the written word. In the media world, it is the visual that breathes life into the text.

Our children exist and clearly revel in a world of magazines, of DVDs, of video games, and of sitcoms, and as educators, we should recognize their interests and in doing so compel them to understand, on practical and ideological levels, how this complex communicational landscape works and how media subsume and promote arts-based education. Children face a fusillade of color, movement, animation, sounds, fonts, and interface that guide and navigate their understanding of their community and their place in it. Whether we like it or not, children inside and outside of school have become demanding producers and viewers of multimedia and multimodality. The world is no longer neatly divided into fiction and nonfiction texts, but instead filled with all kinds of texts, intertexts, and hypertexts serving a variety of functions.

Media as Arts Exploration

In order to understand, analyze, and describe the new social landscape of communication we will have to move towards a new way of regarding language as not only linguistic, but also as visual, as tactile, as having movement, style, and composition. What is more, we should learn to understand how and why these texts are used. As Anne Haas Dyson astutely notes in *Writing Superheroes*, just as we need to understand the artifacts students use inside and outside of school, so too a new curricula "must be undergirded by a belief that meaning is found, not in artifacts [like print media] themselves, but in the social events through which those artifacts are produced and used" (p. 181).

Popular media play such an influential role in shaping our children's perception of the world that they are similar to the storytellers or bards of older tribal societies. But what are media and media literacy? Media subsume television, film, radio, music of all sorts, photography, and print. They are at one and the same time an art form uniting diverse artistic domains, and they represent a variety of different fields of mass media and popular culture. Media literacy is concerned with the process of understanding and using mass media. What is more, media and media literacy are all encompassing, important areas that permeate all facets of the curriculum and all levels of education.

As an art form and forum for children, television, film, radio, and rock videos are accessible vehicles for promoting the arts in education. By crossing domains such as music, art, drama, and dance, media are a lens for the arts. The arts have the capacity to evoke emotions, and equally, media resurrect and channel emotions from watching the final scene in *Cinema Paradiso*, to listening to Leonard Cohen's "Hallelujah" in the film *Shrek*. The key point here is that our students respond to media.

Media in an Arts-based Curriculum

Where does media sit in an arts-based curriculum? For many, the tie between media and the arts is less tangible than, say, visual arts or drama. Media influence the arts as much as the arts influence media. What lies beneath popular media is a complex hybrid of sound, of movement, of animation, of written text, of visual images, and of illustration. Popular media fuse each strand of the arts into one medium, and media makes them accessible. What is essential when incorporating media in the arts is regarding media in terms of production and consumption, making, viewing, and listening.

Activities that are presented later in the chapter are premised on a belief that making media is always in conjunction with *analyzing* media. Students create and read media texts daily whether they are texting on their cell phones, writing code, reading e-mails, surfing the Net, or playing video games or Game Boy. Questions arising from media are: What is the message of a particular medium? How does the medium transmit such a message?

Media elicit responses from audiences as do music, visual arts, dance, and drama—they can elicit empathy, compassion, angst, and joy that unite audiences. As Peter Greenaway expresses it, "A painting or photograph taken as a creative response by someone who wishes to express an opinion or emotion could be displayed in a gallery or be used as part of a media, such as the cover of a magazine." Even Leonardo da Vinci's 500-year-old sketchbook has been photographed digitally and can be flipped through on your computer screen, and by clicking, you can zoom in on details. Media on TV screens and monitors have made the arts accessible to everyone all of the time.

Media, therefore, are no less powerful than more traditional artistic forms such as drama or painting. The Internet values the visual over the oral or the written,

In a culture like ours, long accustomed to splitting and dividing all things as a means of control, it is sometimes a bit of a shock to be reminded that, in operational and practical fact, the medium is the message.
—*Marshall McLuhan*

Modes of communication, other than language, are becoming increasingly prominent and even dominant in many areas of public communication in which language was formerly used exclusively or dominantly. This is true of visual images in particular. We are, it seems, entering a new age of the image, a new age of hieroglyphics; and our school system is not prepared for this in any way at all. Children live in this new world of communication, and on the whole seem to find little problem with it.
—*Gunther Kress*

but film predominantly places equal emphasis on the visual and the oral. Media share a goal with other artistic domains presented in other chapters in this book: to entertain, to enlighten or enrich, to inform, and to educate. *Textuality*, that is, the mixing and melding together of such media as newspapers reviewing films, or daytime television commentary shows discussing other television shows, and *multimodality*, that is, the fusion of sound modes, visual modes, spatial modes, audio modes, and movement of all kinds within media, point to skills that children can master in their engagement with multiple media.

Some educators and theorists regard media, happily or unhappily, as the "first curriculum," as Neil Postman put it, because virtually all that we know about the world is filtered through the media. Our schools and teachers need to educate children about the impact of media. Media shape our values and perceptions. They can be used as a powerful vehicle to connect with the interests of children and adolescents.

Key Components of Media in the Arts

To embed media in your program, you will need to ensure that certain components are in place. These key components include understanding media genres; viewing and building on interactivity in media; designing media; and incorporating media into your program.

Experiencing the Media as Audience: To entice more student interest in the arts, we need to appeal to a medium or media they use on a regular basis. According to scholars such as Donna Alvermann and Carmen Luke, in our teaching, we must encourage students to consider, reflect on, and critique the very texts that they find pleasurable and therefore interesting. To do so, we should guide them as readers, writers, viewers, and users through a reflective process of looking critically at such media texts as rock videos and building them into their reading and writing. Although many educators are now incorporating new media and popular culture into their programs, there still remains some resistance to doing so. More than that, there is some resistance to looking at ideas and the ideologies underpinning them. Alvermann argues that, as teachers and scholars, we have to be amenable to become more like *learners* and less like *teachers* when it comes to media literacy. Our students have more savvy with these texts than we do and we have much to learn about their use and enjoyment of them. For example, with a primary audience, we need to view a television show like *Blue's Clues* as a source of enrichment for students.

Encourage your students to consider these questions when they experience the media they enjoy.

- What is the meaning behind the message?
- What is this text, print or electronic, trying to say to me?
- How does it do this—through words and through images?
- How does it make me feel?
- How do the visual effects have an impact on the reader?
- What are the producers trying to communicate?
- What are the motivations of the producer? How did I receive the text as a reader?

- How does the text, print or electronic, reflect social, political, economic, or spiritual reality?
- What metaphors are used to create a particular message?
- How did the producer construct such a metaphor?

Understanding Media as an Interactive Art

In *What Video Games Have to Teach Us About Learning and Literacy*, James Paul Gee analyzes the effect video games have on our children's learning and literacy development. Video games such as *The Sims,* a computer game in which you control the trajectory of a story by choosing specific characters with singular traits and dispositions and the premise of the story line, have an impact on how children learn in their present and future lives. Indeed, Gee identifies primary areas of cognitive development: how one forms identity; how one acquires language in general, but sign and symbol systems specifically; how one comes to accept and understand ideas and concepts; and how we interpret culture and our "cultural models" (culture affecting our interpretation of events).

Gee speaks of video games as "new forms of art. They will not replace books; they will sit beside them, interact with them, and change them and their role in society in various ways, as indeed, they are already doing strongly with movies" (p. 204). Although we may not appreciate the appeal of popular media, it is clear that our students do. By considering the value of media texts used inside and outside of classrooms, we might find ways of fostering academic learning by incorporating both media texts or the practices students use with them (e.g., writing code, awareness of fonts and symbols).

In this way, media serve as supports to the arts—as a way of extending an artistic experience beyond the moment. As well, media make the arts accessible to those who do not have access to more traditional artistic venues. Many of our students opt for media above other artistic domains because they prefer to listen to popular entertainers such as Eminem or Christina Aguliera, or to watch *Toy Story* or *Dora the Explorer* over other forms or genres of music, dance, and visual arts. Media intersect the domains of print, film, video, TV, radio, and electronic texts of all shapes and sizes.

Jackie Marsh and Elaine Millard talk about looking critically at popular culture texts. In particular, students need to be aware of such issues as racism, sexism, and violence in the media. As they say, "Teachers need to work with children to analyse critically the messages given in ways which do not undermine their pleasure."

Creating Media, Creating Art: Media are on an equal footing with other arts. They are the means by which we make meaning—as producers or as reviewers—from signs, signals, codes, and graphic images. Topics featured in this chapter derive from a belief that children, as viewers and makers of media, need to understand the makeup of film, print, and electronic texts. That is, who is the target audience? And what is the message behind the medium? We have to understand the medium—a powerful transmitter of the arts—as much as we understand the message. For our children, the media *are* the arts.

Recognizing Media in the Classroom: The centrality of the media in our lives is manifested in countless ways in our classrooms, from *Pokémon* or *Digimon* cards handled and traded by our students to their reading and viewing of *Jimmy Neutron* books and CDs. Using media as a way of exploring the arts has been fraught with controversy, given that many parents and educators are concerned that television hinders cognitive and interpersonal development and, perhaps even worse, purveys questionable values. Kate Pahl (2002) explores how *Pokémon* cards allowed children in her research study to work with different modes—written, visual, gestural—in their meaning making. What is more, these cards and games offer a fantasy world in which they can take on different identities and understand the stories behind each one. Students thereby develop an enhanced perception of character development and characters emerging from different cultures and, as Gee corroborates, different cultural models.

Our children are increasingly exposed to media of all sorts, and as educators we have to be equipped with ways to make media meaningful for our students. Part of the solution lies in fostering a critical and creative awareness of media of all kinds. If we are to equip students with the skills they will need to tackle media of all kinds as future workers and users of media, we need to understand more about the medium itself: its relationship to the arts specifically.

Our students need to be discerning viewers and producers of media and, in turn, translate the enterprise of viewing and using media into active and meaningful learning. They need to engage in the processes of design-production-reception, and incorporate these processes into their own learning.

In my work, I have focused on awareness and understanding of media through the production process and its implications on us as viewers and as readers of media texts. Students will create these same sorts of texts over the course of their schooling and their lives as future workers. Our children already carry with them the skills necessary to create modern media: they use the Web as a research tool, they word-process, they create images, they scan, they format text, they recognize and can write code. These are all sophisticated media practices and students fulfill these rites on a daily, if not hourly, basis.

Developing media literacy in students means providing them with opportunities to

- construct meaning from different media
- construct artifacts from media
- produce work—written or visual—out of media
- develop an appreciation and aesthetic understanding of media events, as well as the skills, knowledge, and attitudes necessary to interpret the ways in which media construct our reality
- interpret and understand media texts in order to identify and examine the cultural practices, values, and ideas contained in them
- recognize that those who construct media products are subject to a multiplicity of motivations, controls, and constraints, which include economic, political, organizational, technical, social, and cultural factors

Checklist for Designing a Media Classroom

❑ Have TV and VCR or DVD player in the room.
❑ Create a computer centre in a prominent place with a user list (for rotations).
❑ Plan for the full range of teaching methods.
❑ Plan for change and flexibility.
❑ Make space for movement and dramatic work.
❑ Focus on an exchange of ideas and acquisition of knowledge.
❑ Provide space for different types or styles of instruction: lecture, discussion, audio-visual delivery of lecture, computer-based group instruction and self-paced learning. Ideally, there could be space in the school for camera-equipped classroom suites.

In cases like "media literacy" or "information literacy" we sometimes find implications that we need to learn to "read" media or information sources being "taken in." This is the idea that there are ways of deciphering media and information more or less wittingly or critically as an "insider" or, at least, as an effective receiver or producer within the media spaces in question. To some extent this implies the ability to identify strategies and techniques being used to produce particular kinds of effects on what we think, believe, or desire.
—Colin Lankshear and Michele Knobel

- ❏ Display environmental print that relates to student interests.
- ❏ Have a media centre, which features popular media chosen by students.
- ❏ Consider gender when grouping students for technology-related activities.
- ❏ Choose engaging and relevant topics and activities.
- ❏ Develop content applications that use technology for teaching specific subjects.
- ❏ Infuse technology across disciplines and subject areas.

Media as a Forum for Arts Discussion

What children produce needs to be valued by parents, educators and teachers. An untidy home is the bane of some parents' lives, as children make dens, draw or scribble on scraps of paper or cover the living room floor with bits of cut out magazines, but if we can see this as the way that children come to their making activities, it becomes easier to tolerate the mess.
—Kate Pahl

In the next section, I provide classroom close-ups, extension activities, and teachings strategies and ideas for your use of media in the classroom. The classroom close-ups derive from work with students in classrooms and students in the bachelor of education program. They provide classroom moments when media were used effectively and serve as a source of ideas for you in your planning. Ideas, strategies, and extension activities offer more ways of meaningfully embedding media in your program.

Artifacts of Identity

Media are comprised of movement, of graphics, of text, of illustration, and of animation, and each mode transmits different kinds of messages. In the lesson below, students will reflect on multimodality in such everyday artifacts as a poster as an artifact of self or as a reflection of their individuality. First, a classroom close-up indicates how students can make personal connections with modes of media.

Kinships with Works of Art

Sasha taught a media lesson to a group of Grade 8 gifted students. She began the lesson by presenting a quilt her sister made years ago out of bits of fabric from different stages in her life. Sasha told the class that the quilt embodied her interests and important parts of herself and was, in many ways, an artifact of her past, present, and future.

After presenting the quilt, Sasha handed out postcards of famous works of art and photographs. Each student chose two postcards that interested them and reflected parts of their identity.

The students presented the postcards. As they did so, I remarked at the diverse interpretations and kinships they had and felt for the works of art. The activity was an effective way of connecting art and the aesthetic—an awareness of design and how things look around you—back to their experience.

Ask your students to bring in three texts that represent artifacts of them. They can bring in a CD, a picture, a poster, a magazine, a family artifact, a photograph, a quilt, and so on. The important thing is that the text or object reflects their interests and their individuality. As the teacher, bring in three objects that reflect your interests and your individuality and present them to the class. Discuss what makes the objects unique and how their aesthetic reflects your interests and individuality. Speak of the color of the object, the shape of the object, the type of music (if it is a CD), the texture of the object, what a picture or illustration depicts and why you like it, and so on.

Have students write a reflection piece on one of the artifacts explaining how it is tied to their identity.

The purpose of the exercise is to encourage students to appreciate that our environment and things that engage us are made up of visual, written, and tactile modes that affect us in different ways. As well, students from different cultures are able to feature their cultural aesthetic. The overall aim of the lesson is to demonstrate that multimodality opens up our means of expressing identity beyond the linguistic.

Extension Activities:

- Have students develop a story from a picture or a photo essay, or write a story based on a picture or photograph.
- Invite students to write a biography about a songwriter, rock star or musician, writer, poet, or other artist.
- Suggest that students interview someone about a cherished artifact or an artifact with a story.
- Have students write about a family artifact—how is it tied to your family's history?
- Suggest that students base writing about their families around photographs.
- Ask students to reflect on identity in a piece of music or art. They can write about how identity places a role in the artifact.

Computer-designed Advertisements

This work is multimedia and multimodal, and is done across the curriculum. Present to the class several examples of advertisements and how the ethos, mood, or composition of a visual derives from the unique mixture of color-font-illustration style—photography—ultimately product promoted. Have the class analyze different advertisements and visuals to evaluate how and why a graphic designer created a particular image. Review some of the terminology they could use: predominant mode (e.g., written, visual, tactile), type of text, end user/audience, color palette, landscape versus portrait, fonts (typefaces), and rationale for design. Have students discuss images in terms of "landscapes of communication" so that they do not concentrate overly on written words; they should account equally for the visual, the tactile, and the dramatic, *as well as* the written. We communicate in a multitude of ways, through images, words, and gestures, and our students should appreciate different landscapes.

Ask students to use their production and design skills to design an advertisement. The assignment should be done in-class for those students who do not have a computer at home.

Extension Activities:

- Have students do a text analysis of an advertisement. What is the advertisement promoting? Who would be interested? How have they designed the advertisement for a certain audience? What does the text actually say? What do the visuals transmit?
- Have students analyze the interface of a Web site. Who is the audience? What are the visuals? What color scheme have they used? Is there any animation? If so, what is it? Is there text? If so, what is it?
- Have students interview someone involved with either graphic design or sales and marketing and discuss the design and production process. What is

each stage in the process? What thought goes into it? How did they write the copy? How do they create designs? How much has to do with personal choice or company choice?

Virtual Field Trips

Many institutional Web sites, like the Andy Warhol Museum, the Louvre, or the Royal Ontario Museum, feature field trips to their sites. There are certain steps you need to take in order to plan and go on a virtual field trip.

Organizing and Planning:
- Always tour the target Web site in advance to identify the most accessible pathways to the areas of study or interest for your students. Given that many of these sites are extensive, you will save time in class by having a set pathway, which will also prevent students from getting led astray.
- Keep the Web site's site plan on-hand as a resource.
- Do the advance tour close to the time of the planned trip (sites are often updated and changed).
- As part of this phase, you can create advance planners and information sheets as print supports during the trip.

Before the Field Trip:
- To set the stage for the virtual field trip, present and discuss the site and its importance (e.g., Andy Warhol, his art and how his art had an impact on the art of the day).
- Students can brainstorm different themes, ideas, or people they will look for in the site.

During the Field Trip:
- Students can explore a site in-depth navigated by the teacher.
- You can set up an LCD projector or a large-scale monitor to move through the site. After following your pathway, students are invited to ask questions that will allow them to move around the site.
- Students can return to the site and relate it to other subject areas (e.g., mathematical principles and Warhol's art).
- If students write a follow-up assignment, they can consult the site at various points to add to their repository of information.

After the Field Trip:
- You can hold a debriefing about the field trip: Did students like it? Would they return to the site on their own? Would they have navigated around the site differently? How would they have designed the site? What did they learn from the site? How does it relate to their in-class work?
- You can encourage your students to plan and orchestrate their own virtual field trips.

Questions to consider when students use the Internet:
- Is the site up-to-date?
- Who created the site?
- What is the expertise of the person entering the data?
- Is the site tied to an institution or company?
- Is the information at the site accurate or correct?
- How much time is spent hunting for information?

Planning a Production for Film

As an assignment, have students write out how they would execute a specific role in a film. For example, if a student is the director, how would she or he interpret different scenes and explain the interpretations to actors? If a student is the costume designer, how would she or he select outfits for particular characters? Or, if a student is an actor, how would she or he get into the mind of a given character? The classroom close-up below describes how students can come to understand how necessary and closely related the various roles are.

An Interdependent Structure

Every year, David puts on a play in which every member of his Grade 6 class has a part. David wants to create a drama and theatre community and does not want any student to feel outside of the process. As part of the planning and producing of the play, David asks his class to plan the production of a film and everyone takes on a different role: casting producer, director, actors, and so on. He posts a list of roles at the front of the room and invites students to choose a role. If they have difficulty selecting, they can try out two roles and choose which one suits them best.

> It's fantastic to be creative in a total, unconscious trance, but then there comes a moment when you have to wake up and try to decipher—no, to detect—what is in that obscurity, what is the meaning of everything. I knew that one of the major reasons why I made movies is therapeutic. Doing a movie, if I'm in a bad moment, is the real way to banish demons and nightmares. Making a movie is a great form of therapy.
> *—Bernardo Bertolucci in conversation with Eleanor Wachtel (CBC Radio)*

Students will present their role and responsibilities to the class. The activity should consolidate more of an understanding of production and what goes into the inner-workings of film, television, and drama.

Extension Activities:
- You can modify this activity by asking students to explore the production of other media, like creating a Web site and what goes into the process.
- Ask students to write a paper on being in the film business. If they were in film, what role would they like and why? What part of the process would they like best?
- Ask students to storyboard parts of a scene in a movie. How would they have filmed it differently? Who is their favorite character? How did the director play on aspects of the character's personality? Who is their least favorite character? How did the director play on aspects of this character's personality?
- Ask students to revisit a film and talk about changes they might want to make to the script. Would they change the casting? If so, how and with whom? Where would they film the movie? Would they use animation?
- Ask students to read a few film reviews to develop a sense of the genre of film reviews. Then ask them to review a film or, to make the assignment less onerous, review a music video. They can comment on how they might have changed the video.

Stories in Different Media

Review with your students the terms that are used to describe different sections and functions in a story—introduction, complication, rising action, turning point, climax, and denouement. Construct a plot graph of a short story or novel that you are reading with the class.

Note that there are television narratives that follow a similar format. Television shows such as *Law & Order* follow a predictable, short-story linear pattern, whereas sitcoms, such as *Friends*, have a few sometimes related, sometimes unrelated stories going on at once. To illustrate your point, ask your class to chart the trajectory of a recent sitcom episode as a homework assignment and perhaps even compare the format of a more traditional, linear narrative.

Ask primary students to describe the different parts of such TV shows as *Blue's Clues* or *Arthur*. For instance, *Blue's Clues* follows a certain structure—find clues, get mail, figure out what clues mean, and so on—and with sitcoms, like *Friends*, there are themes or issues that are resolved.

Extension Activities:
- Ask students to write a paper on adapting television shows. If you were to adapt a television show to another medium, what would it look like?
- Ask students to think about genre. What genre is their favorite television show? (Examples: Reality TV, documentary, sitcom, detective or action, game show)
- Ask students to reflect on the appeal of a genre. For example, what is the appeal of reality TV?
- Ask students to think about the target audience of a television show.

Viewing and Constructing Meaning

Discuss the genre of rock videos with students. How do they represent a song or a particular band? What are some examples of good-quality and poor-quality rock videos? How do you differentiate them? Who plans and executes a rock video? What is the purpose of rock videos? In a group discussion, consider some of these questions, and for homework ask the class to analyze one rock video and to consider what went into its planning and executing.

Storyboarding a Rock Video: In the next media lesson, put several sheets of large paper on the board and chart one of the rock videos that the students watched. Choose a student who has thought about the questions and has a general sense of the sequence of rock videos.

Explain to the class that rock videos follow a visual narrative with an overall theme and visuals to represent the theme. Shots in a video are combined to produce scenes, and scenes are combined to construct a narrative. Typically, narratives are set up with a beginning-middle-ending structure, although rock videos take a slightly different take on this in that they begin the song and explore some element of sound or story or character. Next draw a rough outline of a story structure by creating a storyboard of a rock video (or have a student at the front of the class drawing what another student describes). Explain that a storyboard is a succession of images that form a narrative. Have students include such visual features as faraway, or long, shots versus close-up, or short, shots. Talk about choreography and the role of dance in videos. You will also want to discuss characterization and what the rock video says about the artist. (Is the artist featured alone or in a group? Does the video tell a story? If so, what is the story? And so on.)

Extension Activities:
- Ask the class to analyze shots in a rock video, television show, or film. Be sure to reinforce common film terms, for example, shot (a short take of

something or someone), scene (a longer take in a show or film as part of the whole production), and sequence (a series of actions). Students will also have to consider different types of shots: long, medium, close-up, and zoom. How a character or scene is filmed can be key to understanding the content, theme, and ethos of a film or show. Directors can play on close-ups and landscape perspectives to depict characters and moments. An understanding of angles—normal/frontal, high, and low—is important too. As well, students will need to consider the camera profile, or what the camera frames, for example, a person or setting. Is the camera profile objective (further away) or subjective (closer in)? Does the camera fade in, fade out, dissolve, cut away, or cut in? Have students re-create a scene by changing shots in a movie, rock video, or play of their choice.

- Ask students to analyze a rock video in terms of images and lyrics. Is the video a literal or metaphorical interpretation of the song? Does the video convey the image of the band? Does it tell a story?
- Ask students to compare and contrast two videos in the same music genre (e.g., hard rock, rap, folksy, pop, hip hop, blues).

Thinking Beyond the Image

In his Grade 6 class, Mark wanted students to use media as a prompt for writing a story. To begin the class he presented an image of two soldiers in Iraq holding hands—one on a gurney and one sitting beside him offering water. One of the soldiers was American and one was Iraqi. Mark asked the students to reflect on the photo and imagine what was going on. He then began a class discussion about the multitude of ways a reader could view and construct meaning around the image. As a drama exercise, he called upon volunteers to act out the scene. The drama exercise clearly demonstrated that there were many different ways of interpreting the image.

Making a Story List: Mark then asked students to choose a photograph from different forms of media (fashion magazines, Hollywood magazines, newsmagazines, computer magazines, car magazines, and so on) and bring them in the next day. During their language arts period, students were asked to compile a story list to chronicle the story behind their chosen photo. A story list could be as simple as

> tall, African-American woman, early twenties, thin, successful, tired, unhappy about lifestyle, and living in New York City loft

Constructing a Story: As an assignment, Mark asked the class to write a story based on the photo and their story list. Some students brought in fashion images and created a story about a model and her frenetic and at times unhappy existence. Other students contrived stories from images in newsmagazines around key news stories around the world.

The exercise of constructing a story around a photograph allows students to think beyond the image, reflecting on both the motivation of the producer and what could grow from the motivations.

Cameras are the antidote and the disease, a means of appropriating reality and a means of making it obsolete.
—*Susan Sontag (Personal correspondence with George Goldsmith)*

Using Print Texts as Media

Stacea Campbell, Evita Strobele, and Cheryl St. Elier, two exemplary primary teachers and a principal, devised the following lesson for a primary classroom. Send home a letter asking parents to help their child to select a favorite text that deals with the topic of make-believe and bring it to class to share with the other students. After sharing books that children brought, ask students to brainstorm what the word "make-believe" means. Ask students what kind of make-believe things they have always dreamed of doing.

Preview the book *Olivia Saves the Circus* by Ian Falconer and point out the illustrations and how they tell the story. Predict what will happen next in the book. Is this a real story or make-believe? Then read the book to the children and pause at surprises and antics in the book.

After reading the text, ask students various questions about illustrations and written content. "What was the biggest surprise in the book? What did you like or dislike? What was funny in the book?" Ask students to role-play different scenes in the book. Create a class Big Book of how students saved the school one day (the way Olivia saved the circus). Students can create illustrations to match their make-believe attempts at saving the school. Put the Big Book in the reading centre beside *Olivia Saves the Circus* for students to read later. Have students draw or write journal entries based on their own make-believe story. Show a video of a make-believe journey (e.g., the movie version of *Where the Wild Things Are*).

Print Media Collage

In her Grade 3 classroom, Theresa uses and recycles magazines and environmental print and asks her students to create images or collages out of print media. At the beginning of a visual arts lesson I observed, she presented a series of magazines, newspapers, and a variety of signage, and focused on the use of font, graphics, composition, and color palettes in the texts. She then discussed how the form of a text often mirrors the function of the text. As a group, the students discussed how the aesthetic composition and format of texts has an impact on readers and how all of this reflects back on the medium.

After the discussion, students got into groups and created a print media collage around a theme (e.g., environmental concerns, materialism). Some students decided to create an image of a person out of print media.

Extension Activities:

- Have students compare and contrast three different newspapers. How are they different? Who is the readership? How do you know this? Is it evident in the written text? Is it evident in the visuals? Why would someone read it?
- Have students analyze two different fashion spreads. Who is the designer? What does the spread say about the designer? How does the photographer achieve this effect? Why did they choose this model? What is happening in the photographs?
- Have students analyze the tone of a news story in a magazine like *Maclean's* or *Newsweek*.
- Have students create an image for the Web and an image for a magazine. How are the images different and how are they the same?

Triceratops: Exploring Intertextuality

Dorothy began her lesson, part of a whole science unit on dinosaurs, with a clip from the film *Dinosaurs*. The clip shows how a dinosaur egg made its way to a family of lemurs and how they decided to rear the baby triceratops. The students discussed their favorite dinosaurs and most of them discussed the movie, having seen it already.

Dorothy then displayed a chart showing different types of dinosaurs—stegosaurus, tyrannosaurus rex, velociraptor, apatosaurus, and triceratops. She revisited the previous lesson in which she had discussed dinosaurs that eat plants and those that eat meat. To incorporate language into the lesson, Dorothy asked the students to break apart tri-ce-ra-tops into syllables and discuss the sounds in each syllable.

As a final component to the story, the children learned a song about triceratops and some children were chosen to do a dance to the song while others sat around them and sang. The dancers pretended they had three horns like a triceratops and danced to the song. Dorothy concluded the lesson by reading a storybook about a dinosaur who is preparing to meet his friends for an outing.

A Key Link to Students' Lives

Based on the habits and predilections of our students, it is clear that media represent a bridge to our students' interests. The source of our knowledge today can be seen on the Web, on radio, on television, and in print, and popular media in all of its manifestations sustain much of culture. Although media have different sorts of social communication compared to more traditional artistic domains like drama, they are no less artistic or powerful in expressing and in representing human experience and in enriching people's lives.

The question remains, why has there been a relative absence of media in our arts programs? Admittedly, there has been a shift in mindset, but we need to use media as a vehicle to teach art, to celebrate dance and movement of all kinds, to enjoy music, and to integrate arts in general. Without doing so, we do our students a disservice and forget, to return to Picasso, that media form our new canvas: "A picture lives a life like a living creature, undergoing the changes imposed on us by our life from day to day. This is natural enough, as the picture lives only through the man who is looking at it." Reading response theory tells us that the reader interprets the reading. Media provide our link to young learners and as such they need to be a part of an arts program and need to be explored and discussed.

> In my own professional work, I've always held, very insistently, that in the domains that are important for our lives, we generally learn a lot more about people from art and literature than from the most sophisticated work in the sciences, including my own special areas of interest, and probably always will.
> —*Noam Chomsky in conversation with Eleanor Wachtel (CBC Radio)*

....

Virtual Art Galleries
—*Ludmila Shantz*

Electronic sites such as art museum Web sites provide both complementary and unique educational possibilities for arts education, enabling a multitude of meaningful learning experiences which can support arts curricular requirements and help integrate arts into the classroom. They can also "bring" the art gallery or museum to the classroom, since, similar to physical museums, museum Web sites are custodians of artwork and information about it. As such, they represent a key resource of arts information for classroom research and learning. School art programs can be enriched and expanded with art-related Web sites, which can provide material for teacher preparation and classroom use, create opportunities for individual and cooperative/collaborative student learning, and enable students to do research, to investigate and explore, and to pursue various art-related activities. All of the above make children think and develop their ability to learn and grow in their knowledge of art.

How Teachers Can Benefit

- One of the primary ways that electronic sites are useful for art education is by providing material that supports the school curriculum. Web sites can supply teachers with specialized art-based information that they might not have time or expertise to gather themselves. The fact that they are accessible at any time and place and for any length of time is an attractive feature.
- Electronic sites provide forums for sharing and information exchange among teachers, and with educators and art experts; they also offer the possibility of teachers sharing their resources and lesson plans.
- They are a powerful resource for planning instructional activities. They can help teachers gather resources and ideas for thematic units, provide them with lesson plans and information on how to use the lessons in the classroom, and enable them to create a library of activities (such as artwork and questionnaires for tests).

How Learners Can Benefit

- Electronic sites enable learning that integrates seeing, hearing, and doing. Information can be accessed by sending messages or documents through e-mail or obtaining rich sources through text, music, video, audio, animation, color, graphics, and software programs. These multiple sources of information provide stimulating learning experiences that accommodate different students' learning needs, as well as age and grade levels, and help students perceive the subject from different angles. In addition, interactive features (i.e., 3D virtual exhibitions; panoramic views; virtual tours; movies; image magnification—"zoom-in" and "zoom-out"—and side-by-side viewing of artwork) can greatly enhance the learning experience.
- Electronic sites are a powerful tool for locating and linking information, serving as an encyclopedia with extensive information and resources. For example, many sites provide "searches," allowing the student to search for keywords of interest.
- They provide opportunities for sharing and collaboration by students worldwide, as well as communication with museum experts (e.g., curators, artists, art historians) throughout the world. This exposes students to a wide range of viewpoints. Students can ask questions, conduct interviews, compare and share ideas, and learn from one another both nationally and internationally; they can also participate in collaborative projects, both in the physical classroom and in the online classroom, and publish them on the Web for others to read.
- One of the major functions of a museum Web site is in providing the classroom with a resource for primary source material, which can enhance

the curriculum, instigate inquiry, inspire and motivate students to learn about art. Electronic sites can also provide contextual material for artwork, including correspondence, photographs, and acquisition records, enabling students to obtain the context within which the work was created, and thus create their own understanding and develop their own interpretations. In this way students can participate in the actual excitement of the process of discovery (similar to the curatorial process).

- Other possibilities of electronic sites include the following: A virtual exhibition can be viewed long after an exhibition is over in the museum. It also helps students become more informed before visiting a museum or art gallery, by providing pre-gallery visit preparation, as well as resources about what to do during and after gallery visits. A museum Web site may contain information about current and past exhibitions, as well as the most recent material (some sites have daily updates or new information, thus enabling students to experience something new with each visit), as well as in-depth information about artwork, its subject, content, and so on. Site information can be used as a reference while walking through exhibitions by copying information relating to specific works prior to a visit. By placing art in its larger historical and other contexts, the Web site can enable students to understand the complexity of interconnections; and by bringing artwork together from various sources such as from different collections or countries, it can allow for comparison, showing the network of relationships among artwork. Museum Web sites also provide "guided" tours of the art collections, led by curators or other knowledgeable staff. Electronic sites enable a multidisciplinary approach to the study of art.

Multiple Approaches to Learning

Electronic sites also provide recognized learning strategies for different levels of the study of art and for different ages.

- For beginning students, certain sites provide basic art knowledge and skills. They provide foundational concepts and skills, a vocabulary of terms, and a repertoire of concepts.
- Sites may allow students to gain experience with a wide range of media and methods of artistic production; opportunities for looking at and talking about art from different cultures and different historical periods; and a means of studying artists and contexts within which the artists created.
- For the advanced student, sites develop greater complexity of interpretations, such as engagement in dialogue about aesthetic issues and issues of artistic freedom.
- Electronic sites also employ strategies of learning appropriate for children, such as play that contributes to cognitive development; activities involving problem solving that require time, attention, and engagement; "hands-on" physical activities; and practical art-making activities, as well as questioning techniques which, when directed to critical portions of works of art, help students cue to important information.
- Other learning approaches include involving students personally through interactive tours; comparing and contrasting works; and discussing the process of creating artwork (how it was made, what materials were used, etc.).

- As a result, art-related electronic sites allow students to observe more sensitively, look more closely at detail, comment on it, compare, contrast and articulate opinions, thus becoming more discerning and able to appreciate art and verbalize ideas and thoughts about it.
- Furthermore, Web sites help develop specific skills, such as enabling students to reflect and develop an aesthetic awareness; practical art-making; describing, analyzing, and interpreting artwork; and learning not just to look but to know how to see, observe, and apply knowledge gained.

Recommended Sites Representing Artwork

Montreal Museum of Fine Arts
> http://www.mmfa.qc.ca/en/musee/

Art Gallery of Greater Victoria
> To the Totem Forests: Emily Carr and Contemporaries Interpret Coastal
> Villages
> http://www.emilycarr.org/

Karma of the Dragon: The Art of Jack Wise
> http://www.jackwise.net/

Mansion Madness: Mystery at Gyppeswyck
> http://aggv.bc.ca/mansion-madness/index.html

Canadian Museum of Civilization and the Winnipeg Art Gallery
Panoramas: The North American Landscape in Art
> http://virtualmuseum.ca/Exhibitions/Landscapes/

Canadian Museum of Civilization
> http://www.civilization.ca/indexe.asp

Smithsonian American Art Museum
> http://americanart.si.edu/index3.cfm

Metropolitan Museum of Art
> http://www.metmuseum.org/home.asp

Metacentres, or gateways, provide teachers and students with educational networked cultural resources. Examples:

Art Museum Image Consortium (AMICO):
> http://www.amico.org/

Gateway to Educational Materials:
> http://www.thegateway.org/

Canada's SchoolNet:
> http://www.schoolnet.ca

Education Network Australia (EdNA):
> http://www.edna.edu.au/

ADAM, the Art, Design, Architecture and Media Information Gateway:
> http://adam.ac.uk/

Building Blocks for Programming: Technology in the Arts

☐ **Computer Arts**
- ☐ Web sites
- ☐ Virtual field trip
- ☐ Video games
- ☐ Blogs
- ☐ _____

☐ **Media for Story Making**
- ☐ Transposing stories in different media
- ☐ _____

☐ **Using Popular Media Texts (*Pokémon*, comics)**
- ☐ _____

☐ **Graphic Design**
- ☐ Print or media collage
- ☐ Using recycled magazines and environmental print
- ☐ _____

☐ **Creating Media Art**
- ☐ Film clips, charts, illustrations, songs
- ☐ _____

☐ **Producing Visual Texts**
- ☐ Planning a production
- ☐ Storyboarding
- ☐ _____

7 When Teachers and Artists Hold Hands

Partnerships in Arts Education

By Suzanne Stiegelbauer

Suzanne Stiegelbauer is an associate professor at OISE/UT. Her career includes being a teacher, a writer, a visiting curator for the Royal Ontario Museum, a field anthropologist in the American Southwest, a researcher on school issues, a coordinator of OISE/UT's Preservice Elementary program, a professor of art education, and a board member and advocate for First Nations organizations.

Artists in the school programs help the school community to experience the value of arts education and build parental support for arts programming in schools.
—Kathy Broad

There are many ways to think about the arts. One way is to consider the arts as a reflection of our culture; they contain information about culture as it *is* or comment on it as it could *be*. Another way to think about the arts is that they are an expression of our bodies and our senses, in other words, that each of the arts reflects the capacities of a particular sense—music from hearing, visual arts from vision, drama from speaking, dance from movement—as well as the interaction of the senses. In fact, many artists would say that the arts, whatever the medium, *are* the senses expressing themselves. This is an important kind of communication both to give and to receive.

When we work with the arts, we are working with the body and the mind. The body might be the vehicle of expression, and the mind, the integrative and imaginative force that makes expression meaningful. This concept is fundamental to working with the arts and with artists. When we ask students to experience what artists have to offer them, we must also ask them to imagine what artists are doing with their bodies, with their minds, and how students might interpret that experience for themselves. Sometimes this task is for the body, in "doing" something like the work they are experiencing; sometimes the task is for the imagination, in "understanding" what the work might mean.

This chapter is about teachers and artists working together. With cutbacks to the arts, teachers are called upon more and more to enrich their curriculum by teaching with and through the arts as art teachers as well as teachers of every other subject. I would like to emphasize that the arts are a very important part of school life for students: the arts are about play, imagination, the making of connections, bodies in action, and other processes that tap into the different ways that children learn and that allow them to express themselves and their understandings of the world.

Teachers may work with artists themselves or with artists as represented by what they create, be it objects, pieces, or performances. What is presented here are three theme areas to think about and six concrete ideas about ways to work with artists, at least as a beginning for your classroom. The emphasis here is on why we need artists—a term encompassing artworks, art spaces (like museums), artifacts, arts performances, artists at work, and art inquiries—within and without the school walls (including the Internet) in ways that connect to the curriculum and to the imagination.

Themes on Why Students Need Exposure to Artists

The arts, as the basis for an integrated curriculum, will choreograph students' acquisition of knowledge and skill in a way that their intelligences find most effective, will confront them with the most challenging questions about themselves and the world they live in. That is the ideal both teachers and artists must come to espouse as professionals.
—*Walter Pitman*

To prompt student reflection about a work of art, ask as many informational questions as you can.
- What is the work about?
- When was it made?
- Who made it and what do you know about the artist?
- What do you know about the time period and how people lived and thought then?
- What did they do at night?

1. *Looking:* Representations of artists—paintings, sculptures, plays, musical pieces— all tell a lot about the world, especially the time and context in which the art was created. Most people experience works of art in a passive way. Either they like it or they don't; the museum docent tells them about the color, the shapes, or the context, but it is essentially "over there," not a part of the viewer's everyday world. While representations might be works of beauty, they are also historical and social documents. Experiencing a work of art becomes a form of inquiry. What can we say about the artist and the time in which he lived? What did people "know" then that is different from what we know now? What is this picture or play or story really telling us about the people that made it? In doing this we are thinking about it consciously, not just aesthetically, and asking how we are different now. This kind of thinking can be done at any grade level. It asks students to "look" with their minds, not just their eyes, and if they don't know, to ask questions about the context.

This "looking" can be done with sounds or music, or any art form. For example, begin by playing the music of another country, something different from what students are used to. Ask: What do you hear? What kind of instruments? What kind of rhythms? Can you beat out the tempo with your feet or hands? The point of this exercise is that teachers can bring artists into their classrooms through artifacts and then use those artifacts to learn about the arts, but also, to use the arts to learn about other things. What would a unit on Native people be without looking at the arts? And why would that be useful as information about other people in other countries as well? In teaching a graduate course in educational foundations about the early days of schooling, I asked students to look for images of 1820 and what those images communicated about how people lived or thought, and what schools were like. They were able to tell me more about schools from those paintings than from the history books they had read. When we use the arts as a form of inquiry, we learn things we don't expect.

2. *Doing:* As Ellen Dissanayake writes in a 2002 *Orbit* article, "10 Reasons Why the Arts Are Important," the arts allow us to express our feelings and "give us something to do" in times of uncertainty, fear, sadness, or even happiness. They allow us to express those feelings with our bodies and senses and, in that way, release them. In helping students learn to use their bodies to express their feelings, the arts help them to be healthier people. In a sense, the arts are a form of emotional exercise.

Many art spaces and visiting artists have programs that ask students to "do" something: *work* with clay, *create* a dance, *develop* a "scenario" for a play. When we have to "do" something, or interact with a medium in a physical way to express what we want to say, we learn that expression is not limited to words and that sometimes we think or feel things that we only understand later. In talking about our work, we are able to understand it better after, rather than before.

As most teachers do not have background or facilities to provide for an in-depth "doing" experience, art galleries, museum programs, artists' spaces, theatres and artist-in-the-school programs provide guided opportunities in the physical elements of expression. They teach students how to "do" for themselves and model the artist's role in being the vehicle of a particular kind of artistic expression. Even Michelangelo, in carving the "Pieta," had to force the image and the feeling from the stone: sometimes the stone cooperated; sometimes it didn't.

115

But the end product communicates more about the feeling of a mother for a child, and the grief of a mother, than even he could have imagined at the beginning of his work.

3. *Experiencing:* Students deserve to see artists at work. Whether it is going to see a Shakespearean play or the symphony, seeing what can happen when artists perfect their skills can be an inspiration, something students will not forget. In the midst of a good performance, all the senses are in tune. From the atmosphere to the performance venue, to the sounds and sights, the senses are taking it all in. If students get a chance to talk about it or to connect it to something else—a poem, a math problem—then that taking-it-in builds to other understandings.

Whether you are listening to a musical performance in a theatre or watching an artist work in your classroom, it is a primary experience. People learn from watching others, from the modelling, from the association, even in fantasy. What child watching a ballet hasn't wanted to be graceful like that ballerina? Provincial and state departments, school systems, home and school groups, museums, and even individuals will sponsor artist visits or performances in schools. Now and again, an excursion will offer other benefits—the stage, the opening, the performance in all its glory.

Model Activities Based on Experiences with Artists

Given the three themes we have just talked about—teachers being involved with artists in terms of the artifact or "piece," in terms of making art or "doing" something with our bodies in relation to a creative work, and in terms of "experiencing" artists at work in performance—the following ideas give some support to ways teachers might put this in place in their classrooms. They are organized according to attributes of the arts and classroom approaches that emphasize those attributes.

Using the Arts to Place Ourselves in Time
A Social History Lesson: Go to a museum to deconstruct a painting as to what it says about how people lived and thought at an earlier time in the country's history. Take the deconstruction back and deconstruct it further: clothing, housing, ideas, interactions, science, math, other arts. Suggested paintings and examples: Something from revolutionary days, something from the Renaissance, something contemporary. Start with the early days, then try something modern for comparison.

Using the Arts to Tell Others Who We Are
Self-portraits: Many artists paint pictures of themselves. They color or add images to the pictures that convey more than their faces, that tell something about how they feel or think or like to dress. Examples: Freida Kahlo, Vincent Van Gogh, multicultural contemporary. See how many self-constructed images of artists, even musicians, that your students can collect from magazines. These can be starting points for organizing collages based on themes, styles, or content.

Using the Arts to Get What We Want to Say out of Our Bodies
Work with Clay: Part of the visual arts includes physical media, like clay or sculpture. When we work with a physical medium, our bodies have to work as

In this era of accountability, let's not forget that artists first showed the wide range of alternative assessments that we now see in schools. Visual artists gave us the idea of portfolio assessment, musicians gave us the idea of performance assessment, and for years, dancers have used the culminating task in their work.
—Jim Giles

The arts facilitate joyful learning as no other process can, simply because they build on the innate individual and collective desire to express profound ideas and feelings in dance, song, story, or picture.
—Walter Pitman

well as our heads—we have to interact with the medium in a physical way to express what we want to say. For example, students can create pre-Columbian style sculptures after working with potters and teachers at a museum such as the Gardiner Museum of Ceramic Art in Toronto. (There, students make their own figures, pressing clay through garlic presses to make hair and headdresses, cutting little pieces of clay to create decorative clothing, forming and shaping the clay to create a figure.)

Using the Arts to Be a Part of Our Community

Community Projects: Artists do not have to be famous or even work as individuals. Many works of arts are made by communities. In creating something together, people tell a story of themselves or comment collectively on something they feel strongly about. Examples: AIDS quilts, books by Faith Reinhold who uses different materials to make collages, art for celebrations.

The Joy of Creating: The School as an Artistic Community

—Marni Binder

In January 2004, approximately 340 students from Junior Kindergarten to Grade 8, at Lord Dufferin P.S., took part in a whole-school project with visiting artist Allycia Uccello from Art for Children of Toronto. The motif—The Many Faces of Our Community—reflected the vibrant diversity of our community. The colorful images that emerged resonated symbols of significance from the many cultures of the school population—words in different languages, flags, religious icons, musical instruments, people of importance, animals, and masks.

A unique artistic community was created, as the project brought together students from different grades over a five-day period. The room was buzzing with excited chatter. The little heads and arms of JK children reached over the boards to paint pictures of themselves. Older students helped the younger ones don paint shirts and gave them brushes and paint. All students responded to the artist's skill and instruction in using acrylics, and how to create their image using the elements of form, line, shape, texture, and color. Though an open-ended project, the experience was one that revealed the critical role of visiting artists in the schools.

Every Student Involved: A whole-school approach engaged all classes in the process of preparation. Prior to Allycia's visit, teachers discussed the project with the students. The visual arts teacher, who was assisting with the organization, generated a list of images that would relate to the community theme. Books were available in the library to assist in the dialogue process, as well as spark ideas for the students. Each student drew an image of significance. Although only 7 to 10 students from different grades took part in the actual painting, this process provided an inclusive approach for the artistic endeavor.

Images of Personal Significance: The first day of the project arrived. A group of Grade 7 and 8 students helped in setting up the room and painted the background colors on the mural. Allycia spoke about the importance of using a pastel background with designs to push the images out for the eye to see. Allycia worked with two groups each allotted period, focusing on specific elements of design, depending on the age group.

The arts are uniquely educative in character in that they link on so many ways to civilization and provide so many opportunities for individual development. And it is difficult to argue that they are not basic.
—John Goodlad

117

As the images began to emerge from the panels, the creative process unfolded. An aesthetic environment shaped the artistic engagement. Brush strokes and color embodied the imaginative and original voice of the students. The interrelationship of learning and experience was visibly portrayed as inner landscapes were crystallized within images of personal significance. As one Grade 2 student reflected: "I enjoyed doing the artwork on the wall because I love art. I wanted to do more art. I drew Shiva because it is a god of ours and we are Tamil."

Art as Play and Work: Experiences with this project raised the issue of the importance of artists in the school. When thinking about art and the curriculum, teachers often recall their earliest memories of how art was done when they were young. They also struggle with ideas when approaching art. There is the question of the visibility of other subjects and there seems to be the perception that one needs mastery in the subject. As Allycia commented, people tend to "separate art as a mystical process outside of themselves." Instead, we should see that children naturally connect play and art and that art really needs to be viewed as other subjects are.

Allycia stressed the critical element of role modelling—being an artist is a job. When artists come into the schools, they reflect the credible importance of this work: the training and knowledge an artist must have. It is no different from specializing in science or math. They can take the artistic experience and translate it into classroom practice. "There is a method and science to the visual arts," she stated.

Teachers were delighted with our mural project. They felt it was an experience that they could not bring to their classrooms. They were impressed by the quality of the student work. Parents showed a sense of pride when viewing the completed installation.

Using the Arts to Express and Shape Our Feelings

Interpretations of Events: As noted earlier, the arts "give us something to do" in times of uncertainty, fear, sadness, or even happiness. They allow us to express our feelings consciously and unconsciously, and to give form to them for reflection. We can use the idea of "feeling" and what it means to create and interpret works of art. Examples include Dr. Seuss's book on colors, the abstract paintings of Mark Rothko, Picasso's painting "Guernica," and musical pieces and dances that describe war. We can also share how children responded to the horror of 9-11 through writing, drawing, and painting by using Shelley Harwayne's *Messages to Ground Zero*.

Using the Arts to Understand the Relationships That Weave Us Together Physically, Spiritually, and Emotionally

A Museum Visit: A visit to a museum that offers hands-on creative experiences may allow students to better understand how they share something in common with people in other cultures.

A specific illustration follows. Standing within the Gardiner Museum's exhibition of pre-Columbian figurines, students identify with the animal sculptures, feel in awe of the warrior figures, and wonder about the painted surfaces and what they mean. What they really enjoy, however, is looking at how the figurines are decorated, what kind of jewellery or clothes they wore—how ornate, how elaborate—all in clay.

Students are fascinated by the objects they see, but even more than the objects, they are fascinated with the clay. The museum guide explains what the objects mean and how they were used. Then the museum's resident potter suggests to students that they might like to go back to the gallery and look specifically at what people are wearing. The potter models how the figures were made and clothes them like the figures in the gallery. As noted above, students then create their own figures. They come to understand something of how the pre-Columbian maker approached the task so many years ago; in the same way as those artists, they bring the clay to life.

The final product here goes beyond a clay statue. In visiting the museum, students have learned about a culture, a material, and the process of being an artist. They have also felt the satisfaction of making a unique finished product.

Artists for Inspiration

My observations of students actively engaged in artistic encounters have led to deeper insights into the crucial role the artist in the school can play. As Maxine Greene puts it, the arts, if well taught, provide "occasions for reaching out toward the universal, the truly good, or to images of grandeur that might restore the soul." It is important for schools to recognize the importance of the arts as an enhancement for learning. Projects involving artists can encapsulate what is important to students: community building, personal expression, engagement, and creativity. As one Grade 1 student engaged in the mural project reflected: "I like the artist because she inspired me."

Planning for a Museum Visit
—*Sarah Willett and Honoré Marchant-Kelly*

Why should the classroom teacher plan a museum field trip? The reasons are many. Museums offer experiential learning; are fun; are appropriate for any age group; function across subject areas; offer current, well-researched information; can work for learners of various levels and needs; help children in the development of cognitive skills; strengthen communication skills; develop social skills and personal values; encourage lifelong independent learning; and, above all else, offer curriculum support and outreach for the classroom teacher. Museums successfully and evocatively complement classroom learning and serve to remind school educators about the value of multi-sensory, experiential, object-based education. As Genean Stec explains in his book, *The Field Trip Handbook*, "rather than replacing classroom learning, museums are interested in awakening students' interests, stretching their minds, engaging their senses and stimulating them to go back to school to learn" (p. 1). Thus, the museum–school partnership is an exciting and significant relationship that should not be overlooked.

Museums can be valuable and dynamic arts spaces for use by classroom teachers. Teachers at urban schools have a plethora of cultural institutions from which to choose when planning a field trip, including art galleries, natural history museums, science centres, and historical homes. However, museums can also be a valuable tool in rural areas. Smaller community museums or historical homes often provide an engaging and informative means of learning about an area's history, development and diversity. Thus, whether you live in a rural or urban area, a museum field trip can enhance any school curriculum.

To illustrate how this might best be done, we will be using the University of Toronto Art Centre exhibition *20 Pieces—4 Cultures—1 Space* as a case study. The exhibition was a temporary show featuring folk furniture constructed by the Doukhobors, Hutterites, Mennonites and Ukrainian peoples in western Canada between 1870 and 1930. Themes explored during the exhibition included questions of value, function, style and form, as well as immigration experiences and the cultural traditions or adaptations of these four groups in the Canadian West. The exhibition was curated by the University of Toronto Master of Museum Studies program specifically to this particular exhibition; however, the concepts can be applied in other museum or gallery contexts.

Pre-visit Activities

Before the field trip takes place, you should prepare your class with a number of pre-visit lessons. These lessons should include activities that will stimulate student observational skills and establish an understanding of general concepts relating to the exhibit. Following are selected pre-visit activity suggestions:

1. To develop students' observational skills

Observation 101: Have each student think of three questions to ask a partner. Give the students five minutes to interview one another. Be sure to remind students to pay close attention to their respective partners. After you announce that the five minutes have passed, have each student turn around so that their backs are to each other. In this position, each student repeats what he or she has learned in the interview back to the partner and describes what the partner is wearing.

2. To develop students' understanding of material culture

Show and Tell: Have students think of an object that they feel reflects who they are or where they come from. Stress that this object can be anything they want, from a book, to a baseball, to a work of art. Ask them to bring it to class, take a picture of it, or draw a picture of it. After students have had sufficient time to complete the assignment (about one week), ask them to pair up and tell their partner what their choice was and why.

This activity can be structured to reflect the focus of the upcoming field trip. For example, in the case of *20 Pieces—4 Cultures—1 Space*, a teacher could ask his or her students to think of a piece of furniture that reflects who they are.

The museum or gallery you will be visiting may offer a number of pre-visit resources for classroom teachers. These might include teacher workshops (that provide instructors with information on the museum's collections and programming) and loan programs (that provide teachers with a "kit" containing materials, guides and potential pre-visit activities related to a particular exhibit). Beyond this, some museums will send trained interpreters or staff members to a classroom before a field trip to prepare the teacher. Make sure to check with museum or gallery administrators and educators to see what is available to you. In addition to pre-visit activities, be sure to inform your students of proper museum behavior and brief your chaperones on the educational objectives for the trip.

During-visit Activities

It is best to take the museum field trip, with its emphasis on hands-on experiences, as you begin a unit and then plan to follow up with more learning activities in your classroom. As a teacher, think about what you want your students to gain from a particular exhibit prior to visiting the museum and also consider what aspects of an exhibit best tie into your classroom curriculum. If possible, try to visit the exhibit or museum beforehand. Always prepare a student activity, whether you will be participating in a guided tour or viewing on your own. Museum activities should encourage deep consideration of the materials on display and enliven the experiences. In the museum, the following activities will allow students to become comfortable with the subject matter of the exhibit and facilitate an understanding and appreciation of culture. As Genean Stec records in *The Field Trip Handbook*, these activities "encourage object-based teaching" and also "help to sharpen the students' cognitive and perceptual skills" (p. vi). They should be adapted to reflect your students' needs and skills and to meet the objectives of your museum field trip. Following are some during-visit activity suggestions:

1. To encourage students to pay attention to the materials on display

Scavenger Hunt: Before the museum visit, choose five pieces from the exhibit that you would like students to pay particular attention to. Without specifically naming each object, describe them. Provide each of your students with a worksheet with these descriptions as you enter the exhibit. Encourage them to work independently, or on teams if they prefer, so as to determine what objects are being described. After the activity, ask students to explain why they felt a particular object matched with a particular description, whether or not their guesses are correct.

For example, in the exhibit *20 Pieces—4 Cultures—1 Space*, you could ask your students to locate different pieces of furniture by describing the color, shape, and design elements.

2. To encourage personal interaction with the exhibition collection and to teach students that their individual responses are as valid as the curator's vision

The Exhibit and You: Once in the exhibit, have your students move freely around the space. After an appropriate amount of time, given the size of the exhibit and your students' attention span, ask them to reconvene at a specific spot in the exhibition space. Once there, ask them to comment upon their favorite part of the exhibit and how it made them feel.

The museum or gallery you will be visiting may offer programming, activities and guided tours designed specifically for school groups. Make sure to check with museum or gallery administrators and educators to see what is available to you. In addition, inform the museum about the activity you have planned for the visit. If possible, provide the appropriate museum staff with a detailed description of your planned activity and any handout.

Post-visit Activities

These activities should be done in the classroom, after the students have returned from their field trip. They will serve to summarize the students' learning. Beyond this, they will provide the classroom teacher with the opportunity to measure the educational value of the field trip. Following are select post-visit activity suggestions:

Cross-cultural Links: Have your students reflect upon one particular object from the show that was produced by a specific cultural or ethnic group. Discuss with your students if there is a corresponding item in other cultures. Facilitate a discussion where students can compare an object and its counterpart, noting how they are both similar and different.

For example, in the exhibit *20 Pieces—4 Cultures—1 Space*, students could compare the Mennonite cradle with examples of cradles from their own or different cultural backgrounds.

Classroom Reflection: Have students think about the museum visit activity and then write a letter or compose an e-mail to a friend or family member describing their favorite piece from the exhibit, how they felt about it when they were in the exhibit space, and how they feel about it now.

Upon returning to the classroom, you may wish to evaluate your museum visit. It is suggested that you compile responses from students and chaperones, in addition to making your own critique of the field trip. This summary will benefit you, the class, *and* the museum.

The Role of Arts in Self-definition and Communication
—Suzanne Stiegelbauer

As an anthropologist and social scientist, I would say that the arts are important because of their critical role in communication and self-definition as a social and biological entity. Some anthropologists even believe that the arts play a major role in survival of the species and in the success of cultures. Think of the cultural dissemination evident in the profusion of McDonald's arches around the world—those large, yellow, sculptural symbols. As an artist, I feel that the arts are important to self-fulfillment, self-expression, and feeling "good" about life. As a human being, I can't imagine a world without feeling a conscious sensitivity to sunlight coming through the window, to appreciating a room arranged "just right," to hearing my favorite music on the radio, to picking out a new pair of shoes, to talking with a friend about somebody's hairdo, to snuggling up with a hot cup of coffee.

How do I define art? Compared to some, I'm not very discriminating. I consider the arts to be a form of consciousness at play, something constructed, formulated, or appreciated by means of the senses, that has some meaning in individual or societal terms. Given this definition, arranging a room, choosing the colors, and considering the space could be an art or art activity as much as painting a picture or composing a piece of music is. The conditions for this being a form of art is that the individual utilizes some type of aesthetic comparison, has a sense of what is effective, subjectively and objectively, and creates or puts things together in a way that means something to him or her, or to somebody observing.

When I was a child in Watertown, New York, my grandfather had a spring water business. He would take one of his 35 grandchildren along with him in this big, rattling water truck to the spring. I loved to go. There are lots of stories about my grandfather, his truck, and that spring, but one memorable "image" from those trips is that of a house we passed as we drove out of town. This house had a yard full of statues. Made of wood and plaster, the statues were rough, bumpy and not very well put together. There was Jesus on the cross, a clown, an abstracted Venus DiMilo. Some were white, some colored. I couldn't wait to get there to see if there were more. I wondered what made that person make those statutes and continue to make them until the yard was full.

As an adult, I continued to wonder about who and why and what inspired artists, from traditional quilt makers and Zuni potters, to a contemporary women's art collective in Texas, to storytellers and fiddle players, to Hispanic home altars and Mexican toys. Whether the art form was traditional, practical, or just was, it made me think. In an educational world that wants to return to "scientific rationalism" and the filling up of human vessels with the practical three Rs, the arts are just as important in making us think. And, as Maxine Greene would say, they offer the potential of transformation at the moment of contact. I like to think of people as multi-dimensional with multi-dimensional needs—cultural beings, personal beings, learning beings, and artistic beings. The arts allow the expression of those dimensions in ways that many other subjects might not.

Building Blocks for Programming:
Partnerships in Arts Education

☐ **Festivals and Celebrations**
- ❏ _____

☐ **Class-to-Class Sharing**
- ❏ _____

☐ **Displays and Installations**
- ❏ _____

☐ **Partnerships with Arts Organizations**
- ❏ Community projects
- ❏ On-line partnerships
- ❏ _____

☐ **Guests**
- ❏ Artists
- ❏ Performers
- ❏ Storytellers
- ❏ Plays
- ❏ Musicians
- ❏ Dancers
- ❏ _____

☐ **Excursions**
- ❏ Museum, gallery (pre-, during-, post-activities)
- ❏ Theatre visits (pre-, during-, post-activities)
- ❏ _____

Finale

Voices from the Arts Community

By David Booth

As the contributors to this book have shown, the arts appear in almost every aspect of our lives. In our schools, students bring with them varied experiences from their homes and their communities, and we see these revealed in their artistic endeavors each time they express or interpret or reflect within classroom arts events. As teachers, we have the joy of participating in our students' lives as we share in their experiences in arts-making, arts-viewing, and arts appreciation. Our classroom community is richer, more vibrant because of the nature of the arts processes, where participants are encouraged to voice and portray their feelings and ideas, illuminated and stimulated by their own individual life stories. Through our programs in the arts, we add to their storehouse of techniques and strategies, offering them ways and means for giving form and shape to their *felt thoughts*.

As teachers, we are in constant search of opportunities for giving students authentic arts experiences, as well as finding useful resources and activities for developing particular skills to support their attempts at making and interpreting aesthetic meanings. Of necessity, we look to the greater community for assistance with the different arts that our students need to explore in their school lives.

- The children themselves may have useful ideas for enriching the classroom and school programs, from their own after-school lessons to family or cultural events.
- Colleagues on staff may want to share a particular expertise, exchange an arts period, or work in partnership to broaden the scope of an arts unit.
- The school administration may have special resources for promoting or contributing to the arts program during the year.
- A resource teacher or consultant can offer specific workshops exploring one facet of arts education that can support your program.
- The Internet and chat lines present ways of finding information, reading and conducting interviews with artists, visiting virtual sites for the arts, and serving as media for arts-making.
- Picture books, novels about the arts, scripts by professional playwrights for children, illustrated information books about both the artists and the arts, books, photographs of artifacts and antiquities—all add to the children's background.
- Artists can visit the classroom as guests, often supported by grants or parent groups, and present a performance or a workshop that enriches and extends the classroom curriculum.
- Excursions to theatres, galleries and museums offer opportunities for both viewing and hands-on workshops with arts professionals.

- Volunteers offer their time at different arts venues out of a commitment to the arts and to promote the arts with young people. They are often widely experienced in arts education and can offer a great deal to students.
- Guests, such as parents, secondary students, student teachers, graduate students, retired teachers, friends and family, may have special arts hobbies or talents to include in the program in order to initiate or wrap up a unit of classroom work.
- Researchers and writers offer us different perceptions and findings about the arts in school settings, and often stimulate discussion of how we might change, restructure, or extend our arts programs to benefit the students.

In this section of the book, we have included the voices of some of the participants that have been part of our work in the professional community in our attempts to present the widest frame possible for arts education for children. Their words resonate with the arts experiences and training that have given them wide and extensive backgrounds in the different forms that art takes; their reflections can help us move towards arts-based schools that enrich and extend our students' lives in more ways than we ever thought possible.

A Parent's Voice

My four-year-old daughter attends Junior Kindergarten at an innovative school where experiences in the arts are provided to enrich young people's intellectual development and develop their communication skills. Earlier in the year, the Kindergarten teacher assigned a project in Social Studies on the children's own heritage. As part of their inquiry, the students were challenged to learn about their cultural background by collecting photographs, locating maps, conducting interviews, examining artifacts, and using other primary sources to gather information. After learning about their own heritage, the children were able to express their knowledge in creative ways. The teacher encouraged the students to design sculptures, produce models, develop structures, create collages, draw pictures, use photos, and prepare oral presentations as part of their project work. Together with the students, the teacher designed a project around a meaningful topic that related to children's own lives, families, and communities.

As the weeks passed, I saw my own daughter's interest in this personal topic grow as she became aware of her cultural background and learned to use authentic inquiry methods with success. After conducting an interview with family members, she examined photographs, pictures, maps, and artwork to learn more about her culture and ethnic heritage. Together, we listened to folk songs and popular music from our family's country of origin. Later, we prepared ethnic foods from traditional cookbooks and old family recipes. Finally, she created a collage, filled with drawings, photos, and pictures, that demonstrated the many facets of the cultural background she had grown proud of. The context and nature of the assignment enabled her to study and use the arts as a way to explore and express her heritage. With great delight, she carried her artwork off to school to share with others.

Soon the classroom was filled with the creative sculptures, impressive models, innovative structures, and artistic visuals that the children and their parents had produced together as a celebration and expression of their heritage. In the weeks that followed, my daughter returned home to reveal interesting facts and experiences she had learned about other cultures and places in the world from the projects shared and the artwork on display. Through her creative efforts, innovation, and encouragement, the classroom teacher found a way to provide the children in my daughter's Kindergarten class with new lenses to view the world, appreciate the arts, and understand others. This impact remained so powerful and rewarding that months later it prompted my four-year-old to ask, "Mom, where is my Italy project?" My reply was a simple one: "In your scrapbook along with the other special things you have made." Content with that, she walked off with a smile recalling her experiences and remembering with pride the work she had done.

A Student's Voice

—*Naima Akhter*

"ABCDEFGHIJKLMNOPQRSTUVWXYZ . . . Now I know my ABCs, so next time won't you sing with me?" Sound familiar? Almost every one of our talented and magnificent civilians in Ontario has sung this particular song when young. The "ABC" song is a perfect and accurate example of how music can provide our education with a special and exciting touch. A small five-year-old couldn't learn all 26 letters of the alphabet without the song supporting it and amusing the child. It is especially hard to believe that due to budget cuts, the government and school boards in my province are thinking about cutting off our valuable art and music programs. Many treasurable skills are enhanced by music instruction. Music gives kids an academic edge in school and a competitive edge in the working world. According to significant research conducted all over Canada, results clearly demonstrate that music education improves a child's development and aids the student in achieving higher grades in all subjects. Music is a way to make things more enjoyable and stimulating. It has the powerful ability to facilitate any hard concept that the child might not comprehend. Taking away the art and music programs is simply disadvantaging innocent children. In conclusion, the art and music programs are ideal to create well-rounded, confident, and successful individuals to lead our community. We need well-educated people in our country, and in order to have that, the teachers have to teach them in a way that will urge them to learn more and more. Keeping these valuable programs will result in coherent, polished, and intellectual humans. So remember, "Making Music Makes You Smarter!"

A Student's Voice

—*Nusrat Zahan*

To live a prosperous life without the arts is like living in a crumpled sea with no sinuous waves. Are the arts in our existence just for diversion, or for facilitating us to achieve an important role in life? The arts benefit us, allowing us to develop and improve in many ways such as teamwork, goal setting, hand-eye coordination, memory skills, quality of life, self-confidence and self-esteem, communication, and much more. We should understand the impact of arts education in the lives of everyone. Art *does* make a difference in our lives. When students study arts, they discover focus and expression. They develop the ability to draw, understand, and use symbols in the everyday world. They can discover and lead the power of personal creativity and self-expression by words or actions.

Arts can provide students with a competitive edge. Research on intelligence and cognitive function points to the possibility that music can be a form of intelligence. Everyone deserves a right to arts education. Current budget cuts have created a situation in which the arts are seen as an extravagance, not a right. Private schools actively lure those who can afford their schools by promoting top-quality arts programs. That is not fair. All students must have equal access to arts education. There are several scientific reports that relate the teaching of arts to students to improved progress in areas such as math, science, and more. All students deserve the musical advantage. In conclusion, arts programs make students more academically accomplished. The most important achievement to me is developing skills in understanding the importance of quality of life. Every student deserves the right to an arts education and to grow up with many abilities. Not abolishing arts from the curriculum can lead to a much more beneficial life.

A Teacher's Voice

—*Wendy Agnew*

"Can we paint on the wall?" This is the first question raised after we move to our new school. The grounds are shielded from the highway by a mighty barrier that runs for about 120 m (400 ft.) on the north side of a large field. Approximately 6 m (20 ft.) tall, it is non-textured concrete. We had already established a pattern for using art to transform our environment by installing three 4' x 8' environmental murals on the walls of our previous school and creating a sculpture garden there. We had dealt with the hazards of non-sympathetic elements when our garden was sprayed with pesticide, cut down, and finally used as a parking lot. Through these experiences, we'd developed some resilience and a sense of humor about the obstinacy of established "regimes."

In a discussion with our principal, I asked if we could paint some modest flowers on the foot of the barrier and she agreed. The next day a group of 20 nine- to ten-year-olds came to me for art class from a geography lesson on the nature of the earth's crust. We began to discuss minerals and fossils—the preliterate storytellers. The ensuing discussion wrapped us in relation to the elements of matter—the calcareous nature of our bones, resonating connection to both humble and colossal ancestors. "Are there dinosaur bones in the barrier?," someone asked. A fascination for the reptilian age seemed to predominate in this class, so I suggested we follow the thread of our discussion with a creative visualization. It went something like this:

"Find a comfortable position and close your eyes. Keep them closed and take deep slow breaths. Imagine that you are deep inside the body of the earth; that the earth is not only a part of you, but that you are a part of it. Linger in that knowledge for a moment. Keep your eyes closed. Now allow your consciousness to wander back in time. You have all the time in the world. On the way back you might notice great thundering herds of bison dissolving among the masted forests of tall ships. You're going back and back. You may sense the whisper of sand swirling around the feet of the pyramid builders . . . see the flicker of fire animating the paintings on cave walls of prehistoric tribes . . . back and back to the time of the mammals and then further into the golden age of reptiles. Nature is all around you. It is your home. You are perfectly safe here because you belong. You are inside a wonderfully leathery egg, sleeping deeply and warmly under the sunny sand. But . . . " etc., etc.

The children were led to choose a reptile and become it; feel the texture of their new skin, notice their breathing patterns, the way the warm sand was absorbed and became their body temperature, the shape of their claws (if any), the length and feel of their tails, the quality of rotation of their eyes, the position of their knees and elbows. *"How do you think now?"* I asked them. *"What do you dream about?"* The class was utterly quiet and then after a pause and a cue to remember these sensations, we came back to being human. *"But you still have the whisper of that reptile inside your paintbrush."*

We went outside and drew the outline of a giant brontosaurus on two sections of the barrier with a felt pen. Inside its body, the children drew the reptiles they had just simulated with pencil-crayons. Then we got out the acrylic paints and set to work. Because the creature was so tall, a stream of children went back to the school to get chairs and a table to stand on. As the mural progressed they would spontaneously run back and shout, "It's beautiful, it's beautiful!" from the top of the field. There was much sharing of paint and invitations to improvise on the reptilian environment they were creating. The only directive I gave was to leave nothing inside the body of the mother reptile unpainted and to stay within her confines. Two hours later we were looking at a finished work. I applied a coat of UV inhibiting varnish to protect it from fading and went home to dream of color.

Now every class wanted to do a mural, and so, through consensus, we paired the remaining classes of vertebrates to the remaining classes of children. Montessori uses vertical age groupings to promote community, mentoring, and intellectual flexibility so the classes in our school are delineated by age, not grade. Three classes of six- to nine-year-olds each created a mural of an eagle, a tadpole changing into a frog, and an elephant dancing with a human. The remaining class of eleven- and twelve-year-olds designed and painted a giant swordfish.

A Principal's Voice

Kathleen Fraumeni

In a time when the benefits of arts education are often undervalued and misunderstood, it is a rare occurrence to discover that there are elementary schools, thriving in our midst, dedicated to teaching and learning through the arts. Equally as rare is the privilege to be a principal in a school where the curriculum is anchored in the arts, where the students' learning is defined by their expressions of ideas through music, drama, dance, and visual arts. St. Mary School, in London, Ontario, has been providing an arts-based education to students for almost 40 years. In the early years of its existence, the school was highly unusual in its ability to offer vocal and string instruction to all its students, Grades 5 through 8, while setting goals for academic excellence and fine training in liturgical music traditions. Today, the school continues to fulfill its original mandate to provide a choir and orchestra program and has further evolved in its arts focus by incorporating all the areas of the arts into daily classroom learning.

It is one thing to have arts education endorsed by policy makers; it is quite another to bring arts into the real life of the school as a valid and valued vehicle for learning. It becomes the responsibility of the principal to ensure that the staff and the students are provided with an abundance of opportunities to incorporate arts-based learning activities in all areas of the curriculum in order to move the theory of arts education into practice.

Before any arts programming can effectively take place, the school must forge a well-connected network of supportive partnerships. Clearly, the district school board must step forward with support for arts-based learning in both financial and philosophical ways. A board's commitment to a school for the arts is a public statement of belief that the arts are valued as tools for improved student learning and as credible avenues for the expression of ideas. Such a board should be commended for its leadership in education. School councils and community partnerships, including the community's artists, are also invaluable pillars of support for a strong arts program. The principal is called to play a pivotal role in establishing a valuable and meaningful relationship among all the stakeholders of the school. The common goal among all these partners must be that the students become lifelong learners, educated to be contributors to and appreciative of the cultural life of the community. Once all partners are secured and the belief systems are in place, the possibilities for student learning through the arts are endless. It then becomes the role of the principal to develop and deliver a curriculum rich in artistic perspective and unique in its ability to promote learning in music, drama, dance, and visual arts for all the students.

One of the greatest challenges in the life of an arts school is the task of setting realistic and attainable goals for continued improvement. It is not enough to merely sustain the existing program with proper staffing and sufficient funding. Rather, it is critical to the life of the school to build on the achievements of the past to ensure growth for the future. The overall school improvement plan needs to contain strong statements about the arts focus across the curriculum and the plans for promoting learning through the arts at all grade levels. Plans for literacy improvement need to be articulated in language that embraces the arts such as *writing in role* to improve student writing and *in-role* activities to promote stronger oral language. The principal must encourage staff to embrace the arts when planning at the classroom level. Look for opportunities in music to draw a visual image of a symphonic piece. Look for moments in history class where *speaking* as the immigrant might teach more than *reading* about the immigrant. As curriculum leader, the principal must demonstrate a vision for learning through the arts that is true to the guidelines of the curriculum and provides for arts-enriched teaching strategies in the classroom every day.

It is essential to the success of the arts programming that there be trust among the school community's key players. Teachers need to feel that they can take risks when designing the learning activities that will best display their students' creative talents. The principal can demonstrate support by providing resources and funding for additional materials, by bringing in guest artists, and by seeking out professional development opportunities for teachers. Students also must be given latitude when they demonstrate their learning and express their ideas. In any given classroom, the skilled teacher will recognize the varied learning styles and different intelligences of the students and allow for many unique responses to learning. In a school dedicated to the arts, the infusion of music, drama, dance, and visual arts encourages the students to explore an even broader range of responses to learning through artistic expression of their ideas. Dance may be an appropriate response to a passage of poetry. A diary entry may be the best way a student can come to an understanding of the character in a novel. A charcoal sketch may be the best way to show understanding for the starkness of Canada's rugged northern landscape. Learning looks very different in an arts-based classroom, and the principal must provide a culture within the school that welcomes that difference.

A Consultant's Voice

—Suzanne Horvath

The Visual Arts Instruction Department at the Toronto District School Board wanted to support Sir Samuel Steele's development as an arts-influenced school on a deeper level. Besides presenting workshops after school and during the day for teachers, there was a desire to create a teacher centre to serve many schools throughout the board. Centres have the advantage of offering an opportunity for informal and formal exchanges among peers and of enabling a stable ongoing resource base of both people and materials to form. The North Arts Centre began as a way of reaching out to new elementary teachers in the board. Schools, including Sir Samuel Steele, were chosen to become a part of a pilot project to launch a new model of professional development. The idea was to assist teachers in the process of visual arts unit development and implementation with the aid and support of instructional leaders and professional artists. Working in pairs within their schools, teachers created an integrated visual arts unit and visited the North Arts Centre studio to begin the process. Along the way, ongoing contact with instructional leaders took place on a teacher electronic conference exclusive to North Arts Centre teachers. The aim was to create expert teachers who could not only share their units of study with other teachers in their school, but also provide guidance and instruction to their family of schools.

One of the classes that attended from Sir Samuel Steele was a special needs primary class whose teacher was in her first year of teaching. Initially, concern was expressed by both the teacher and parents that perhaps the students would be uncomfortable trying something different from their usual routine in the classroom. Honoring the many concerns, the instructional leaders worked closely with the teacher and education assistants on visual arts content development, delivery, and alternative activities. They found that content-rich lessons provided more language experience and a familiar medium for the students.

On Sir Samuel Steele's first visit to the Arts Centre, the teachers, artists, and instructional leaders all took part in class routines. The visual arts lesson and activities were incorporated into their usual practices to provide comfort for the students. In creating landscapes, the class discussed and described familiar settings (their backyards) and then looked at photos and paintings of landscapes from a variety of artists. From there, landscape drawings and mono prints were created using printing inks and various papers. An intense concentration and desire to create many prints was an indicator of the success of the experience for the students. The pride they felt in their work was later celebrated at a school board exhibition in February, where students, parents, and friends came to see the work on display. Despite the initial concern, one of the teachers involved commented: "Although I was nervous about the arts visit it turned out very well and was a great experience . . . I learned that art is and can be a way to communicate with the exceptional children in my class."

Although only in their second year of implementation, the staff at Sir Samuel Steele has a strong commitment to arts integration benefiting every student in their school. As Principal Peach said in a personal interview: "Parents and teachers want to prepare their children for the future. Creativity, imagination, and emotional expression are skills that are required in the workforce of the future and are all fostered in an arts-based program." It is this commitment to the arts and student achievement that has fostered the success this school has had thus far.

An Artist's View

—Vicki Kelly

I pondered upon what it means to see, to know, to shape, to show. I recognized that each act is a step taken in the unfolding process of the artist. These acts designate the events that lie along the songlines of the soul in the process of creating. They point to the places—sacred spaces—in which the artist must move in the enactment of the mysteries of becoming. They are the signposts along the well-worn and ancient pathway traversed by all artists throughout all time. They indicate the stepping stones or springboards that ultimately launch all aspiring creators following in the footprints of the quintessential creator.

The first act is to see. To see is to perceive with the eye or to apprehend as if by the sense of sight. To see also means to have a mental image of or to see in the mind's eye and thus to visualize in the imagination. Perhaps most important, to see is an indication of a sense of understanding or a movement toward comprehension and thus knowing. The artist endeavors to perceive or to become aware of directly through all the senses. Artists take intense notice of phenomena and observe. To observe is to step over the obstacle of oneself in order to serve or attend to the other; in other words, observing is an act of selflessness. In so doing, artists perceive so exactly that they ultimately re-create or re-form an experience through inner images and through an active seeing or perceiving in their imaginations.

The second act is to know. To know is to have a clear perception or under-standing. It is to perceive, to be aware of or so cognizant that one is well informed. One is firm in the mental grasp of something or so secure in the skill, study, or experience that there is a certainty in the act of knowing. Ultimately the artist endeavors to know or to identify that which was the origin and intention of the creator and to recognize the idea, image, or creative imagination out of which an object was created. This idea, ideal, or archetype is encrypted into the very nature and substance of the created world.

The third act is to shape. To shape is to create, to fashion, or to mould. It is to carve a contour or form, characteristic of a person, thing, or class of things. To shape is also to arrange, to devise or to give expression to a definite form or condition. In the creative act, it can also mean to adapt, adjust, or edit so that all the unessential is removed like a discarded chrysalis. In the final analysis the work of art is shaped according to an inherent order or imagination. The artist endeavors to create an artistic representation which honors the essential truth of being through the media of sound, color, form, and lines, and combine the colors so that through the work of art the most quintessential part—the essence of the human being that the artist has glimpsed—is revealed. The distinguishing forms and the shade or hue of color blend to reveal how the individual's gaze eloquently greets one through the portal of the eyes—this elusive reality is captured or portrayed by the artist.

This is the fourth act: to show. To show is to cause or allow something to be seen or viewed—it is displayed or made visible. Artists, in showing, make something present for public exhibition; they make it manifest or reveal through the work of art. Artists attempt to re-present an aspect of personal experience and to make it eloquent for others. They show or guide others by pointing out or indicating some aspect of life through their representation. The act of creating or shaping reveals, and in so showing, it reshapes or informs the imagination of the artist. Thus, in the shaping and showing artists adjust for the making visible of one aspect of their perspective, which in turn facilitates a broadening of their own viewpoint and a furthering of their understanding. In art the act of forming informs.

For me this almost Haiku-like phrase speaks with the barest simplicity and with the most elegant eloquence what it means to create and what it means to stand in the world as an artist. The artist *endeavors*: "To see, to know, to shape, to show." It is also true that by following in the footsteps of the artist we are led: to see, to know, to shape, to show, and thus come to recognize, humble or small, the artist in us all.

An Arts Student's Voice

—Masayuki Hachiya

During my early childhood, when I was eager to work in a variety of ways to express my feelings and ideas, artwork was my favorite pastime. I spent many hours at home making different kinds of pictures and crafts. While attending elementary school in Japan, I loved each visual arts class, held 1½ hours a week. I was happy to make my own artwork, encouraged by my teachers' and classmates' comments. The art lessons gave me immeasurable pleasure and self-confidence.

At school, curriculum subjects were regularly scheduled and students received free textbooks for most of the subjects, including art. Teachers were supposed to follow the guidelines of these books, but art was an exception. They preferred their own methods in teaching art. Still for me, the art textbooks were interesting enough to arouse my curiosity and spark inspiration. These books were almost like small art catalogues containing pictures of paintings and sculptures, as well as various types of designs and crafts created by artists and students of my age.

In junior-high school, my classes in visual arts became more advanced. I was always anxious to receive the teacher's evaluation of my work. When my pictures were displayed on the wall of the school corridor along with some other students' artwork, I felt proud of my accomplishments. By this time, though, some of my classmates seemed to have difficulty with their artwork. Perhaps their work was stifled by the teacher's comments, as many of their decisions were based on the subjective judgment of the teacher.

But I did not enjoy the final art exams held at the end of each semester in junior-high school. They made art seem to be an exam-based subject. The questions were generally based on art history. I began to wonder whether it was necessary to have written exams for this subject. What was the purpose of written testing? This issue must have made an imprint on my mind. At the level of graduate school, the issue of assessing student artwork became a major interest to me, eventually propelling me to write a thesis on the subject.

When I was in a senior-high school, my program did not include any visual arts lessons. I was allowed only one credit course in the arts. That seemed to me unfair, but I chose music because I was more enthusiastic about it than visual arts at that time. My life became so involved in music during those years. I had been selected a leader and a conductor of the school wind orchestra. By the time I reached university, though, my interest began to shift back to visual arts.

When I was in Grade 12, I went to an art institution after school, taking a university preparation course. I had the aim of becoming an architect who specialized in art design and its environment. However, during the prep course, I found that my objective changed. Since working on visual arts at this school, I came to know the limitation of my competence and talent in art. The students who attended the course were all excellent artists.

Then, I began spending my time on plaster drawings in a dark art room, hoping to acquire the ability to see an object and to represent it on a white piece of paper. It was the intensive, independent learning after school that gave me an essential landmark of art and education. While doing plaster drawings, many thoughts came to my mind: What kind of reality can I understand in art? What is the role and meaning of art in my life—self-achievement?

My four-year B.Ed. program at university in Tokyo included teacher qualification courses as a generalist and specialist dealing with pedagogy, educational theory, practice, and formal art training. These courses also included creating paintings and sculptures, making prints and graphic and product designs, doing metal and wooden craft arts, and studying art history. Several art professors whose works were well known and appreciated in our society taught this program. Students had to audition to be accepted into this specific program, where we were fortunate to learn craftsmanship and apprenticeship.

Besides visual arts activities, I gained experience in drama education, calligraphy, and music by taking courses. Also, I was constantly busy in arts-related activities—visiting art galleries and museums, and attending performances of dance, music, and plays. My involvement with these arts courses and activities gave me opportunities to meet new friends, many of whom shared a vision of the arts, as well as similar interests, and to think about the nature of the arts and their unique contributions to a larger society.

At university, I was swamped with doing artwork. Although it required self-discipline and patience, I was obsessed with making my art productions. At the beginning, since I was eager to be good at sketching, I practised repeatedly. But at the end of the day, I often felt that work still needed to be done on my sketch. One day, I saw a sketch by Leonardo da Vinci in an art gallery, and I felt his amazing talent was beyond excellence.

The thoughts and feelings that emerged while I worked on my art and looked at da Vinci's have been truly important for me as a student in pre-service education. Good artists are not always good art teachers. You don't need to be an artist, but rather you may want to have an experience in the arts and to be familiar with materials. Artwork requires patience and apprenticeship, time, and energy, as does art teaching. Education cannot be achieved by just a one-day workshop with a simple hands-on activity, a fun time.

An art teacher candidate is often asked to provide a portfolio of his or her artwork in a job interview. What does this imply? Through my experience as a student and novice researcher in arts education, I came to wonder whether the degree of your artistry is regarded as a qualification for teaching art. Of course, your artwork should help your teaching in some way. But it is probably more important to experiment with various modes of art expression and to know materials, tools, and each student's potential and developmental stage in art.

From my years of being an arts student, I learned how difficult it is for many elementary teachers to cope with teaching art; I also learned that they feel, "I don't teach art well because I'm not good at art." Teaching art is not dependent on what you have made, but how you instruct students in art and respond to their artwork. It is a communication between you and your students. This process is much more complex than just creating your own artwork: you must interact with every student to help each to grow within the arts.

A Volunteer's Voice

—*Michael Seary*

Our project at the museum was to make "alternative worlds."

"I know," said a student, "like the red planet."

Or perhaps painted dioramas. No one knew what they were so I produced a corrugated cardboard box, placed it on its side, and facilitated a discussion about what could be inside. A bedroom, perhaps, or a stable, or the ocean floor, or the desert, or outer space—like the red planet?

And what would be on the outside? We talked about doors that would open, how the top could be the sky and you could make slits in it and hang clouds from it—or airplanes, or rocket ships, or birds, or fish. And then you could glue another box on top and add an attic or a loft for the barn. And you could add cardboard walls, or trees, or fences in front of the box or around it.

"Does everyone have the idea?"

Everyone had the idea long ago and they all rushed to claim boxes. . . .

Sophie, who kept telling me she didn't know what she was doing, painted and constructed all afternoon. She started with some abstract expressionist-style paintings that she glued onto the walls of her place. The walls were painted black to enhance the effect. Between them and the open space at the front of the box, she draped a cobweb made of string. Glued above the main room there was a second, smaller box. It had a window on one wall which, when opened, pulled out a paper head of a cow with the caption "hello" printed above it. The opposite wall had slits with paper pictures you could slide back and forth or up and down in and out of the room. This room had a trap door in the middle of the floor which led to a wiggly paper staircase that took you to the floor of the main box. The outside of the two boxes was undecorated. "I want people to say, 'Oh, these are just two boxes,' and then when they see the inside, 'Wow, this is something really different.'"

Another project was made by a youngster who was so quiet that he only whispered his thoughts. But he'd got to the boxes first and his was the biggest. He made the inside of his box into a cave by painting paper sheets black and brown and then crunching them against the back and side walls and the floor. Stretching across the box he made a platform also painted black. Then he indicated to me that he wanted to have a slit on the roof above the platform and another short slit near one of the side walls. I wanted to know what the slits were for. "Back'n forth, up'n down," he whispered.

"Draw them," I said. So he drew two box-like, car-like, machine-like objects, one to go back and forth, the other to go up and down. He then wanted a door "for the up'n down." I looked doubtful, so he said with a happy smile, "Or, I can just imagine the door." No need. I cut a door he could open and shut.

When the parents came, I noticed the boy demonstrating his alternative world by making the one box go up and down and the other slide back and forth.

And we did get the red planet. It started with a composition of red blobs of wet paint sponged onto a blackened background which was then crunched and glued onto the floor of the box. The four sides and inside top were covered with shiny white cardboard. The whole thing was sealed shut except for one small hole on the side that you could look through and another one on the top that let in some shadowy light shining on . . . the red planet.

An alternative world.

(Source: *Children Making Art*)

Appendix A: Developing a School-based Arts Policy
—Jane Cutler and Lee Willingham

Excellence in art education occurs when the school is committed to equity and excellence in arts programs for all students.

Every student receives a balanced and comprehensive arts program. Arts education is linked to the overall learning of the student.

Every teacher receives support for professional growth as an educator in, through, and about the arts.

The school is also committed to finding ways to link the learning process in school with arts organizations in the community, to involve professional artists to complement and enrich school programs.

An arts policy includes dual dimensions: (a) clearly stated outcomes for student learning and (b) a range of responsibilities for all who are involved in children's education, including administrators, elected officials, teachers, students, parents, and the community at large.

Expectations

The following are some expectations that might serve to form an *arts policy* for a school.

As learners, we

- are introduced to and develop the skills and abilities within each of the art forms
- create, present, and experience art in many forms
- promote arts initiatives within our community
- apply critical and analytical skills in our arts experiences
- express ourselves in verbal and non-verbal ways
- appreciate diverse perspectives, openness, and flexibility in thinking
- develop a high level of self-awareness and self-confidence
- enlarge our capacity to take risks and solve problems creatively
- build on ideas learned from visiting artists
- work with a variety of media and techniques to gain insights about cultural and historical issues
- use a rich and healthy sense of beauty and imagination in our everyday lives

As teachers, administrators, parents, and community members, we

- ensure that schools provide facilities and resources for working creatively and safely in all of the arts
- ensure that arts specialists teach in our schools
- allocate sufficient time for regular, continuous arts instruction
- continuously develop our skills and knowledge in order to provide an effective and balanced arts program
- provide "hands-on" experiences for students in the arts
- teach so that the arts are connected to one another, to other disciplines, and to our everyday lives
- display and make public a wide variety of artwork throughout our schools

136

- go out of the school to be an audience for performances or participants in a gallery
- use technology and multimedia to support learning in, through, and about the arts
- know the potential of the arts to address student learning through the *multiple intelligences*
- provide students with learning activities that will enable them to develop personal skills, means of expression, and appreciation for the arts and for creative approaches to life
- demonstrate an interest in the artistic expressions of our students
- support the development of students who will become performers, audiences, and workers in various areas of the arts
- have a staff Arts Committee to plan curriculum development and school-wide arts activities
- work together to create special celebrations in the arts

Further Considerations

It is important to make an arts policy *explicit* in order to determine the effectiveness of existing policies, and to identify the needs and solutions. It is also important to take a *realistic* approach and to establish a *critical path* for the development and implementation of an arts policy. Two causes for failure are attempting too much and leaving too little time.

Approval and *implementation* are key parts of the policy process. It is necessary to include all levels of administration, teaching staff, elected members, and community in the development process. Discussions, the circulation of draft outlines, feedback, and public forums all help to ensure the acceptance of an arts policy.

We are reminded that we have some fundamental beliefs about students and the arts, and these beliefs inform our decisions about the arts and learning. We believe that *all* students are artistic. We believe that the arts are experienced in a variety of ways. We believe that the study of the arts promotes critical and reflective thinking. We believe that artistry contributes to an overall better life. We conclude that experiencing art-making as part of our educational journey is essential to developing deep understanding, appreciation, and enjoyment.

Appendix B: Research and Resources in Arts Education
—Barbara Soren

. . . research provides compelling evidence that the arts can and do serve as champions of change in learning. Yet realizing the full potential of learning in and through the arts for all . . . children will require heroic acts from all segments of our society. With the 21st century now upon us, we, too, must be champions of change; we must meet and exceed the challenge of giving our young people the best possible preparation we can offer them. To do so, we must make involvement with the arts a basic part of their learning experiences. In doing so, we will become champions for our children and their children.

> Champions of Change: Executive Summary
> What the Arts Change about the Learning Experience
> (http//aep-arts.org/Champions.html)

New evidence of enhanced learning and achievement when students are involved in a variety of arts experiences was reported in *Champions of Change: The Impact of the Arts on Learning* (Fiske 1999). With the support of the GE Fund, the John D. and Catherine T. MacArthur Foundation, the Arts Education Partnership, and the President's Committee on the Arts and the Humanities, seven major studies examined the role of arts education on the academic, behavioral, and thinking lives of children. The studies revealed that the arts

- reach students who are not otherwise being reached
- reach students in ways that they are not otherwise being reached
- connect students to themselves and each other
- transform the environment for learning
- provide learning opportunities for the adults in the lives of young people
- provide new challenges for those students already considered successful
- connect learning experiences to the world of real work
- enable young people to have direct involvement with the arts and artists
- require significant staff development
- support extended engagement in the artistic process

Since 1999, researchers in Canada, the United States, and the United Kingdom have further demonstrated that arts experiences in classrooms enhance learning and achievement, and enrich the lives of young people and their families, as well as those of teachers and school administrators.

The balance of this report highlights research findings and resources in the following areas:

- the impact of the arts on student academic and socio-cultural development
- the arts as meaning makers
- arts assessment and standards
- the arts and the creation of mind
- multiple settings for learning and approaches to understanding

The Impact of the Arts on Student Academic and Socio-Cultural Development

Two groups promote a group of studies called *CRITICAL LINKS: Learning in the Arts and Student Academic and Social Development* (Deasy 2001). The Arts Education Partnership (AEP, formerly the *Goals 2000 Arts Education Partnership*) is a U.S.-wide coalition of arts, education, business, philanthropic, and government organizations. AEP demonstrates and promotes the essential role of the arts in the learning and development of every child and in the improvement of America's schools (http://www.aep-arts.org). The second group, Americans for the Arts, boldly states on their Web site and in ads in the *New York Times*:

A Little Art is Not Enough!

There's not enough art in our schools or in our children's lives. But ask almost any parent, and they'll say that arts education is very important to their child's well-being. Which makes it so surprising that the arts have been allowed to virtually disappear from our children's learning experiences.

(Source: National Arts Education Public Awareness Campaign at
http://www.artsusa.org/public-awareness)

These *CRITICAL LINKS* studies focus on understanding the cognitive capacities (thinking skills) developed in learning and practising the arts, and the relationship of those capacities to students' academic performance and social development. They also examine achievement motivations, attitudes, and dispositions towards learning and fostered through learning and practising the arts. The studies suggest that for certain populations—including young children, students from economically disadvantaged circumstances, and students needing remedial instruction—learning in the arts may be uniquely able to advance learning and success in other areas. For example:

- Certain forms of arts instruction enhance and complement basic reading instruction aimed at helping children "break the phonetic code" that unlocks written language by associating letters, words and phrases with sounds, sentences and meanings.
- Young children who engage in dramatic enactments of stories and text improve their reading comprehension, story understanding, and ability to read new materials they have not seen before. The effects are even more significant for children from economically disadvantaged circumstances and those with reading difficulties in the early and middle grades.
- Learning in individual art forms, as well as in multi-arts experiences, engages and strengthens such fundamental cognitive capacities as spatial reasoning (the capacity for organizing and sequencing ideas); conditional reasoning (theorizing about outcomes and consequences); problem solving; and the components of creative thinking (originality, elaboration, and flexibility). For instance, music instruction, such as training in keyboard skills, develops spatial reasoning and spatial-temporal reasoning skills, which are fundamental to understanding and using mathematical ideas and concepts.

- Learning in the arts nurtures motivation, attitudes, and dispositions to pursue and sustain learning through active engagement, disciplined and sustained attention, persistence, and risk taking.
- Studies of student learning experiences in drama, music, dance, and multi-arts activities show student growth in self-confidence, self-control, self-identity, conflict resolution, collaboration, empathy and social tolerance.
- The arts help to create the kind of learning environment that is conducive to teacher and student success by fostering teacher innovation, a positive professional culture, community engagement, increased student attendance and retention, effective instructional practice, and school identity.

How a Comic Book Project Helped Improve Literacy

A project with urban youths in New York City is an excellent example of how involvement in the arts can have an impact on socio-cultural development (Bitz 2004). In 2002, 733 students from fourth to eighth grade sketched, plotted, wrote, and designed original comic books. The Comic Book Project offered students in an inner-city after-school program an alternative pathway to literacy through visual arts. Research has shown that children's creation of comic books can help improve literacy through an engaging artistic process in which words fit intuitively with pictures (Morrison, Bryan, & Chilcoat 2002). Most of the children were identified as low performing and more than half of the children participating in the project were identified as English as a Second Language (ESL) learners.

An equally important outcome was that children used the comic book format to depict their lives as urban youth. The comic books illustrated what they experience, how they respond to extraordinary circumstances, and how they struggle with daily hardships. The project demonstrated how artistic process can engage and empower children and teachers. This project was intended to reach the many inner-city children who may not have been identified as talented, and may never have been exposed to making art. Some of the comic books had a moral, such as "don't do drugs," and some were "tales of futility in which the main characters were doomed despite bold efforts to overcome struggles" (p. 34). Scenes generally occurred on street corners or schoolyards. The most prominent themes were gang violence, drug abuse, and opposite-sex relationships. The comic books tended to be mirrors of urban life and "serve as a wakeup call to society as a whole" of how "urban youth tend to view themselves and their prospects for success" (p. 39). Bitz concludes: "Art can be a pathway to understanding one's extraordinary surroundings, and a way of enabling others to learn from and hopefully act upon the messages that urban youth put forth" (p. 39).

The Arts as Meaning Makers

The Arts as Meaning Makers by Claudia Cornett of Wittenburg University (see also Cornett 2003) and Katharine Smithrim (2001) richly describes how teachers can enrich their teaching *with, in, about,* and *through* the arts. The goal of the book is to help teachers *meaningfully* integrate literature, art, drama, dance, and music throughout curricular areas by providing "a basic art knowledge base, clear reasons for integration, and specific arts integration principles" (p. vi). Hands-on activities and ideas, daily routine ideas, integrated unit ideas, and adaptable classroom structures provide "how to's" for using the arts throughout the curriculum in K–6 classrooms—in social studies and science, in reading and language arts, and in math. In the foreword to the book, Rena Upitis, then dean of education at Queen's University, commented on the timeliness of this publication. In spite of research evidence about the importance of the arts to brain development, academic achievement in other subject areas, and success in school, there is generally declining support for arts education.

Upitis and Smithrim (2003) provided research evidence in support of arts education in their report on a national assessment for the Royal Conservatory of Music's Learning Through the Arts™ program (LTTA) from 1999–2002. The report describes the effects of the program over a three-year period on 6,675 students in schools at six Canadian sites. The focus of the report is students who were in Grade 4 at the beginning of the study and at the end of Grade 6 at the conclusion of the study, as well as beliefs and practices of parents, artists, teachers, and administrators. The study highlighted how the arts motivated children, and that there were emotional, physical, cognitive, and social benefits of learning in and through the arts. Most parents (90 percent) reported that the arts motivated their children to learn. Artists in the classrooms observed a wide variety of benefits, "including the development of arts skills, exploration of curriculum topics through the arts, and laying the foundation for a lifelong love of the arts" (p. 2). At the end of the three-year period, teachers involved in the program believed the arts were an effective way to teach language, science, and math. The LTTA teachers showed increased commitment to teaching through the arts, as well as growing skills and confidence in embedding the arts in their teaching practice. Principals in these schools also tended to consider the arts as "very important."

Arts Assessment and Standards

The National Standards for Arts Education outline what every K–12 student should know and be able to do in the arts. Arts Education Standards in the United States were developed by the Consortium of National Arts Education Associations, through a grant administered by the National Association for Music Education. The Standards are published on-line by ArtsEdge, the National Arts and Education Network that supports the placement of the arts at the centre of the curriculum and advocates creative use of technology to enhance the K–12 educational experience. ArtsEdge empowers educators to teach in, through, and about the arts by providing the tools to develop interdisciplinary curricula that fully integrate the arts with other academic subjects. It is a program of the John F. Kennedy Center for the Performing Arts, and a consortium of national education organizations, state education agencies, and the MarcoPolo Education Foundation. The vision for the Arts Education Standards is as follows:

> . . . a future worth having depends on being able to construct a vital relationship with the arts, and that doing so, as with any other subject, is a matter of discipline and study. The Standards must usher each new generation onto the pathway of engagement, which opens in turn onto a lifetime of learning and growth through the arts. It is along this pathway that our children will find their personal directions and make their singular contributions. It is along this

pathway, as well, that they will discover who they are, and even more, who they can become.

(Source: Standards: Discovering Who We Are
at http://artsedge.kennedy-center.org/teach/standards)

As articulated in this document, the Standards can make a difference because they help ensure that the study of the arts is disciplined and well focused, and that arts instruction has a point of reference for assessing its results. In addressing these issues, the Standards insist on the following:

- that an arts education is not a hit-or-miss effort but a sequenced and comprehensive enterprise of learning across four arts disciplines, thus ensuring that basic arts literacy is a consequence of education
- that instruction in the arts takes a hands-on orientation (i.e., that students be continually involved in the work, practice, and study required for effective and creative engagement in all four arts disciplines)
- that students learn about the diverse cultural and historical heritages of the arts (The focus of these Standards is on the global and the universal, not the localized and the particular.)
- that arts education can lead to interdisciplinary study—achieving standards involves authentic connections among and across the arts and other disciplines
- that the transforming power of technology is a force not only in the economy, but in the arts. (The arts teach relationships between the use of essential technical means and the achievement of desired ends; the intellectual methods of the arts are precisely those used to transform scientific discovery into technology.)
- that across the board and as a pedagogical focus, the development of the problem-solving and higher-order thinking skills necessary for success in life and work is taken seriously and
- that taken together, these Standards offer, for the first time in American arts education, a foundation for educational assessment on a student-by-student basis

The Arts Education Standards help define what a good education in the arts should provide. Students must acquire a thorough grounding in a basic body of knowledge and the skills required both to make sense and to make use of each of the arts disciplines. This includes the intellectual tools to make qualitative judgments about artistic products and expression. The Standards can help weak arts instruction and programs improve and help make good programs even better. They are expected to advance both quality and accountability and to help the nation "compete in a world where the ability to produce continuing streams of creative solutions has become the key to success" (Standards: The Difference Standards Make).

In 1992, anticipating that education standards would emerge as a focal point of the reform legislation, the Consortium of National Arts Education Associations successfully approached the U.S. Department of Education, the National Endowment for the Arts, and the National Endowment for the Humanities for a grant to determine what the nation's schoolchildren should know and be able to do in the arts. In an on-line publication of the U.S. Department of Education, there is a *Summary Statement: Education Reform, Standards, and the Arts*, which outlines what students should know and be able to do in the arts (see http://www.ed.gov/pubs/ArtsStandards.html).

- Students should be able to communicate at a basic level in the four arts disciplines—dance, music, theatre, and the visual arts. This includes knowledge and skills in the use of the basic vocabularies, materials, tools, techniques, and intellectual methods of each arts discipline.
- They should be able to communicate proficiently in at least one art form, including the ability to define and solve artistic problems with insight, reason, and technical proficiency.
- They should be able to develop and present basic analyses of works of art from structural, historical, and cultural perspectives, and from combinations of those perspectives. This includes the ability to understand and evaluate work in the various arts disciplines.
- They should have an informed acquaintance with exemplary works of art from a variety of cultures and historical periods, and a basic understanding of historical development in the arts disciplines, across the arts as a whole, and within cultures.
- They should be able to relate various types of arts knowledge and skills within and across the arts disciplines. This includes mixing and matching competencies and understandings in art-making, history and culture, and analysis in any arts-related project.

Summary Statement: Education Reform, Standards, and the Arts concludes: "As a result of developing these capabilities, students can arrive at their own knowledge, beliefs, and values for making personal and artistic decisions. In other terms, they can arrive at a broad-based, well-grounded understanding of the nature, value, and meaning of the arts as a part of their own humanity."

The Arts and the Creation of Mind

Elliot W. Eisner, one of our most prolific and persuasive arts educators, argues that the arts are critically important for developing complex and subtle aspects of the mind. In *The Arts and the Creation of Mind*, Eisner (2002) wants to "dispel the idea that the arts are somehow intellectually undemanding, emotive rather than reflective operations with the hand somehow unattached to the head." The arts have tended to be "at the rim, rather than at the core of education" (p. xi), considered to be a minor part of a curriculum that challenges students to think. However, work in the arts evokes, refines, and develops thinking, argues Eisner. The arts have distinctive contributions in the development of thinking skills, the expression and communication of forms of meaning that only artistically crafted forms can convey, and experiences that are treasured for their intrinsic value.

Eisner discusses the contribution that standards can make to arts education (p. 173). Standards can be used as aids if they do the following:

- represent in a meaningful and non-rigid way the values arts educators embrace and the general goals arts educators seek to attain
- provide those who plan curricula with an opportunity to discuss and debate what is considered important to teach and learn
- suggest criteria that can be used to make judgments about arts educators' effectiveness

Defining standards provides an opportunity to describe and examine conceptions of arts education and to deepen the dialogue about what the arts can teach us. Discussion about the meaning of standards in arts education can provide a motivation for thinking about the possibility of different standards for different populations, different schools, and different students.

For Eisner, meaning is not limited to what words can express. "Humans are meaning-making creatures. All of us wish to create meaningful experiences" (p. 230). The arts provide a spectrum of forms—through visual arts, music, dance, and theatre—and multiple sources of learning through which meanings are made, revised, shared, and discovered. In his concluding chapter, Eisner revisits the 13 important ideas in his book. Two particularly empowering ideas are these:

- Among all the fields of study in our schools, the arts are at the forefront in the celebration of diversity, individuality, and surprise (p. 235).
- The possibilities for growth in and through the arts cease only when we do (p. 240).

Multiple Settings for Learning and Approaches to Understanding

Howard Gardner (1991) strongly supports the need for environments that promote deeply motivating experiences. In the area of visual arts, for instance, Gardner believes that more intuitive ways of knowing will operate for young children without the need for anything except rich opportunities for learning. Children's discovery museums provide opportunities in which people can clarify these more intuitive conceptions or, in Gardner's words, confront "those habits of the mind that tend to get in the way of a thoroughgoing understanding" (p. 179). Beyond six years of age, it is essential to create experiences and learning situations that help people to be actively involved in artistic activities, deepen knowledge, and work towards higher levels of understanding so that the sense of creating and reflecting continues to evolve throughout one's life.

Gardner has identified eight distinct intelligences—linguistic, logical-mathematical, musical, spatial, bodily-kinesthetic, interpersonal, intrapersonal, naturalist—that all human beings have to some extent (see, for example, Armstrong 2000). His Theory of Multiple Intelligences proposes that each person has capacities in all eight intelligences and that they function together in unique ways in each individual giving people a "jagged profile of combined intelligences" (Gardner 1997, p. 25). On-site and on-line visits to museums, for example, offer school visitors experiences in which they can use multiple intelligences and develop a range of literacies as they explore resource-rich environments, interpretive materials, and interactive exhibits.

Gardner (1999) also elaborates on three approaches to helping people understand "rich topics," which can be applied to planning for classroom and museum experiences (e.g., Project MUSE, Davis & Donahue, 1996):

- Multiple points of entry into a topic can include narrative, numerical, logical, existential, foundational, hands-on, or interpersonal entry points.
- Powerful analogies and metaphors enable us to make connections and associations, which make experiences personally meaningful.

- Multiple representations of core themes provide interpretation in different ways and in different media (e.g., natural language, logical analysis, graphic form, audio/video, film, arts media, or live interpretation).

Gardner wrote the Foreword to a book by Terry Marks-Tarlow (1996), *Creativity Inside Out: Learning through Multiple Intelligences*. Marks-Tarlow believes that creativity "thrives in the soil where two or more intelligences mix" (p. x). Creativity is in "fullest bloom" when individuals are internally motivated by, for instance, curiosity, determination, and passion, rather than expecting external rewards like praise, recognition, and good grades. Activities in this book are rich in creative expression, risk-taking, exploring curiosity, nurturing self-esteem, and promoting cooperation, communication and harmony. Activities enhance creativity from the perspective of differences among the children and across subject matters.

Since the late 1990s, there has been an increasing focus on how students build or construct personal meaning. Piaget (e.g., 1967) argued that knowledge is never acquired passively because new knowledge can be handled only through assimilation to a cognitive structure an individual already has. In social constructivist thinking, learners are active and adapt to the world by forming and reforming categories and structures that work to explain the phenomenal world and allow the learner to interact with it effectively (O'Connor 1998). Therefore, learners are thought to be active creators of their knowledge. They build up, or scaffold, piece by piece, an internal mental structure that is made up of pieces that pre-existed. Individuals rely on this structure in reorganizing their activity on the basis of further experience. Glasersfeld (1993) explains that knowledge has to be built up by each individual learner. It cannot be packaged and transferred from one person to another. Learners are always assimilating information from the world and accommodating to the world by creating new knowledge structures. O'Connor describes how Vygotsky's work (e.g., 1978) and that of other Soviet psychologists on socio-cultural or sociohistorical analyses of mind and learning have been interpreted and extended by constructivist educational researchers interested in how participation in the social world influences higher cognitive abilities. Vygotsky's term *zone of proximal development* is also cited by museum educators as a concept important to the kind of lifelong learning experiences museums provide. As described by Vygotsky (1978, p. 86): "The zone of proximal development . . . is the distance between the actual developmental level as determined by independent problem solving and the level of potential development as determined through problem solving under adult guidance or in collaboration with more capable peers."

Eilean Hooper-Greenhill, at Leicester University, United Kingdom, explains how museum and gallery visits can help school visitors construct meaning. "Individuals search for meaning, look for patterns, try to invest their experience with significance" (2000a, p. 118). Visitors interpret objects in museums through a reading or looking combined with sensory experiences (e.g., touching or smelling), resulting in both spoken and unspoken cognitive and emotional responses. In *Museum and Gallery Education* (2000b), Hooper-Greenhill explains that learning experiences offered by museums and galleries in the United Kingdom are designed to be complementary to those offered in classrooms. But students can be exposed to alternative ways of learning, and to a variety of active ways of working with objects or material evidence. Hooper-Greenhill has found that the museum environment can enable some children to demonstrate abilities and skills that are not visible in the more formal environment of the classroom. For all students visiting a museum or gallery: ". . . going to a new place, meeting new people, experiencing new approaches to gathering information and encountering real things can be very stimulating and motivating, and can put the knowledge they have gained at school into perspective" (p. 152).

Many museums and galleries in the United Kingdom also organize an outreach program to schools that might include a mobile museum, workshops in schools and community venues. Loan services have also been well established in the United States and Canada with cased objects, discovery boxes, teaching aids such as charts, specimens, reproductions, models, and replicas. Some art galleries in the United Kingdom organize artists' residencies in schools in which each project is carefully planned and the artist and school carefully matched. Artists and students meet in the gallery, sometimes visit the artist's studio, and work together in the classroom.

In *Learning the Arts in an Age of Uncertainty*, Walter Pitman (1998) suggests that a trip to a museum or an art gallery can give students insights and offer new relevance to information they gather from textbooks on disparate subject areas. A romp through a Greek gallery at an interdisciplinary museum like the Royal Ontario Museum can help students experience all they "could have imagined about the literature, the mathematics and science, the sculpture and architecture, the games and drama of the ancient world without isolating any single one of the these elements" (p. 3). Pitman's final words aptly sum up why the arts belong in classrooms:

> *The arts . . . are the ultimate form of equality, of joy and delight. They are of the moment, to be grasped and celebrated. They are a way of knowing what can be shared with children and adults who have very different intellectual and physical capacities . . . the arts are, above all, how we express the finest elements of our humanity—our understanding, our compassion, our caring, and our love.* (p. 263)

References Specific to This Appendix

Armstrong, T. (2000). *Multiple intelligences in the classroom* (2nd ed.). Alexandria, VA: Association for Supervision and Curriculum Development.

Bitz, M. (2004). The comic book project: The lives of urban youth. *Art Education, 57*(2), 33–39.

Cornett, C. (2003). *Creating meaning through literature and the arts: An integration resource for classroom teachers* (2nd ed.). Englewood Cliffs, NJ: Prentice Hall.

Cornett, C. E., & Smithrim, K. L. (2001). *The arts as meaning makers: Integrating literature and the arts throughout the curriculum.* Toronto: Pearson Education Canada.

Davis, J., & Donahue, D. (1996). *The Muse (museums uniting with schools in education) book (building on our knowledge).* A report on the work of Project Muse. Cambridge, MA: President and Fellows of Harvard College.

Deasy, R. (Ed.). (2001). CRITICAL LINKS: Learning in the arts and student academic and social development. Washington, DC: Arts Education Partnership. Retrieved March 10, 2004 from http://www.aep-arts.org/PDF%20Files/CriticalLinks.pdf

Eisner, Elliot W. (2002). *The arts and the creation of mind.* New Haven & London: Yale University Press.

Fiske, E. B. (Ed.). (1999). *Champions of change: The impact of the arts on learning.* Washington, DC: Arts Education Partnership, the President's Committee on the Arts and Humanities, the GE Fund, and the John D. and Catherine T. MacArthur Foundation. Retrieved March 10, 2004 from http://aep-arts.org/Champions.html

Gardner, H. (1991). *The unschooled mind: How children think and how schools should teach.* New York: Basic Books.

Gardner, H. (1997). Integrating learning styles and multiple intelligences. *Educational Leadership,* 55(1), 22–27.

Gardner H. (1999). *The disciplined mind: What all students should understand.* New York: Simon & Schuster.

Glaserfeld, E. Von. (1993). Learning and adaptation in the theory of constructivism. *Communication and Cognition,* 26(3/4), 393–402.

Hooper-Greenhill, E. (2000a). *Museums and the interpretation of visual culture.* London: Routledge.

Hooper-Greenhill, E. (2000b). *Museum and gallery education.* London & Washington: Leicester University Press.

Marks-Tarlow, T. (1996). *Creativity inside out: Learning through multiple intelligences.* Menlo Park, CA: Addison-Wesley.

Morrison, T., Bryan, G., & Chilcoat, G. (2002). Using student-generated comic books in the classroom. *Journal of Adolescent & Adult Literacy,* 45(8), 758–67.

O'Connor, M.C. (1998). Can we trace the "efficacy of social constructivism"? In P. D. Pearson & A. Iran-Nejad (Eds.), *Review of Research in Education,* Vol. 23 (pp. 25–71).

Piaget, J. (1967). *Biologie et connaisance.* Paris: Gallimard.

Pitman, W. (1998). *Learning the arts in an age of uncertainty.* Toronto: Arts Education Council of Ontario.

Upitis, R., & Smithrim, K. (2003). *Learning through the arts^{TM}: National assessment 1999–2002. Final Report to the Royal Conservatory of Music.* Kingston, ON: Queen's University. Retrieved March 10, 2004 from http://www.discussionzone.ca/press/LTTAjun03-ResearchReport.pdf

Vygotsky, L.S. (1978). *Mind in society: The development of higher psychological processes.* (M. Cole, V. John-Steiner, S. Scribner, & E. Souberman, Eds.). Cambridge, MA: Harvard University Press.

Appendix C: A Checklist for Assessing Growth in and through the Arts in Education

Arts-Making: Expressing and Communicating Ideas and Feelings through the Arts Forms

- ❑ Accepts the teacher as an arts instructor and an arts maker
- ❑ Demonstrates a willingness to discover, experiment with, and explore different arts forms and materials
- ❑ Selects, shapes and presents ideas and feelings through a variety of arts forms and materials
- ❑ Expresses inventive and innovative ideas through an arts form
- ❑ Finds satisfaction in making and creating artistic products and events
- ❑ Is emotionally and intellectually engaged in the arts work
- ❑ Is willing to revise, shape and work towards improving and completing the arts work
- ❑ Expresses ideas and feelings freely and without fear of judgment
- ❑ Is willing to take risks when working independently or with others
- ❑ Sustains involvement from initiating, following through, to completing arts work
- ❑ Applies a developing knowledge of the elements of the arts form
- ❑ Applies prior learning (skills, concepts, techniques) and draws on personal background in the development of the arts form
- ❑ Demonstrates continuing growth in the ability to communicate ideas and feelings through arts forms
- ❑ Incorporates a variety of multimedia and technology in arts learning
- ❑ Transfers knowledge of the ideas explored in curriculum areas into personal arts work
- ❑ Transforms ideas represented in one arts form into another composition using a different arts form
- ❑ Uses metaphor, symbolism and abstraction in arts making
- ❑ Demonstrates an understanding of the basic elements of the different arts forms
- ❑ Discriminates and makes effective choices for specific artistic purposes
- ❑ Elaborates ideas in arts works by adding, omitting, distorting, and/or exaggerating
- ❑ Experiences the arts of different cultures
- ❑ Uses tools, equipment, materials appropriately and effectively
- ❑ Explores a variety of sources for ideas for arts making
- ❑ Investigates a variety of possibilities for using different arts forms
- ❑ Researches information for artistic compositions
- ❑ Seeks possibilities, finds alternatives and explores ideas in-depth through the arts
- ❑ Accepts and supports the contributions of others in creating an ensemble arts work
- ❑ Creates arts events as a member of an ensemble
- ❑ Develops and shares ideas and materials
- ❑ Is able to discuss the process involved in producing the arts work
- ❑ Is aware of audience, adopting appropriate style and content
- ❑ Is receptive to advice from others
- ❑ Presents arts work publicly

Arts Literacy: Demonstrating Awareness and Knowledge about the Arts Forms

- ❑ Appreciates and interprets the arts work of peers and professionals
- ❑ Appreciates different ideas, styles and products
- ❑ Appreciates the effects of form on the meaning of what is seen and heard
- ❑ Defines the elements and principles of the arts form, and uses them when responding to arts works
- ❑ Describes how artists representing various periods, styles, and cultures have used materials, tools, elements and the principles of the arts form for a variety of purposes
- ❑ Identifies and describes types and genres of arts events
- ❑ Identifies factors that affect our understanding of the arts
- ❑ Identifies ideas evoked by the artist or the work
- ❑ Recognizes the implications of commercial arts forms
- ❑ Sees similarities and differences in a wide range of artistic styles in each arts form
- ❑ Understands how the ideas in arts works relate to their own knowledge and experience
- ❑ Demonstrates appropriate viewing and listening behaviors in response to an arts work or event
- ❑ Appreciates displays and installations in school
- ❑ Participates in arts events with guests and during excursions
- ❑ Communicates understanding and knowledge of the arts form in appropriate ways
- ❑ Demonstrates knowledge of aspects of the historical context of an arts product or event
- ❑ Describes products, performances and events, and distinguishes between the types or styles used
- ❑ Differentiates between stereotype and truthful interpretations in arts products and events
- ❑ Makes and understands artistic and aesthetic choices
- ❑ Recognizes the value of arts experiences, both as maker and viewer, and as interpreter and critic
- ❑ Uses the terminology of the arts form
- ❑ Reflects upon and assesses own work orally and in writing
- ❑ Demonstrates a growing understanding of overall effect of arts forms (elements, principles, techniques, styles)
- ❑ Has an awareness of unity and coherence in the arts forms
- ❑ Explains key ideas, concepts and personal connections that emerge in the arts work
- ❑ Explains a preference for specific arts works
- ❑ Reflects on personal learning and growth in an arts form
- ❑ Shares connections, ideas and insights with others
- ❑ Applies artistic and aesthetic learning to other areas and aspects of life
- ❑ Demonstrates empathy and consideration for the work of others
- ❑ Keeps an arts portfolio of arts products, reflections, and resources
- ❑ Examines ideology and values presented in the arts forms
- ❑ Listens, reflects on, and thinks critically about the arts works of others
- ❑ Gives personal and informed opinions about an arts event
- ❑ Responds affectively and cognitively to arts works and events

Biographies of Feature Contributors

Carmen Alvarez is a classroom teacher in an inner-city school in Toronto. She has recently worked with students in the junior division and completed qualifications in drama courses. She has taken the initiative to weave drama extensively into her program.

Bob Barton has been involved in teaching children and teachers as a classroom teacher, language arts consultant, drama instructor, and author for more than 40 years. He has authored and co-authored several books, including recent titles *Telling Stories Your Way, Poetry Goes to School,* and *The Bear Says North.*

Marnie Binder is a primary teacher in an inner-city school who uses the arts as the basis for her classroom program. As well, she lectures and writes about her philosophy of arts-based education for teachers, student teachers, and parents.

Shosh Brenner is a classroom teacher and a conference presenter with interests in literacy, numeracy, foreign language, and the arts. A mother of three young adults, she is a lifelong learner who has completed her Master's degree from the Ontario Institute for Studies in Education, University of Toronto (OISE/UT).

Paola Cohen is an art teacher in an elementary school who recognizes the importance of visual arts in early childhood education and in elementary school. She has also taught courses in art education at OISE and at the Institute of Child Study, University of Toronto.

Catherine Combs has been a classroom teacher in downtown Toronto for the past 20 years. She is a drama consultant in Toronto and an instructor of dramatic arts courses at OISE/UT.

Jim Giles has been a classroom teacher and consultant for the past 20 years. He is a strong advocate for arts education, as well as a popular speaker on the topic of equity issues.

Jacqueline Karsemeyer is a resource teacher specializing in early childhood education. She has extensive background in movement and dance. In her Ph.D thesis from OISE/UT, she described her personal philosophy of kinesthetic knowledge.

Christine Jackson is a dance and drama consultant for the Toronto District School Board. She is an instructor for dramatic arts courses at OISE/UT, the co-author of language arts documents and handbooks for her board, and a reviewer of drama course profiles for Ontario's ministry of education.

John Mazurek is an experienced classroom teacher and an instructor in the elementary preservice program at OISE/UT. He is a TRIBES trainer who frequently presents sessions throughout Ontario.

Sheena Robertson has worked extensively as a teacher in inner-city schools for the Toronto District School Board. Sheena currently works as a freelance arts consultant and presents drama workshops that integrate curriculum areas.

Ludmila Shantz is an educator at the McMichael Canadian Art Collection, developing educational programs, giving tours of gallery exhibitions and teaching studio sessions. Her MA thesis topic was art museum electronic educational sites. She is a practising artist and has taught art classes in a variety of settings.

Barbara Soren is an independent consultant who focuses on museum and arts education. She has worked with schools, community organizations, museums, and performing arts organizations. She was the coordinator of Arts Forum at OISE. Barbara is an adjunct instructor in the Faculty of Fine Arts, York University, and in the Museum Studies program, University of Toronto.

Sarah Willett and **Honoré Marchant-Kelly** are museum educators who are completing their graduate degrees in Museum Studies.

Meguida Zola teaches in the Faculty of Education at Simon Fraser University. The focus of his work is on language learning and children's literature. He has compiled anthologies of Canadian writing for children and edited a language arts series for schools. His own writings for children encompass picture books, novels, poetry, and biography.

Annotated Recommended Resources

1 Implementing an Arts-based Curriculum: Why the Arts Matter

Cornett, C. E., and K. L. Smithrim. 2001. *The Arts as Meaning Makers: Integrating literature and the arts throughout the curriculum.* Toronto: Prentice Hall.

> This book helps teachers integrate literature, art, drama, dance, and music throughout the curriculum by providing an underlying arts knowledge base, a rationale for integration, and specific arts integration principles. It offers a historical and theoretical background supporting the benefits of arts education.

Edwards, L. 1997. *The Creative Arts: A process approach for teachers and children.* Upper Saddle River, NJ: Prentice Hall.

> This book conveys the importance of the process of creativity in the arts and broadens our understanding of how teachers acquire knowledge and skills when actively engaged in the creative arts process. The author emphasizes that it is the human being, not the art activity that should be the centre of the experience and provides a comprehensive survey of professional research to support her views.

Eisner, E. W. 1998. *The Kinds of Schools We Need.* Portsmouth, NH: Heinemann.

> Eisner is an internationally renowned authority on how the arts can be used to improve education. This book reviews Eisner's groundbreaking theories on aesthetic intelligence to help us understand the connections among art, literacy, research, and evaluation.

Greene, M. 1995. *Releasing the Imagination: Essays on education, the arts and social change.* San Francisco: Jossey-Bass.

> Maxine Greene argues that imagination opens our eyes to worlds beyond our experience, enabling us to create, care for others, and envision social change. This book provides a vivid portrait of the possibilities of human experience and education's role in its realization.

Piazza. C. L. 1999. *Multiple Forms of Literacy: Teaching literacy and the arts.* Upper Saddle River, NJ: Prentice Hall.

> This book challenges teachers to address a curriculum that includes viewing and representing literacy by collaborating with arts specialists in the schools and community. The author provides a survey of communicative choices available to students that extends language symbols to that of multiple symbol systems offered by the arts.

Pitman, W. 1998. *Learning the Arts in an Age of Uncertainty.* North York, ON: Arts Education Council of Ontario.

> This book provides a solid and rich reasoning about the centrality of arts in education. Each essay provides clear rationale and insight into the arts in our schools. Chapters include The Arts and the World Our Children Face, The Arts as a Process of Learning, and Artists and Teachers, Parents and Community.

Roberts, B. A., ed. 1997. *Connect Combine Communicate: Revitalizing the arts in Canadian schools.* Sydney, NS: The University College of Cape Breton Press.

> The National Symposium on Arts Education '97, hosted by the Canadian Music Educators' Association, provided an opportunity for arts educators, professional artists, and government representatives to discuss common concerns to develop strategies for strengthening the arts in schools.

Smith, S. L. 2001. *The Power of the Arts: Creative strategies for teaching exceptional learners.* Baltimore, MD: Paul H. Brookes.

> This book provides the arts as an alternative method for teaching academic subjects to students with disabilities. Interviews with teacher-artists, case examples, and step-by-step instructions are offered to build students' individual strengths and interests through the art projects they engage in.

2 Finding Yourself in the Painting: Visual Arts in Education

Barrett, T. 1997. *Talking about Student Art.* Worcester, MA: Davis.

This book is a collection of diverse voices that enhances thoughtful reflection about student artwork. Its focus is to improve students' thinking and talking about the art of their peers. It includes models and suggestions to facilitate dialogues about art.

Herberholz, D., and B. Herberholz. 2002. *Artworks for Elementary Teachers.* 9th ed. New York: McGraw-Hill.

This book offers introductory experiences in art-making and art-viewing. It helps teachers understand art through production, history, criticism, and aesthetics. A practical and detailed source, it helps teachers introduce experiences for creating art and responding to it.

Hume, H. D. 2000. *A Survival Kit for the Elementary/Middle School Art Teacher.* West Nyack, NY: The Center for Applied Research in Education.

This practical handbook provides more than 100 art projects to help elementary teachers implement art activities. It offers guidelines and reproducible resources for building and managing the art program. Art projects that include painting, drawing, printmaking and three-dimensional design are outlined in detail.

Schirrmacher, R. 2002. *Art and Creative Development for Young Children.* 4th ed. Albany, NY: Delmar.

This comprehensive book is written for teachers who work with primary-aged children. The resource guide includes theory and research with practical applications covering issues of creativity, cultural diversity, and developmentally appropriate practice for young children.

Steele, B. 1998. *Draw Me a Story.* Winnipeg, MB: Peguis.

Bob Steele uses children's drawings to describe the connections between art and language. As students create these drawings, they express ideas, emotions, and feelings through these visual images. This book demonstrates how children's drawing can encourage verbal and written communication and how we can find meaning in those drawings.

3 Joining in the Singing: Meaning Making and Music Education

Campbell, Patricia Shehan, Ellen McCullough-Brabson, and Judith Cook Tucker. 1993. *Roots and Branches: A legacy of multicultural music for children.* Danbury, CT: World Music Press.

This resource contains a book and audiocassette or compact disc, including 38 musical memories shared by men and women of 23 different cultures, including selections from China, England, Israel, and Cambodia, as well as African-American and Navajo traditions.

Choksy, Lois, and David Brummitt. 1987. *120 Singing Games and Dances for Elementary Schools.* Englewood Cliffs, NJ: Prentice Hall.

A classroom teacher's bible, this resource contains songs for moving in place, circle games and dances, line games and dances, clapping and passing games, and how to create games and dances. It also features a glossary of musical terms and a bibliography of other valuable resources.

Goodkin, Doug. 2002. *Play, Sing & Dance: An introduction to Orff Schulwerk.* Miami, FL: Schott Music.

This book is an exercise in re-envisioning the timeless ideas of Orff Schulwerk, a dynamic approach to music and movement education that began more than 75 years ago. Though practical suggestions are included, the emphasis is on generating ideas.

Montgomery, Amanda P. 2002. *Teaching towards Musical Understanding: A handbook for the elementary grades.* Toronto: Prentice Hall.

> Age-appropriate music, classroom activities, and teaching strategies are provided for all aspects of elementary school music. The handbook covers singing, playing and improvising with instruments, listening, moving, reading and writing music, assessment and evaluation, and short- and long-range curriculum planners.

Wiggins, Jackie. 2001. *Teaching for Musical Understanding.* New York: McGraw-Hill.

> With its emphasis on real-world teaching, this book ensures that students learn both the theory and practice of music education. A 16-track audio CD featuring music by composers such as Grieg and Stravinsky is available for purchase with the text.

4 Learning "in Role": Drama in Eudcation

Barton, Bob. 2000. *Telling Stories Your Way.* Markham, ON: Pembroke.

> This comprehensive handbook provides practical how-to support for choosing stories, telling stories, and using stories for language and drama learning in the classroom.

Booth, David. 1994. *Story Drama.* Markham, ON: Pembroke.

> David Booth argues that role-play is a natural way in which young people can explore the world around them. *Story Drama* offers classroom models and frameworks for creating a safe, interactive, enriching environment that includes a number of ways of deepening stories to enhance language growth, writing, problem solving, and decision making.

Neelands, J., and T. Goode. 1990/2000. *Structuring Drama Work: A handbook of available forms in theatre and drama.* Cambridge, UK: Cambridge University Press.

> This practical handbook offers teachers a wide range of drama conventions to develop, shape, and extend drama work. Jonothan Neelands and Tony Goode provide 72 key conventions, with examples, and provide advice to teachers for planning drama to maximize involvement and learning.

Swartz, Larry. 2002. *The New Dramathemes.* Markham, ON: Pembroke.

> This resource offers more than 100 games and activities using themes as a springboard for drama work. Opportunities for exploring literary sources, including the picture book, novel, rhyme, folktale, poem, and script, are suggested. This book provides accessible frameworks for structuring drama and features planning guides and profiles for assessment.

Winston, J., and M. Tandy. 1998. *Beginning Drama 4–11.* London: David Fulton.

> This book provides an introduction for elementary teachers, offering step-by-step guidance to help teachers and students grow in confidence in their use of drama. A range of strategies is offered to help with planning, guiding, and controlling a drama lesson.

5 Moving in the Circle: Dance Education

Grant, J. M. 1995. *Shake, Rattle and Learn: Classroom-tested ideas that use movement and active learning.* Markham, ON: Pembroke.

> This book explores the relationship between movement and language learning. Dance activities that promote important concepts in rhythmic, spatial, and language expression are highlighted.

Kaeja, A. 1999. *Express Dance.* Toronto: Dance Collection Danse.

> *Express Dance* provides teachers with an overview of dance language and techniques. Practical strategies and frameworks for implementing choreographic conventions are featured in this useful guide.

McGreevy-Nicols, S., and H. Scheff. 1995. *Building Dances: A guide to putting movements together.* Champaign, IL: Human Kinetics.

This how-to book helps teachers to introduce, develop and assess the basics of choreography. More than 230 step-by-step ideas are presented as blueprints to create and facilitate dance and movement in the classroom.

Rooyackers, P. 1996. *101 Dance Games for Children.* Alameda, CA: Hunter House.

101 Dance Games for Children encourages children and adults to use body language to develop creativity, sociability, and physical coordination. The games here combine dance and play in ways that release a child's spontaneity and self-expression.

Wiertsema, H. 2002. *101 Movement Activities for Children.* Alameda, CA: Hunter House.

These non-competitive games focus on pure movement that promotes coordination, self-confidence, and physical expression. Each game is described in detail, including variations.

6 Plugging in the Arts: Media and Arts Education

Dyson, Anne Haas. 1997. *Writing Superheroes: Contemporary childhood, popular culture, and classroom literacy.* New York: Teachers College Press.

The author offers a detailed picture of the impact of popular culture, especially superhero stories, on learning inside and outside of school. Using her ethnographic research in classrooms, Dyson explores how children inhabit the worlds of superheroes and how that shapes their understanding of writing, genres, character development, and ultimately, of identity formation.

Gee, James Paul. 2003. *What Video Games Have to Teach Us about Learning and Literacy.* New York: Palgrave Macmillan.

The author offers an in-depth look at what goes on when children use video games. Rather than viewing them as a bad influence or as an anathema, Gee argues that there are 36 important learning principles built into video games that support current research on human learning in cognitive science. His book will open educators' eyes to what takes place when a child plays a video game.

Kress, Gunther. 2003. *Literacy in the New Media Age.* London: Routledge.

Kress offers a robust theory of literacy, covering such core areas as shifts in how we read texts (printed and electronic); how genres work and how to work within them; how to critically frame the texts we read and view; and how to build on children's awareness of visual communication in texts.

Moline, Steve. 1996. *I See What You Mean: Children at work with visual information.* Markham: Pembroke.

In *I See What You Mean*, teachers of all subject areas learn how to help students understand and present pictures, timelines, maps, graphs, tables and many other forms of visual information. Hands-on activities and more than 100 student examples illustrate how students can communicate concepts better with visual texts.

Pahl, Kate, and Jennifer Rowsell. 2005. *Understanding Literacy Education: Using new literacy studies in the classroom.* London: Sage.

Understanding Literacy Education provides a road map for using new research and practice in literacy and media education. At the heart of the book is a belief in building on students' communicative practices—from their use of media to their awareness of technology and cultural histories—and it is offered in an accessible way that will allow you to use it in planning and assessing literacy development.

7 When Teachers and Artists Hold Hands: Partnerships in Arts Education

Dissanayake, Ellen. 1998. *What Is Art For?* Seattle, WA: University of Washington Press.

This book is designed to answer the question "What is art for?" and reveal other questions: What is art? Is art necessary? Where did art come from? What effects—on individuals and on societies—does art have? In answering these questions the author helps us understand and recognize the significance of creating art for museums, for communities, and for school curricula.

Ehrenworth, M. 2003. *Looking to Write: Students writing through visual arts.* Portsmouth, NH: Heinemann.

The author appreciates the meaning and inspiration that the visual arts can afford the writing process. This resource offers examples of historical artworks and provides strategies for using visual prompts to help students locate significant things to write about and to craft beautiful writing in response.

Eisner, E. W. 2002. *The Arts and the Creation of the Mind.* New Haven, CT: Yale University Press.

Eisner invites readers to celebrate the uniqueness of art education and to explore the rich connections between thinking and learning in other areas. This book reimagines the kind of reforms needed in education through Eisner's notions of arts-based research and understanding the mind as process, a way of being in and acting upon the world.

Freeland, Cynthia. 2001. *But Is It Art?* New York: Oxford University Press.

Cynthia Freeland explains why innovation and controversy are valued in the arts. She weaves together philosophy and art theory as she discusses beauty, culture, money, museums, and politics. The book also helps to clarify contemporary and historical accounts of the nature, function, and interpretation of the arts.

Jensen, E. 2001. *Arts with the Brain in Mind.* Alexandria, VA: Association for Supervision and Curriculum Development.

To push for higher standards of learning, many policy makers are eliminating arts programs. To Jensen this is a mistake. Based on what we know about the brain and learning, this book presents the definitive case for making arts a core part of the basic curriculum and thoughtfully integrating them into every subject.

References

Ackroyd, Judith. 2000. *Literacy Alive! Drama projects for literacy learning*. London: Hodder and Stoughton.

Alexander, J. 2000. *Command Performance: An actress in the theatre of politics*. Cambridge, MA: Da Capo Press.

Bartel, Lee, and Lee Willingham, eds. *Canadian Music Educator Journal*, various issues.

Barton, Bob. 1993. *The Storm Wife*. Kingston, ON: Quarry Press.

Blom, L. A., and L. T. Chaplin. 1988. *The Movement of Movement: Dance improvisation*. Pittsburgh, PA: University of Pittsburgh Press.

_____. 1986. *The Intimate Art of Choreography*. Pittsburgh, PA: University of Pittsburgh Press.

Booth, D., and H. Reynolds, eds. 1983. *Arts: A survey of provincial curricula at the elementary and secondary levels*. Toronto: Council of Ministers of Education, Canada.

Booth, David. 1994. *Story Drama*. Markham, ON: Pembroke.

Brooks, M., and M. Hunter. 1986/1995. *I Met a Bully on the Hill*. Toronto: Playwrights Union of Canada.

Buckingham, D. 1998. *Media Education in the U.K.: Moving beyond protectionism*. UK: International Communication Association.

Burningham, John. 1996. *Cloudland*. New York: Crown.

Cannon, Jan. 1995. *Trupp*. San Diego, CA: Harcourt, Brace and Company.

Cohen, S. J. 1992. *Dance as a Theatre Art*. Princeton, NJ: Princeton Book.

Dyson, A. H. 1997. *Writing Superheroes: Contemporary childhood, popular culture, and classroom literacy*. New York: Teachers College Press.

Edwards, Pamela Duncan. 1997. *Barefoot*. New York: HarperCollins.

Egan, Kieran. 1997. *The Educated Mind: How cognitive tools shape our understanding*. Chicago: University of Chicago Press.

Eisner, E. W. 1997. *Educating Artistic Vision*. Reston, VA: National Art Education Association.

_____. 1998. *The Kind of Schools We Need: Personal essays*. Portsmouth, NH: Heinemann.

_____. 2003. The Arts and the Creation of Mind. *Language Arts* 80(5): 340–44.

Farrell, Susan. 2000. *Tools for Powerful Student Evaluation*. Fort Lauderdale, FL: Merideth Music.

Fowler, C. 1994. Strong Arts, Strong Schools. *Educational Leadership* 52(3): 4–9.

Gardner, Howard. 1988. A Cognitive View of the Arts. In *Research Readings for Discipline-based Art Education: A journey beyond creating*, edited by S. M. Dodds. Reston, VA: National Art Education Association.

Gee, J. P. 2002. Millennials and Bobs, *Blue's Clues* and *Sesame Street*: A story for our times. In *Adolescents and Literacies in a Digital World*, edited by D. Alvermann. New York: Peter Lang.

_____. 2003. *What Video Games Have to Teach Us about Learning and Literacy*. New York: Palgrave Macmillan.

Gibbs, J. 1978/2001. *TRIBES: A new way of learning and being together*. Santa Rosa, CA: Center Source Publications.

Goldhaber, M. 1998. The Attention Economy Will Change Everything. Telepolis (Archive 1998). http:www.heise.de/tp/English/inhalt/te/1419/I.html.

Goodkin, Doug. 1997. *A Rhyme in Time: Rhythm, speech activities and improvisation for the classroom*. Burbank, CA: Warner Brothers.

_____. 1998. Polycentric Music Education. In *Music of the World's Cultures: A source book for music educators*, edited by Barb Lundquist and C. K. Szego, with Bruno Nettl, Ramon P. Santos, and Einar Solbu. Reading, UK: International Society for Music Education.

_____. 2002. *Sound Ideas: Activities for the percussion circle*. Burbank, CA: Warner Brothers.

_____. 1995. Art and Imagination: Reclaiming the sense of possibility. *Phi Delta Kappan* 76(5): 378–82.

Greene, M. 1995. *Releasing the Imagination: Essays on education, the arts, and social change.* San Francisco: Jossey-Bass.

Hackett, Patricia, and C. A. Lindeman. 1997. *The Musical Classroom: Background models and skills for elementary teaching.* Upper Saddle River, NJ: Simon and Schuster.

Halen-Faber, C. v. 2004. *Seeing Through Apples: An exploration into the ethics and aesthetics of a teacher-educator-researcher's arts-based beginnings.* Unpublished doctoral dissertation, OISE/UT.

Hardie, Marilyn, and Elaine P. Mason. 2001. *Music Builders: Grades K, 1, 2, 3, 4, 5, 6.* Markham, ON: Berandol Publishers c/o Mayfair Music.

Harwayne, Shelley, compiler. 2002. *Messages to Ground Zero: Children respond to September 11, 2001.* Portsmouth, NH: Heinemann.

Jenson, Eric. 2001. *Arts with the Brain in Mind.* Alexandria, VA: Association for Supervision and Curriculum Development.

Johnston, A. 2001. Integrating Drama throughout the Curriculum. In *The Arts as Meaning Makers: Integrating literature and arts throughout the curriculum—Canadian edition,* edited by G. E. Cornett and K. L. Smithrim. Toronto: Prentice Hall.

Kress, Gunther. 1997. *Before Writing.* London: Routledge.

_____. 2003. *Literacy in the New Media Age.* London: Routledge.

Lankshear, C., and M. Knobel. 2003. *New Literacies: Changing knowledge and classroom learning.* Buckingham, UK: Open University Press.

Lowenfeld, V., and W. L. Brittain. 1970. *Creative and Mental Growth.* 5th ed. London: Macmillan.

Marsh, Jackie, and Elaine Millard. 2003. *Literacy and Popular Culture in the Classroom.* Reading: National Center for Language and Literacy.

McLeod, J. 1988. *Drama Is Real Pretending.* Victoria, AU: Ministry of Education (Schools Division).

McLuhan, Marshall. 1964. *Understanding Media: The extensions of man.* London: Routledge.

Miller, J. P. 2000. *Education and the Soul: Toward a spiritual curriculum.* Albany, NY: State University of New York Press.

Mills, J. C. 2000. *The Painted Chest.* Toronto: Key Porter.

Moline, Steve. 1996. *I See What You Mean: Children at work with visual information.* Markham, ON: Pembroke.

Neelands, J., and T. Goode. 1999/2000. *Structuring Drama Work: A handbook of available forms in theatre and drama.* 2d ed. Cambridge, UK: Cambridge University Press.

Pahl, Kate. 2002. Ephemera, Mess and Miscellaneous Piles: Texts and practices in families. *Journal of Early Childhood Literacy* 2(2):145–65.

_____. 1999. *Transformations: Meaning making in nursery education.* London: Trentham Books.

Pahl, Kate, and Jennifer Rowsell. 2005. *Understanding Literacy Education: Using new literacy studies in the classroom.* London: Sage.

Rooyrakers, P. 2002. *101 Dance Games for Children.* Berkeley, CA: Hunter House.

Seary, M. 2003. *Children Making Art.* Kentville, NS: Gaspereau Press.

Stec, Genean. 1991. *The Field Trip Handbook: A Guide to Visiting Museums.* Toronto: Pearson Education.

Sterling, S. 1992. *My Name Is Seepeetza.* Toronto: Groundwood Books.

Sullivan, Timothy, and Lee Willingham, eds. 2002. *Creativity and Music Education.* Edmonton, AB: Canadian Music Educators' Association.

Swanwick, K. 1988. *Music, Mind, and Education.* London: Routledge, Chapman and Hall.

Swartz, L., and S. M. Stiegelbauer, eds. 2002. Arts in Education. *Orbit 32*(3).

Tsuchiya, M. 2003. *History and Analysis of Expressions Found in Elementary School Student Pictorial Artwork over 100 Years.* Tokyo: Tokyo Gakugei University.

Wagner, B. J. 1976/1999. *Dorothy Heathcote: Drama as a learning medium.* Portland, ME: Calendar Island.

Wiertsma, H. 2002. *101 Movement Games for Children.* Berkeley, CA: Hunter House.

Wynne-Jones, Tim. 1988. *Architect of the Moon.* Toronto: Groundwood Books.

Index

159